FastWeb.

COLLEGE
GOLD

FastWeb!™ COLLEGE GOLD

The Step-by-Step Guide to Paying for College

Mark Kantrowitz

with Doug Hardy

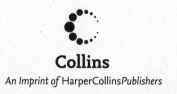

Collins

An Imprint of HarperCollinsPublishers

HarperCollins books may be purchased for educational, business, or sales promotional use. For information please write: Special Markets Department, HarperCollins Publishers, Inc., 10 East 53rd Street, New York, NY 10022.

AP, Advanced Placement Program, College-Level Examination Program, CLEP, College Board, CSS/Financial Aid PROFILE, PSAT, PSAT/NMSQT and SAT are registered trademarks of The College Board.

ACT is a registered trademark of ACT, Inc.

FIRST EDITION

Designed by Joy O'Meara

Library of Congress Cataloging-in-Publication Data is available.

ISBN-10: 0-06-112958-5

ISBN-13: 978-0-06-112958-2

06 07 08 09 10 DIX/RRD 10 9 8 7 6 5 4 3 2 1

This book is dedicated to three groups of people:

The staff at FastWeb, who are continually enhancing and expanding an important free service that helps students pay for college;

America's college financial aid administrators and high school guidance counselors, many of whose voices are heard in this book. The work they do in facilitating access to education is essential to helping students realize their potential;

and most important, the students. We hope this book will enable more students to seek and complete a college education.

Contents

Foreword

FastWeb's *College Gold* is surely the friendliest, most accessible handbook describing the world of financial aid for college. Its practical advice is both authoritative and understandable, and families will find that the book presents the complicated world of paying for college information in an easy-to-find format. I believe *FastWeb College Gold* will also be a most welcome expert resource for libraries, guidance counseling offices, and college financial aid offices around the country. Because the specifics of college financing can change over time, the book is backed up with a continually updated online resource, www.college gold.com. This and updated editions of the book will continue to serve students, families, and college finance professionals for years to come.

For more than a decade, *FastWeb College Gold* author Mark Kantrowitz has provided up-to-date, objective, unbiased advice to students, families, counselors, and financial aid professionals seeking to negotiate the labyrinth of college financial aid. His mastery of the subject matter combined with his availability to grapple with the regulatory, ethical, and practical problems of the financial aid process has made him a trusted resource in our community. *FastWeb College Gold* is the complete handbook of student financial aid—an invaluable guide for students and their families today and in years to come.

Nancy Coolidge
Coordinator of Student Financial Support, Office of the President
University of California
June 6, 2006

Introduction

College is expensive. I mean, really expensive. More expensive than other things you might desire deeply, like a luxury car, a nice new kitchen or a year off from work. More expensive than medical insurance, groceries, utilities and other items you pay for every month. Unless you're truly wealthy, the only thing in your home more expensive than a college education is . . . your home. If you're a parent with several children, it's quite possible that the family education bill will end up surpassing the price of your home.

When you purchase a house, you're not just buying a building. You're also buying into a town, a neighborhood, a school system and a lifestyle. You're investing your money in a decision that will affect much of your daily life. If the home grows in value over time, you're making a long-term financial investment as well.

Attending college is also a long-term investment of time and money, with a strong influence on your (or your child's) eventual wealth, career choices, intellectual habits, social standing and, for many, lifetime friendships. It's a choice that encourages a lifetime of greater opportunity, success and happiness.

It has never been more important to attend college. U.S. Census Bureau data show that men and women with a college degree earn almost twice as much as those with just a high school education, and those with a graduate degree earn almost three times as much.[1] At a time when less-skilled jobs are moving offshore, and the American economy reserves its biggest rewards (outside of professional athletes, rock idols and movie stars) for "knowledge workers," college is clearly the best investment a person can make in his or her future.

Now for the sticker shock: Today's high school students are facing college costs of $50,000 to $120,000 to pay for a college education. College costs are rising much faster than inflation at both public and private institutions. A child born today can expect his tuition to cost three to four times today's price by the time he is eighteen. (That's somewhere between $150,000 and $480,000—not including graduate school!)

If you have no idea how you can afford that number, don't panic. The college financing puzzle has many pieces, but it's a project you can manage. We're going to provide you with a simple, step-by-step program to paying for college. Scholarships, loans, taxes, government help—it's all in here. Whether you're a family facing the problem together for the first time, or a student paying for college on your own, this book will help you break down the challenge into manageable steps, most designed to take twenty minutes or less.

Keep in mind that a college's tuition rate is a list price, but what you will actually pay is likely to be less. Financial aid in all its forms (loans, scholarships and grants, government and employer assistance) makes actually paying for college much more affordable. Net college costs and the total cost of attendance grow much more slowly than the much publicized tuition inflation rate. More than $142 billion in college financial aid is awarded each year in state and federal grants, scholarships, loans and other forms of student aid. Financial aid resources continue to increase with the growth in college costs. Most students—76% in a recent government survey—receive some form of financial aid.

In chapters 1–4 of *College Gold*, you'll create a project plan lasting several months to a year. You'll estimate how much money you'll need, and identify where you'll find it. If college is several years away, you can spread out the work; if college is just around the corner (and we suspect it is for many of you), you'll have to concentrate your effort a little more. If you are a family with several children, we urge you to plan a college financing project for all of your children, combining tasks wherever possible. Many steps can be done once, and then easily adapted for younger children.

Chapters 5–10 lead you through the major components of a college financing plan, including federal and state programs, grants and loans. You'll learn how to work closely with the most important advisors in this process, guidance counselors in high school and financial aid administrators in college.

Introduction

Chapters 11–13 immerse you in the world of scholarships—how to find them and how to win them! Students might want to scan these chapters first because they can start searching for scholarships throughout the process, and even beyond, when they are attending college.

Finally, chapters 14–16 will help students and their families make decisions about the final makeup of their college financing plan, avoid danger zones (like college scholarship scams) and prepare for that big transition to college.

About savings: You'll find an overview of long-term savings plans at the end of this book. *College Gold* has been written for families with a student (or students) close to entering college, which is typically when families start preparing in earnest. College savings plans generally should be started sooner. If you are thinking long-term, or if you have younger children, see the appendix on page 269. (And congratulations for thinking long-term!)

The *College Gold* Survey: As part of writing this book, FastWeb conducted a national survey of students and parents to discover which parts of the college financing process caused the most difficulty. We've cited the survey in several places, and responded to what we learned with specific advice on thorny or confusing topics. Students also shared their best advice about getting the most money for college with the least anxiety. You'll find their comments in boxes labeled "I Wish I Had Known . . ."

Finally, FastWeb provides a companion web site at www.collegegold.com, containing interactive tools, expanded advice and updates. You'll find references to this site throughout the book under the heading "BOOK TO WEB." While this book can be used on its own, we strongly encourage you to take advantage of the free site—it will make you that much better at playing the college aid game. The Book to web references are marked with a code, so you can find the reference quickly on the web site.

The process of paying for college begins with the process of thinking about college in the first place. Ideally, this begins when a child is born (if not before). For many families, however, it begins late in the junior year of high school. Let's consider the situation of the Gordons, a fictional family whose eldest child is now considering college.

Paying for College 101

Following the junior class assembly, Matt Gordon[2] walked through the exit and across the school parking lot. It was the second Thursday in June, and the seniors would graduate on Saturday. Matt arrived at his dented black Bronco, tossed his backpack behind the driver's seat and then positioned his acoustic guitar carefully in the compartment, wedging the case so it would not shift during the drive to work. He paused, momentarily wondering if his enthusiasm for classical guitar would help him get into college. His senior class friends Sherry and Al, both classical guitar players, would attend great music schools in the East in a few months. Matt imagined the transition he'd undergo in the coming year; what would it be like, he speculated, to know what the next four years would hold?

He climbed into the cab, scanned the school exits for his sister Sarah and thought about the bombshell Ms. Breen had dropped on the 163 juniors of Mansfield High School. After forty-five minutes of year-end awards for best this and most improved that, the principal had ceded the podium to Sherry Breen, a financial aid counselor from a local college.

"The seniors are graduating, so you're going to be the big men and women on campus," she had said. "Most of you have already started thinking whether you're going to attend college. Have you thought about which colleges you might attend? Are they in-state or out of state? Should you consider two-year or four-year colleges? What about the armed forces?

"Do you know what you want to choose as a major? Is it okay to change your mind fifteen times before you graduate, or will you have wasted your time and money?

"And speaking of money," Ms. Breen had continued, "do you have any idea how you're going to pay for college?" Dead silence. "That's okay," she had concluded. "The seniors survived, and so will you. Take this seriously, though—and be ready for some major sticker shock."

Matt saw Sarah across the parking lot with two friends. He drummed the steering wheel. Ms. Breen's question wouldn't leave him alone.

Matt had already received literature from a few dozen schools—but the envelopes lay unopened in one of his mother's ubiquitous milk crate organizers. Today, with most of his class, Matt had been stunned by the numbers Ms. Breen had emphatically recited in the M.H.S. auditorium.

"One hundred forty thousand dollars," she had begun. "That's right; let me say it again: One hundred forty grand for four years in the Ivy League. For the state university, more like seventy thousand. Do you have that kind of money? Almost nobody does. Fortunately, there's a lot you can do about the problem."

Now, sitting in the driver's seat, Matt played with the $140,000 figure in his imagination: That's three Lexus SUVs or . . . after calculating some quick math . . . 1,200 pairs of his favorite running shoes. That buys 140,000 songs online . . . at four minutes each would make 560,000 minutes of listening time, divided by 60 equals 9,333 hours. How long would it take to earn that? wondered Matt. At $9.50 an hour for his summer job as a camp counselor that would take more than 14,000 hours or . . . how many weeks of work is that?

"Hey," he said as Sarah opened the passenger door. "If you make $9.50 an hour, how long before you have $140,000?"

Sarah, who loved to display her quick math skills, didn't hesitate. "Okay, $9.50 an hour at 40 hours a week makes $19,000 a year. Delete the thousands, that's 140 divided by 19 which is a little more than 7 years," she said, concluding, "Call it seven-point-something years."

"Wow," said Matt.

" 'Course that's seven-point-something times fifty weeks. Call it 370 weeks. But you wouldn't have $140,000 at the end of that," said Sarah. To Matt's puzzled look she said, "Well, taxes and stuff. You wouldn't actually save $140,000 in seven years. It would be more like nine or ten. Why do you ask?"

Nine or ten years of work to pay for college, thought Matt. Is it worthwhile? Ten years of work—how many cars could I buy with that?

"I'm trying to figure out if going to college is really worth it. We had an assembly today and $140,000 is what it costs. Of course, when you get a college degree you make a lot more money. Twice as much, they said."

Sarah considered the numbers. "So if you go to college, you pay a lot of money but you make it up later."

"Sure," said Matt.

"And because you'd make more money," she continued, "you'd have more money to pay back what you owed for school, and later, when school's paid back, you would be able to afford a better car, and a house and stuff."

Matt started the truck. "I can't keep this all in my head. I need to write it down," he said.

MATT'S PARENTS

Driving home that evening, Lynn Gordon realized the time had come to organize the college search for Matt. This would be the first time she and her husband, Jim, would help one of their children through the process of choosing a college . . . and paying for it. Lynn knew from having managed complicated projects at work that they had to have a plan if they were going to get anywhere.

Matthew's a great kid, she knew, but he wasn't the best at following through . . . what kid was? A schedule would help them all stay on track.

An hour later, Lynn and Jim sat studying the kitchen table, which was now crowded with applications, brochures, catalogs, notepads, a calendar and a calculator. They decided to discuss Matt's college options when he returned from dropping off Sarah at her play rehearsal. Waiting for Matt to return, they scanned the tuition and college cost information.

"Well, we knew it would be expensive," said Lynn. "Look at the range, though: The private schools cost twice as much as Ohio State University, and the branch here in Mansfield is half that."

"He can get into a lot of good schools," said Jim. "I don't think we should take them off the list early just because they're expensive." He wrote figures on a

👍 **RULE OF THUMB**

Private colleges cost roughly twice as much as public colleges (for in-state students).

notepad, saying, "Let's see what it would take if he got into one of the private schools. How much do we have in his account right now?"

"Twenty-nine thousand five hundred," said Lynn. "Ten years at $200 a month, plus interest." She watched Jim write, correcting and adding figures they had discussed occasionally in the past—what portion of the budget could go to education, how long savings would last, and more. The note grew:

MATT

Savings - $ 29,500	$ 7375 per year
School budget @ $500 /mo	$ 4500 per year
(x 9 months)	
Gift from Mom @ $3000	$ 750 per year
TOTAL	$ 12,625 per year
Tuition, fees, etc.	$ 29,350 per year
SHORTFALL	$ 16,725 per year

"Wow," said Jim, underlining the shortfall. "How in the world are we going to pay for this? We have some work to do."

The conversation ranged over dozens of possible tasks and questions.

"The Ford will be paid off in sixteen months. That will free up $400 a month."

"The $200 a month we've been saving in his college fund can continue. We shouldn't forget that."

"We don't want to cut back on your 401(k). That's our retirement. People will lend us money for college but nobody will lend us money for retirement."

"Your mother offered more help. Can you ask her about that?"

"His guitar might help. There has to be scholarship money around."

"We shouldn't forget Sarah in all this. We'll be doing this again in three years."

"It can't be just the parents' responsibility; Matt and Sarah also have a responsibility to help pay."

"We have to find out about loans. Let's check the college web sites for financial aid."

"Isn't there some government loan program for this? Freddie Mac or Auntie Mae or one of those? I think there are grants too."

"Can he get more financial aid if he stays in-state?"

"Wait, we'll have to add travel expenses if he goes east to school."

They heard Matt's truck door slam as Jim said, "Well, wherever he goes, we have a lot to figure out. What should we tell him now?"

Lynn considered. "That this is a project that won't wait. That we'll help but it's up to him, and that we can't pay the whole cost out of savings. But let's find out more before we bring up the money part. Tonight, let's talk about applications."

Matt walked into the kitchen, opened the freezer and stared at the contents in the half-bow of a foraging teenager. He took a container of mint chocolate chip ice cream, then walked over to the cabinet and added a handful of trail mix to the container. Mixing his snack, he recognized the glossy publications on the kitchen table.

"We talked about college in assembly today," he said, trying to sound cheerful. "The guidance counselor said it was time to start. I guess you had the same idea, right?"

• • •

Paying for college is a daunting challenge. In the 2006 *College Gold* survey, 79% of respondents said that financial aid ranged between "important" and "extremely important" to their choice of a college, and 68% rated the process of getting financial aid "stressful, very stressful or extremely stressful." That's a lot of stress!

The cost of college has risen faster than inflation for a generation, doubling about every ten years. In 2005–2006 (the most recent statistics as this book goes to press) one year's average tuition at private colleges topped $21,235. By 2007–2008, that bill will be approximately $23,850 and if the trend continues, by 2010–2011 today's high school freshmen will have to pay $28,400 per year. Since costs continue increasing each successive year, that is at least $124,240 for four years.

Tuition is not the only expense, of course, and the bill climbs as you add living expenses, the cost of books and computers, transportation and so forth.

Paying for college isn't just expensive; it's also complicated. Even at its best, it's a long-term project with many steps, many decisions, many unfamiliar terms and an alphabet soup of acronyms (FAFSA, EFC, SAR . . . see pages 11–12 below). There are numerous loan, scholarship grant and employment programs

Projected yearly costs for four-year private college: today, 5 and 10 years from now		
	2005–2006	2010–2011	2015–2016

	2005–2006	2010–2011	2015–2016
Tuition and Fees	$21,200	$28,400	$38,000
Room and Board	$7,800	$9,900	$12,700
Books and Supplies	$900	$1,100	$1,300
Transportation	$700	$800	$900
Other Expenses	$1,300	$1,600	$2,000
Total	$31,900	$41,800	$54,900

Projected yearly costs for four-year public college: today, 5 and 10 years from now

	2005–2006	2010–2011	2015–2016
Tuition and Fees	$5,500	$7,700	$10,800
Room and Board	$6,600	$8,900	$11,900
Books and Supplies	$900	$1,100	$1,300
Transportation	$900	$1,000	$1,100
Other Expenses	$1,700	$2,100	$2,600
Total	$15,600	$20,800	$27,700

(Stafford, Perkins, PLUS, Consolidation, Pell Grant, SEOG . . .), multiple options for savings (529 College Savings Plans, Prepaid Tuition Plans, Coverdell Education Savings Accounts . . .), and the potential for a significant impact on taxes and other financial obligations and goals. Work-study and/or part-time employment are part of many students' lives.

It's hard to choose which of all these options are most beneficial to you. Yet each family has to create a combination of savings, loans, scholarships and other money that's suitable for them . . . and it will be different from other families' plans.

Many families experience significant time pressure as well. You have to hit numerous deadlines and synchronize them with the competing timetables for college admissions. You often have to complete a lot of work in a short time to get the best deal. It's a yearlong process of moving parts, and sometimes you feel like they're moving a little too fast!

To begin putting the puzzle together, let's look at the three big sources of money for college: Your family (or yourself), financial aid and grants/scholarships. If you consider the national average of sources of money for college, you find it's roughly one-third from family, one-third from government aid and one-third from grants/scholarships. Let's describe those three sources a little more closely.

MONEY SOURCE #1: FAMILY

According to Jim Sumner, Dean of Admission and Financial Aid at Grinnell College, "There are three ways to pay for college: You can pay ahead by planning and saving. You can pay at the time . . . if you've got the required cash flow. Or you can borrow during college and, therefore, pay for it afterward."

As Sumner states, you can marshal your past, present and future resources over the long term to make an investment in college. For most families, it's a combination of all three—savings from the past, income from the present and loans for the future. Because the family is the primary source of college money for most students, you need to understand how colleges, state and federal governments, and others view the family's ability to pay for college. If you're currently an undergraduate student, family matters. If you are a graduate or independent student, "family" means you and possibly a spouse.

There is actually a dollar amount that guides the view of colleges, governments, et al. and it's called the **Expected Family Contribution (EFC)**.[3]

The EFC is a calculation of how much a family can afford to pay for college. The EFC is based on a federal government formula[4] and is used to allocate the money available for financial aid in any particular year. It is not a perfect assessment (a common first reaction among families is that their EFC is set too high), and it's not even the final word on what you will pay (see chapter 15, "How to request a professional judgment review" page 238) but it is a widely used number: The need analysis system assumes that the family has the primary responsibility for paying for college, and provides help only where family finances fall short.

You'll find a worksheet for estimating your EFC in chapter 3 (and on this book's companion web site).

Even if you are personally self-sufficient, keep in mind that the government will still consider the income and assets of your parents until you meet criteria set by the federal government for independence.

Family-based resources start with your family's current assets—including savings accounts, investments and special funds devoted to college, such as so-called 529 plans. (For simplicity, we'll use the term "family" inclusive of any number of relatives, from doing it on your own, to students and parents, to spouses, to grandparents, to having your rich great-aunt Agatha help foot the bill.)

These days, the typical family has not saved enough to pay for college, nor has it taken advantage of every savings opportunity. Studies of college savings habits show big gaps between what families have set aside, what they think they need and what they actually need.

Another big consideration will be your family's ability to pay for college out of current income . . . a tall order when the bill runs into tens of thousands of dollars! To help you pay out of pocket, you might need to take a cool-headed look at all of your spending, cutting back on other expenses to make room in the budget for tuition.

MONEY SOURCE #2: FINANCIAL AID

Financial aid is the second source of college money for most families. It's also the most complex, but for a good reason: Many people, institutions, companies and government agencies see the value of higher education and support it, but with different objectives, priorities and programs.

The two broad categories of institutional financial aid (that is, aid from the college you attend) are *need-based*, which is aid awarded because of a family's inability to pay college costs, and *merit-based*, which means aid that is won without regard to the family's financial strength, such as aid awarded based on academic, artistic or athletic talent.

In 2005, institutional need-based grants were awarded to more than 10% of undergraduate students (almost 2 million individuals), with awards averaging $3,330. Tuition and fee waivers, another form of grant, go to 2.1% of students.

Institutional merit-based grants in 2005 were awarded to 7.9% of students (1.5 million), with an average award of $4,269.

Federal Pell Grants—which we'll talk about in chapter 6—are received by 26.8% of undergraduate students (5.1 million), with an average amount of $2,492 ($12.7 billion). State grants are received by 14.7% (2.8 million), with an average grant of $1,956 ($5.5 billion).

Federally guaranteed loans include several types of programs, amounting to about $60 billion a year. More on those programs, which make up the largest source of higher education funding, in chapter 7.

If you're typical, some college money will depend on your family's ability, willingness and wisdom to borrow for your education. While some borrowing is unavoidable for most students, there are better (and much worse) ways to take on debt, especially if you already have a lot. We'll look at those in chapters 7–8.

☑️ **I Wish I Had Known . . .**

"You'll find out early that each school has different criteria for grants, scholarships and other financial aid. If your student has high grades or high SAT scores, she'll have more choices. Also, as you start the process, think long-term. If your student is going to need an advanced degree, you might consider less expensive state schools for undergraduate work with the goal of attending a prestige school for a graduate degree."

—P.M., a student's mother

MONEY SOURCE #3: PRIVATE SCHOLARSHIPS

Scholarships probably inspire more myths and misconceptions than any other topic in college finance, so let's start with some facts: More than 1 million students receive private (not from government or colleges) scholarships each year, and the average amount received is about $2,000. The raw odds of receiving a scholarship—about 1 in 15 students receives a private scholarship—reflect many factors, including a student's grades, extracurricular interests, leadership abilities, other talents and the sheer number of scholarships for which the student applies.

There are rare cases in which a student pays his or her way through school entirely on scholarships, but for most families, scholarships are just one part of the total plan.

Scholarships are the part of the total plan that is more under the control of the student than his or her parents, because scholarships don't represent "free" money at all: A student earns scholarship awards through an application process that evaluates qualifications and hard work.

Contrary to a common misconception, scholarships aren't restricted to highly specialized circumstances. Even if you're not a vegetarian twin who speaks English, French, German and Klingon, you can find scholarships for which you're qualified.

Scholarships are very competitive—there are many applicants for a limited number of awards. There are also a lot of them, but again, the likelihood of paying your entire college bill with private scholarship money is small. (There are "full ride" awards made by individual colleges, however; we'll discuss those in chapter 11).

Scholarships have an effect on the other components of your college financing plan, and families are surprised to learn that outside scholarship money and some resources can reduce the size of need-based financial aid awards . . . but you should still make them part of your plan (see chapters 11–13).

The good news is that money is available in the form of financial aid. More than $142 billion in financial aid was awarded to students in 2004–2005,[5] and millions of students qualified for aid. The simple truth behind the statistics is: If you're willing to work for it, you can get it.

☑ I Wish I Had Known . . .

It really is not that hard to find financial aid if you have the right people helping you through the process.

—J. Kachelski, freshman
University of Wisconsin-Waukesha

WHAT YOU NEED TO KNOW TO GET STARTED

There are a few background facts to understand as you get your practical program of paying for college underway.

First, a typical financial aid package combines aid from several sources. It usually has several components, including reduced tuition pricing, work-study pay, grants and scholarships, and loans. The federal government, for example, has at least nine student aid programs, and you might qualify for several.[6]

Second, the process of paying for college tracks closely with the admissions process. This means that many deadlines occur close to one another, and also that you must begin the process of applying to college before you know how much the institution will cost you

Third, financial aid decisions are based on four factors: The total cost of attending a year at the school; how much your family can pay; how much aid is available; and how much the institution wants you to attend (and vice versa). These factors vary a lot and are interconnected, so your goal is not just "to get the most money" or "to get the lowest out-of-pocket cost" but to get the best outcome—attending the right college at the right price for the right reasons.

Finally, you must learn a few basic terms that will be used over and over during the process. Here they are:

Cost of Attendance (COA): Also known as the student budget, it includes tuition and fees, room and board, allowances for books and supplies, transportation, and personal and incidental expenses.

Expected Family Contribution (EFC): The annual dollar amount that a family is expected to pay toward a student's educational costs. EFC is based on family income (students and parents are accounted separately), net value of assets, the number of children in college and family size.

Financial aid package: The financial aid package is a combination of various forms of student aid (grants, scholarship, loans and employment) offered by a college and other sources to meet a student's financial need.

Free Application for Federal Student Aid (FAFSA): A single, free application form designed by the federal government that most students must complete to apply for most forms of financial aid. It is the basis of awards by the federal and state governments and (often) colleges as well. It is available online at www.fafsa.ed.gov. Hundreds of private colleges use a similar form called the CSS/Financial Aid PROFILE, available online at profileonline.collegeboard .com.[7]

Merit-based aid: Financial aid based on academic, artistic, athletic or other merit-oriented criteria (not financial need).

Need-based aid: Financial aid based on the student/family's financial need, the difference between the cost of attendance and the expected family contribution. This is the gap between total college costs and your ability to pay.

Need analysis: The process used by government and colleges to determine a student's financial need.

Student Aid Report (SAR): A report that summarizes the information included in the FAFSA, states your EFC and must be provided to your school's office of financial aid.

A FAMILY AFFAIR

Most families treat the college selection and financial aid process as a project involving as many members of the family as can participate, so "all hands on deck." It's a big job, and while it is all about the future of the student, parents, spouses and even siblings can become deeply involved in the process.

The financial aid process is stressful: It's the biggest project most students have undertaken to date; their future is at stake; and the task is complicated and unfamiliar. Between locating colleges, gathering information, taking college entrance exams like the SAT and ACT, and understanding of all kinds of financial aid, there's plenty of work to go around. What's more, the big project of choosing a college and arranging to pay for it comes at a time when the relationship between parents and their children ranges from gently evolving to tumultuous.

Accepting the differences in the parent and student points of view is healthy for the process and the family.

Parents might have a positive, protective attitude, such as:
- I'm totally responsible for educating my child and that continues right through college.
- My child doesn't know what I know.
- I have to protect her/him from the "system"—debt, scams and disappointments.
- This is part of the big picture—siblings, retirement, my aging parents, my whole life.

. . . and they might have more negative feelings, such as:
- This kid isn't performing up to his/her potential; then things would be easy.
- This should be the kid's responsibility; it's his/her future.
- I have to do everything.

- If I made (or saved) more money, this wouldn't be so stressful.
- Are we doing this right? Are we missing anything important?

Students might experience similar mixed emotions—positive ones like:

- This is incredibly exciting; I'm designing my future.
- I'm an achiever and have a world of choices in front of me.
- My friends and I are going through this at the same time.

. . . and negative feelings like:

- Just getting into college is stressful; the financial aid process is excruciating.
- My future is on the line; if I make a mistake now, it will affect me for the rest of my life.
- Why can't my parents just pay for it all?
- Why are my parents on my case to do this? Do I have to work with them on this?
- If I were a better student, this would be easy (Ivy League schools would be offering me lots of free money just to attend).
- Why is everybody looking at me?
- This is overwhelming; how can anyone expect me to do all this plus all my senior year courses?

You're moving from a parent-child relationship to an adult-adult relationship, and this takes a lot of work on both sides. Issues as basic as privacy will come up, such as whether a student has a right to know his/her parent's stock holdings. College can be the beginning of the student's transition from a sheltered existence to the real world. They will choose a major field of study (with or without parental approval). Most students get their first credit card in college. It's an opportunity for parents to support their children without dominating the project.

Parents might be confused about their role versus the role of the student—should they make the student do everything? Should they do everything? Should it be a hand-in-hand process? Should they let the student make mistakes? When should they step in to move the process along?

Families that treat the process of paying for college as a team effort are on their way to a good result, because they are putting all their knowledge, talent and resources together toward a goal that everyone wants—the best terms for attending the best college for the student. The program and expertise of this book is meant to help you in that team effort.

Brian Lindeman, Director of Financial Aid at Macalester College, suggests the value of open communication at the beginning: "Have frank conversations early," he says, "so expectations are understood. Every family makes decisions about the value of education, about how much they're willing to sacrifice financially, and it's always better when everyone in the family has the same expectations."

Good expectations start with separating the facts from the falsehoods, so to set the stage for learning to pay for college, let's get the most common myths and misunderstandings out of the way, in chapter 2.

2

Financial Aid Myths

One afternoon just before summer break, Matt met with his guidance counselor, Sally Becker. Sally started the conversation with a review of the college application process, then asked Matt where he wanted to apply.

"I'm just starting to look," said Matt. "I'd like to check out Ohio University, and I'll probably look at Mansfield State too."

"Any interest in smaller colleges?" asked Sally.

"Oberlin's cool but I don't know if I'm good enough to get there on a music scholarship. That's the only way we could afford it."

"Why do you say that?" asked Sally.

"Well, my family is kind of caught in the middle," Matt replied uncertainly. "We don't have enough money to pay for places like Oberlin ourselves, and we aren't poor enough to qualify for lots of help."

Sally asked, "How do you know?"

"I'm not sure," said Matt. "I heard it or read it somewhere."

Sally sketched several notes on a small writing pad. "I hear that from a lot of students," she said, "But it's more a myth than reality."

"Why would people say it, then?" asked Matt.

"The formulas that determine financial aid are complicated, and it's difficult to know how much aid you'll get until after you've applied. Did you know that a more expensive college will give you more financial aid to compensate?"

"No." Matt said. He realized that there was a lot to learn in the next few months, and some doors he'd assumed were closed might be open after all.

"That's often the case, so don't rule out any college in advance based on the sticker price," continued Sally. She concluded, "There are many, many sources of money for college, and the sooner you get to know what they are, the better. . . . Don't worry, when you get past the myths, there's a lot of good news."

• • •

At this early stage, Matt is not only unclear about how to pay for college; he's also confused by the myths, misinformation and "urban legends" about financial aid and scholarships that get passed around. Before you know the facts about a process like paying for college, it's tempting to listen to these myths.

David Levy, Assistant Dean and Director of Financial Aid at the California Institute of Technology (Caltech), says these myths about financial aid are rampant among families who haven't been through the process, and their net effect is usually to discourage students and families from even trying. (David provided some of the most common myths in this chapter.)

More insidiously, some misconceptions are based on resentment (usually of some other class of people who "automatically" get financial aid, but don't "really" deserve it) or the false assertion that there are piles of unclaimed money just waiting to be found (usually this comes in the form of a sales pitch for the person who's going to find the money . . . for a fee).

Do not let any of the following myths prevent you from applying for the student aid for which you qualify.

My family makes too much money to qualify for financial aid.

This myth is a showstopper for many families. In the 2006 *College Gold* survey, 55% of respondents who did not apply for financial aid used this reason. Don't assume that because you're a member of the middle class, you can't get financial aid. Many factors beyond annual income, such as family size, number of children in college, age of the older parent and the market value of your family's net assets are considered. You may also qualify for education tax benefits. The unsubsidized Federal Stafford loan and the Federal PLUS loan are also available without regard to financial need. Even families earning more than $100,000 a year have qualified for need-based grants, depending on their financial circumstances. Unusual circumstances such as unreimbursed medical expenses, providing support to an elderly grandparent, impending job loss and private elementary or secondary school tuition might increase your eligibility.

Financial Aid Myths

We have lots of equity in our home and retirement accounts so we can't get aid.
Federal and state financial aid guidelines do not consider home equity, and most private financial institutions adjust the value of your home relative to your income. Families with home equity have a resource not available to those without home equity, but they cannot be forced to use it. Most retirement funds are not counted as assets in the need analysis formula.[8]

We will get more aid if we don't save for college.
Financial aid calculations are much more heavily weighted toward income than assets (including savings). Money in retirement funds and the net worth of the family's primary residence are ignored, and the first $45,000 to $50,000 in parent assets are sheltered from the need analysis process, depending on the age of the older parent. Any assets above that threshold are assessed using a bracketed system (similar to income tax returns), with a maximum rate of 5.64%. Overall, only about 10% of families have any contribution from parent assets. So there is only a slight penalty for savings (and significant tax advantages), meaning that you always have more options if you have saved for college. Moreover, if you don't save for college, you will have to take out more loans to help pay for your education, and it costs more to borrow than to save.

I'm a straight-A student; I can do it all on scholarships.
Statistically, few students earn enough scholarship money to cover *all* college costs. Make scholarships one part of your overall plan to pay for college. Having good grades does help.

I'm not an A student, so I won't get any aid.
Although there are many academic scholarships, there are also many grant, employment and loan programs that depend on financial need, not grades. Also, there are many private scholarships that look for students who excel in other ways, such as community service, artistic or writing ability, math and/or science skills, or leadership and extracurricular activities.

Scholarships and financial aid are only available for underrepresented minority students.
Although a few scholarships do take race, gender, disability and/or other factors into account, the overwhelming majority of scholarships are awarded without regard to these factors. The most common criteria qualifying a person for aid in-

clude academic, artistic or athletic talent, financial need and community service. Very few financial aid applications even ask questions about race or ethnicity, and the percentage of all aid received by minority students is similar to their representation in the student population.

I'm not an athlete, so I won't get any financial aid.

Only about 1% of college students receive athletic scholarships. Most scholarships are awarded based on other criteria, and the majority of financial aid is awarded based on financial need or academic merit, not physical prowess.

We're not poor, so it is inappropriate for us to apply for financial aid.

College costs have increased enough that more than two-thirds of all families will qualify for some form of financial aid. There is no shame in applying for student financial aid. Your financial aid application will not deprive a needier or more deserving student of the money they need to pay for school.

Loans are not a form of financial aid.

Everybody prefers to get grants and scholarships. But few families can afford to pay out of pocket for college without some help. So, to the extent that education loans provide cash flow assistance, allowing you to spread the cost over a longer period of time, they represent a form of financial aid. Plus, federal education loans have lower interest rates and fees than most other forms of consumer credit, so they help make a college education more affordable. Federal education loans also offer a variety of flexible repayment terms.

For most students, financial aid means loans and a job, so why bother?

More than half of all students receive some grant aid. Besides federal and state grants, there are also institutional grants and private sector scholarships. It is always worth applying for financial aid, since the more financial aid you receive, the more options you'll have. It would be a shame if you got into the school of your choice, but couldn't afford to go because you didn't apply for financial aid. About 85% of undergraduate student aid recipients receive more than just loans and work.

If my parents don't claim me on their income tax returns, I will get more aid.

This has not been the case since 1992, when the criteria for independent student status changed. To be considered independent, you must satisfy the criteria listed in chapter 5. Even if you are independent, this doesn't necessarily mean you will get more aid.

Financial Aid Myths

The big, prestigious colleges will award more financial aid.
Every college makes its own decisions about how much aid to offer, and in what forms. Big colleges have big expenses, and some colleges with relatively small endowments have significant financial aid resources. Working directly with the colleges that interest you is the best way to learn what they can offer.

If you borrow more for other expenses, you'll get more aid.
This is a classic "my neighbor told me . . ." myth. Debt is debt, and unwise borrowing in the hope of gaining more financial aid (especially in the form of loans) makes no sense in terms of a family budget, priorities and peace of mind. The need analysis formulas do not consider most forms of consumer debt as an offsetting factor. So families who borrow more will find it more difficult to pay for college, not less.

I will have to go deeply into debt in order to pay for my college education.
Most students graduate with less cumulative debt for all four years than the cost of a single year of college. A good rule of thumb is to not borrow more than your expected starting salary when you graduate. If you do this, you will be able to afford to repay the debt within ten years of graduation. See chapter 15, "All those other expenses."

We can't afford the high price of college.
Although newspapers and magazines often report the high cost of education at Ivy League schools and there's a lot of hysteria about faster-than-inflation increases in tuition rates, college is still affordable. Most students attend colleges that charge tuition that is less than a quarter of that of the most expensive institutions, and there is financial aid available to help defray college costs. Only the wealthiest of families pay the full cost of college. Moreover, the highest priced institutions tend to provide bigger aid packages, so your net cost will be about the same, regardless of which college you choose to attend.

Student employment during the academic year will hurt grades.
Studies have shown that a modest amount of work-study during college, no more than ten to fifteen hours per week, actually improves grades. See more about work-study in chapter 9.

Last year, millions and billions of dollars in aid went unclaimed.
The only aid that has ever gone unclaimed is aid that can't be claimed. This myth is based on a thirty-year-old estimate that has never been substantiated and

has nothing to do with scholarships. The unclaimed aid myth is based on a 1976–77 academic year study that estimated that $7 billion of employer tuition assistance was potentially available to employees (i.e., if every eligible employee were to go to college), but that only about $300 to $400 million was being used each year. Subtract one from the other and misreport it, and you get the infamous "$6.6 billion in scholarships went unclaimed last year." If you want information about employer tuition assistance, visit your employer's human resources office.

You need to have good grades to win scholarships.
Every scholarship sponsor selects winners based on some criteria, such as academic, artistic or athletic talent, leadership, creativity or community service. Although there are some scholarships that depend on your GPA and some that depend on athletic prowess, you do have to distinguish yourself in some way from the other applicants in order to win a scholarship.

☑ I Wish I Had Known . . .

The more scholarships you apply for, the more likely you will get money, even if your grades are not perfect.

—*Kristina Salinas, sophomore*
South Texas College

There is less aid available each year for needy students.
The total amount of aid has been increasing each year, faster than even tuition inflation. For example, in 2004–2005 total aid increased by 10% compared with the previous year. The ratio of grant aid to total aid has been dropping, in part due to cuts in government funding on a per-student basis, but even so, grant aid increased by 3%. If you need help paying for college, you can get it, and you won't be taking money away from a student with greater financial need.

If you apply for financial aid, the government will take your home.
Nobody is going to require you to sell your home to pay for college. Federal need analysis ignores the net equity in your home. Even at colleges that consider net

home equity, most of the eligibility determination will be based on income, not the net value (the market value minus outstanding mortgages) of your home.

Colleges cut the amount of support during the junior and senior years.
Although some colleges practice front-loading of grants[9], which yields a higher proportion of grants to loans during the first year in college, most do not. Even among the colleges that do, the family's net cost remains about the same throughout the student's college career, assuming that the family's financial circumstances don't change significantly. (The origin of this myth is the typical scenario in which two children overlap in college for a while, and when one child graduates, the amount of aid granted to the other decreases because they are no longer splitting the parent contribution.)

My neighbor's children did not qualify for financial aid, so neither will mine.
The only way to find out whether you will qualify for financial aid is to apply, and the big step—filling out a FAFSA form—is free (see chapter 5). Your neighbor might have significantly different financial circumstances than your own, all appearances to the contrary. Moreover, the rules governing the federal aid programs change every year, so what was true a decade ago or even last year might not be true this year. If you don't apply for aid, you definitely won't get any.

I shouldn't apply for aid this year because I didn't get anything last year (or my brother or sister didn't get anything last year).
Eligibility for financial aid can sometimes change significantly from year to year. If the student had significant savings, but exhausted them on college bills, this can yield a big change in eligibility for financial aid. Similarly, having more than one child in college at the same time can lead to a dramatic increase in eligibility for financial aid. Federal legislation can significantly alter financial aid eligibility from one year to the next.

You should wait until you've filed your tax returns to apply for student aid.
Families should file the FAFSA as soon as possible after January 1, and not wait until their income taxes are done. There are state deadlines as early as mid-February, so it is best to file the FAFSA in January or February. Some schools use the FAFSA to allocate institutional aid, and may have early "priority" deadlines for the school's own funds. It is okay to estimate your income and taxes when fill-

ing out the FAFSA, so long as the figures are close to the real numbers. You will have an opportunity to provide the correct numbers when you receive your Student Aid Report (SAR).

Prenuptial agreements and trust funds are good tools for sheltering money from need analysis.

A prenuptial agreement is an agreement between husband and wife before they are married. It cannot be binding on a third party who was not party to the agreement (e.g., a college or the federal government). In other words, two people can't agree to change the rules set by a college or government. Likewise, voluntary restrictions established by a trust fund, such as restricted access to income or principal, will have no effect.

Applying for financial aid will hurt my chances of admission.

Most colleges practice need-blind admission, which means they decide who they will admit without regard to ability to pay. They then try to meet the full demonstrated financial need of the students they admitted. From a practical perspective, financial aid packages are determined only after the student is admitted, as the financial aid office wants to avoid the work involved in packaging aid for students who will not be admitted.

If I win a scholarship, they will reduce my financial aid package.

This can be true to some extent, but not entirely. Federal rules called "overaward regulations" prevent you from receiving more total financial aid than the cost of education. So if your outside scholarship pushes you over the top, the school will be forced to reduce your need-based aid package. This assumes that the college was able to meet all of your need. Most colleges apply outside scholarships first toward reducing the gap (unmet need), and second toward reducing loans and/or work-study. To the extent that you are substituting a scholarship for loans, you are benefiting, since the scholarships won't need to be repaid and the loan will.

3

Getting Started

EXPECTED FAMILY CONTRIBUTION

"I'm almost done with this Expected Family Contribution worksheet," said Jim. "Do you have the totals on all the schools there?"

"Four of them," said Lynn. "Before any financial aid, a year here in Mansfield—if Matt lives at home—will cost about $6,000; a year at Ohio University down in Athens will cost around $16,000; and up at the high end, Caledonia and Oberlin are both around $40,000 to $43,000." She flipped a page on her legal pad and added with emphasis, "Per year."

Matt slid a catalog into a folder. "Well, I probably can't get into Oberlin, at least not on music," said Matt. "But I really liked Caledonia." He picked up a purple folder. "Even though it's expensive, I mean. I liked Ohio too. They're really different, but I think I'd be happy at either one of those." Matt stacked a green folder on the purple. In front of him lay printouts of web pages from Ohio State in Mansfield.

Lynn passed a red folder to her son. "Well, let's make up a file for Mansfield, Mattie. Nobody's saying you shouldn't apply to Caledonia or even Oberlin if you want to, honey. We just have to find out where we stand."

Jim, finishing his work on a hand calculator, said, "Looks like each of them will expect us to contribute at least $3,000 every year."

• • •

The Gordons are getting organized—an important early step for families entering the financial aid maze.

Families who organize the process of paying for college early save time and hassle later, but it's easy at an early stage to be apprehensive. Are you taking the right steps? Are you making a costly mistake somewhere? Could some action make you eligible for more financial aid? The process is long and has many overlapping, related and interconnected components. Certain pieces interact and have constraints, such as one piece acting as a prerequisite for another.

The key to managing a complicated project like paying for college is to get organized, so that you are doing the right tasks in the right order at the right time. This involves breaking down the long list of tasks into a sequence of steps, estimating the amount of time each step will take, identifying deadlines for each step and getting started.

In the following section, we'll list those tasks in order, and then show how they stretch out over a number of months. The "getting started" part is up to you, whether you're a student-parent team or a single individual.

If you can handle this project without missing deadlines or pulling a lot of all-nighters, you'll be ahead of the game in your college years, when there never seems to be enough time for class work, homework, work-study jobs . . . while still leaving time for extracurricular activities, dating and college life.

TIMETABLE

Part of the complexity of the college admissions and financial aid process is that there are many tasks that need to be done simultaneously. One not only needs to know how long the tasks will take, but when they can start (e.g., FAFSA cannot be filed before January 1) and when they must be complete.

The timelines for applying to college and assembling the pieces of a financial strategy overlap, but are not identical. Even if you've had a longtime savings plan, and don't know if you'll have to find additional money for college, the junior and senior years of high school are ideally when you have to begin putting all the pieces into place.

Many families start looking for financial aid late in the game, after the student has already been admitted to college, and that's a mistake. "The schools do not save money just in case people file late," says Joseph A. Russo, Director of

Student Financial Strategies at the University of Notre Dame. "Every school has its own set of procedures in terms of forms, verification requirements and timing."

As you will see, many of the documents and steps in the process are standardized, so that colleges use the same information in determining financial aid eligibility. This makes it possible to get a lot of the paperwork done early.

Here's an ideal timetable for the process of paying for college, as it moves forward in parallel with the college application process. This book is not designed to cover every aspect of the college admission process, so note that the college admissions notes below (in *italics*) are limited to the major milestones.

If you are not in a position that fits this timeline (it is past the student's junior year, you are not attending college directly after high school or you are already in college or graduate school), use this as a sequence of tasks still minding the deadlines.

JUNIOR YEAR
(Or two years before planning to attend college)

Begin to think about schools that interest you, but don't worry too much about costs. It is too early to worry about that for two reasons: First, success at college depends on finding the school that's right for you, not the least expensive institution. Second, the more expensive schools tend to have more financial aid available, so your net cost could be about the same, even at colleges with a bigger price tag. Your initial choice of a college should not be based on price.

If parents will be selling stocks to pay for the student's college education, they should sell them by the fall of the junior year in high school to avoid having capital gains artificially inflate income. This can have a significant impact on eligibility for need-based financial aid.

The spring of your junior year is a great time to decide on a list of colleges that might be right for you. Talk to your guidance counselor about your options—public, private, vocational, and four-year and two-year institutions.

There are dozens of factors to consider in addition to cost, such as size, location, reputation and available areas of study. You'll find that as you learn more about different colleges and universities, you'll develop a list of places that seem right for you. Online resources, such as FastWeb's college search, can be very helpful in researching and comparing colleges. Again, even though this is a book about paying for college, not choosing a college, we want to emphasize the importance of finding a school that will be worth all that money!

You can visit colleges in the spring, but avoid spring break, when all you'll see is a lot of empty buildings.

You should take the PSAT during your junior year. Besides acting as a dry run for the SAT, it also serves as a qualifying test for the National Merit Scholarship competition.

This is a good time to ask teachers, coaches, employers or other mentors for letters of recommendation. Most have more time in the summer. You should also start searching for scholarships now, if you haven't already. In the 2006 *College Gold* survey, more than half of all college-bound students reported that they did not think about scholarships until it was too late. There are scholarships available for high school juniors and younger students, and some of the scholarships for high school seniors require advance preparation. By searching for scholarships early, you will be able to fulfill any prerequisites. Some scholarships have deadlines in the beginning of the senior year, as early as September or October.

SENIOR YEAR
(Or one year before planning to attend college)

September

Begin college application process. If you haven't visited colleges yet, do it now. The main differences between colleges are found in the students, not the faculty or facilities, so you'll want to visit when classes are in session. More time is spent learning from one's peers than sitting in a classroom. When you schedule a visit, ask for a quick conversation with a financial aid administrator (see chapter 10). Although you won't know where you're going until the admission letter comes (usually in mid-March and early April, unless applying Early Action or Early Decision), it is best to start the financial aid process now. (Also consider meeting with career placement, talking with current students, sitting in on a class, staying overnight in a dorm room, etc.)

We suggest that students and parents split up on a campus visit. They'll cover more ground, and students can get a better feel for how they'll fit in if parents are not lurking over their shoulders for the entire visit. One trick: Parents can go to the cafeteria and offer to buy a random student lunch if he'll tell them everything that's right—and wrong—with the place.

Calculate your Expected Family Contribution (EFC). This will begin to tell you how much money your family may be expected to pay for college if the school is able to provide financial aid to help meet the full demonstrated financial need.

It's not too early to start your search for scholarship money, which is available all year but subject to strict deadlines. Register at www.fastweb.com and ask your school guidance counselor about local scholarships. Research to know what your options and requirements will be when it's time to apply, and begin applying for scholarships *now*.

Prepare a list of your academic and non-academic accomplishments, in which you summarize your notable achievements. You will find it handy when you are completing your college admissions and scholarship application forms. You can also provide a copy to the people who are writing letters of recommendation for you. They can use it as a source of additional material when they are writing their letters. Here are examples of what you should include:

- Grade point average.
- Brief descriptions of exceptional class projects, such as lab reports, writing assignments or research papers. Have the full projects available if, for example, a scholarship provider wants them.
- Record or describe a performance you gave, bring a portfolio of your art or show a newspaper clipping describing a great athletic achievement.
- Have you won any awards, contests or competitions? For example, this list might include math meets, science fairs and Olympiads, and poetry contests. How did you rank in your school, state, region and nationally? What were your scores and percentile performance? Did you set any records?
- Write a description of your role in community, church, extracurricular, paid and volunteer work or charitable projects you've completed. Later, you'll want to write a full essay about one or more of these experiences, so it's good to start thinking about them now.

This is also the month to go carefully through the exercises in this chapter and use the online calculators. The more you know about your financial situation, the better your chances of putting together a financial plan that works. In paying for college, you can never have too much information.

For college admissions, there's usually an ACT test date in late September. The SAT and ACT are also offered in October, November, December and January. Often the December test is the last one that can be used for regular admission, but some schools will accept the January test results as a supplement. It is generally a good idea to take the September or October test, to allow you time to retake the test in November or December if you aren't satisfied with your scores. Some counselors advise taking the SAT/ACT sometime during the spring semester of your junior year. Unless your score was really bad, we recommend this only if you believe you can improve your score by at least 100 points. September/ October is also a good time to ask teachers, coaches and employers for letters of recommendation for college admissions and scholarships. Give your teachers plenty of advance notice, since it takes time to write a good letter of recommendation.

October

By now, you should be applying for scholarships. You can apply for scholarships throughout your senior year (and beyond). The more you earn now, the less you will probably have to borrow later.

At this point, you should have narrowed down your college choices, so get the combined college admission and financial processes organized.

- Create a filing system for your college admissions and financial aid work.
- It is helpful to keep a file folder for each scholarship to which you are applying. Try using color coding to organize the folders, with a different color for each deadline month. Attach a checklist of application requirements and deadlines to the front of the folder.
- Online applications can save time, so check with your application materials to see if the application can be completed online.
- Ask parent and/or student employer(s) about employer tuition assistance programs. Many employers have programs to help pay for college.

- Keep a central calendar of all the dates for applications, financial aid and scholarships. (FastWeb has an online calendar that may be useful.)

Review the deadlines at least once a week, to make sure you are aware of any that are approaching. If you have questions, call the college financial aid office.

November

Download the FAFSA on the Web Pre-Application Worksheet at www.fafsa.ed.gov or get a copy from your guidance counselor, and fill out as much as possible now in order to save time in January when the schedule gets tighter. (You'll have to wait until January to enter some financial information, such as taxable income.) If you complete the FAFSA online, don't forget to sign it electronically with a PIN or to print, sign and mail the signature sheet.

Some private colleges require financial aid applicants to submit the CSS/Financial Aid PROFILE in addition to the FAFSA. If your colleges use the CSS/Financial Aid PROFILE, you can complete it online at profileonline.col legeboard.com—do not use the "www." prefix.

Try to complete college admissions applications by the end of the month.

December

If you receive an early-admissions acceptance letter this month, take advantage of the extra time to get your financial house in order and get your financial aid information together early, (see "Early Admission" on p. 33).[10]

Before the winter school break begins, go through all your college files to confirm that you are on schedule for the many college admissions application deadlines.

Review individual college and scholarship files for deadlines, from early scholarship application dates to half-finished essays. Finish tasks that can't wait until the new year.

Also, take a deep breath during the holiday season, because the next three months are going to be very busy!

January

File the FAFSA form as soon as possible after January 1. Estimate required tax information using the last pay stubs of the year if you do not yet have your W-2 and 1099 forms. Some states require you to submit the FAFSA as early as mid-February or March to qualify for state aid. Also, if you submit the forms early, you'll be helping your colleges' financial aid administrators beat the rush and possibly get a first shot at the aid they have available. Keep photocopies of the completed forms. Do the same for the CSS/Financial Aid PROFILE if your schools require it.

Complete the process for applying for financial aid at each college (see chapters 5–10).

Many scholarship deadlines occur in late winter and early spring, so keep on top of them. (See chapters 11–13).

☑ I Wish I Had Known . . .

I am not wishing; I am doing. I am going to build a time machine after completing an advanced degree in quantum physics. At that point I will use the time machine to travel into the past in order to tell my past self to file the FAFSA earlier.

—*anonymous college student*

February

About four weeks after completing the FAFSA (sooner if you filed electronically), you should receive a Student Aid Report (SAR) from the U.S. Department of Education. The SAR summarizes the information you submitted on the FAFSA and presents the Expected Family Contribution (EFC). If you do not receive the SAR within three weeks, call the federal processor at 1-800-4-FED-AID (1-800-4-333-243) or 1-319-337-5665. Review the SAR carefully for errors of fact. For example, if your original income estimates were inaccurate, you can correct them now (online using your PIN). If necessary, make any corrections on Part 2 of the SAR and return it promptly to the address listed on the SAR. You will then receive a new SAR. If you provided an e-mail address on your FAFSA, your SAR may be delivered to that address.[11]

If there is something even slightly unusual about your family's financial circumstances, ask your colleges' financial aid offices for a "professional judgment" review of your application (see chapter 15). This is sometimes called a "special circumstances" review. Unusual circumstances include anything that distinguishes your family's finances from those of typical families, or any change in your finances from the tax year that just ended to the upcoming academic year. This can include job loss, unusually high medical expenses, private elementary and secondary school tuition, and one-time events that artificially inflated your income. Anything out of the ordinary that is not reflective of your ability to pay is worth mentioning. Be prepared to provide third-party documentation of the unusual circumstances and their financial impact.

March/April

Admissions letters should start arriving, followed by financial aid award letters. The award letter describes the types and amounts of financial aid for which you qualify, the cost of attendance and your expected family contribution. If your EFC appears to be more than you can afford, talk to the financial aid administrators at your college(s) about additional options.

May 1 is the National Candidate Reply Date, the date most colleges require students to make a decision on admissions and financial aid. Wait until you have heard from all the schools before making a decision.

When you notify the college of your choice that you will be attending, you must also accept the financial aid award package by signing it and sending it in with a copy of your SAR.[12] You do not have to accept every part of the aid package (see chapter 15). Keep a photocopy for your records. The school may also require a nonrefundable deposit to confirm that you will attend.

Study this simple chart of an "ideal" junior and senior year. It shows when tasks begin and end, and also shows which tasks are dependent on each other, For example, you cannot complete the FAFSA form until after January 1 of your senior year, when you know the exact amount of your previous year's income. If you are not currently enrolled in high school, you can use this to estimate your time frame as well.

Junior and Senior Year Planner

Item	J-Jul	J-Aug	J-Sep	J-Oct	J-Nov	J-Dec	J-Jan	J-Feb	J-Mar	J-Apr	J-May	J-Jun	S-Jul	S-Aug	S-Sep	S-Oct	S-Nov	S-Dec	S-Jan	S-Feb	S-Mar	S-Apr	S-May	S-Jun
Capital Gains	█	█	█	█	█	█																		
PSAT				█																				
Research Colleges							█	█	█	█	█	█	█	█	█	█								
Guidance Counselor								█	█	█					█	█	█							
Scholarship Search		█	█	█	█	█	█	█	█	█	█	█	█	█	█	█	█	█	█	█	█	█	█	█
Summer Job, Scholarship Credentials												█	█											
Admissions Applications																Early	Regular	Rolling						
Calculate EFC															█	█								
Scholarship Applications															█	█	█	█	█	█	█	█	█	█
ACT/SAT								█	█	█	█				█	█	█							
Visit Colleges												█	█	█	█									
Ask at Work about Employer Tuition Assistance																█								
FAFSA, CSS Financial Aid PROFILE																			█	█				
College Financial Aid Applications																			█	█				
Receive SAR																				█				
Ask for Professional Judgment if Unusual Circumstances																				█	█	█	█	█
College Admissions Notifications & Decisions																			█		█	█	█	█
Research Student Loans and Providers																				█	█	█	█	
College Bills Arrive																								█

BOOK TO WEB

You can download a color version of this junior and senior year planner at www.collegegold.com. Print it out and put it on your refrigerator!

CODE: 1002

If you are already in school or are starting later in the junior year, take a look at the whole chart and pick up where you can. Some items will not be applicable (such as PSAT testing). Others are tasks to revisit every year, such as applying for scholarships and financial aid.

EARLY ADMISSION

Do early admission decisions have an impact on financial aid? A common worry with regard to early decision (as opposed to early action) is that since the college knows they have you, they can offer less. Although surveys show this worry is unfounded, we generally do not recommend applying early decision because the commitment limits your choices. Things change, even in the short amount of time between the fall and spring semesters. Better to leave your options open.

The "apply early decision to save money" argument is pretty weak. If saving money is a concern, one should apply early admission (no commitment) to a college where one is pretty certain one can get in early, thereby eliminating the need to apply to safety schools.

We also recommend including a *financial aid safety school* in the mix. This is a school which will not only admit you, but where you are sure you could afford to attend even if you get no financial aid.

DON'T MISS ANY OPPORTUNITIES

Are you restricting the colleges you are considering to those you think you can afford? Don't be misled by that big cost of attendance number. When was the last time you paid list price for anything? College pricing is unique in that tuition rates are discounted according to ability to pay. When you apply for financial aid, colleges use the Expected Family Contribution (EFC) as a measure of your family's ability to pay. They offer financial aid to help bridge the gap between the cost of attendance and ability to pay. This means that a college with a big ticket price may be just as affordable as a low-cost community college. Sometimes the more expensive schools will offer an even better mix of grants and loans than the lowest cost colleges.

Guidance counselors advise students to ignore the price of a college when deciding where to apply. In many cases a college that wants a student will find ways to make attendance possible. If you are organized and prepared to work with financial aid administrators, scholarship providers, guidance counselors and others, you'll stand a better chance of affording the best school for you, regardless of the initial price tag.

Colleges differ in hundreds of ways, many of which are relevant to both admission and financial aid. They differ in the kind of student body they seek to admit—areas of study, geographic differences, academic and athletic excellence, personal circumstances and on and on. They differ in the amount of money they can spend supporting students. They differ in their relationships to scholarship providers.

Most of these factors are relevant to whether you can get into a certain school and whether you can afford to attend, and it's nearly impossible to know all these factors early in the process.

Lori Johnston, a guidance counselor at Hastings High School in Hastings, MI, notes, "Most of the time the kids see the dollar sign and think that's the first factor they should consider. It definitely has to be one of the factors, but don't try to make your decision before you've even looked at your options . . . give yourself the opportunity to have all the options laid out."

STAY ORGANIZED

"Part of the challenge in planning the financial aid process is that each college has its own checklist, its own process, its own forms," says Daniel Barkowitz, Director of Financial Aid at MIT. "Families don't simply navigate a single process; if they're applying to eight different colleges, they navigate eight somewhat different processes."

There are a lot of moving parts, so you need some basic organization to manage the process. Take the following steps before your senior year.

- Create a file for each college that interests you, and label them with the name of the college. Expandable folders work great because you can also keep college catalogs and notes in them. Some find it helpful to use different colors for different colleges, so for example, a red file might mean the University of Arizona and a blue file might mean Notre Dame.
- If you want to be very organized, keep two files for each college, one labeled "Admission" and one labeled "Financial Aid."
- Also prepare a file folder for each private scholarship application. (See chapters 11–13.)

- On the cover of each folder, write a checklist of relevant deadlines, including "due date" and "sent date" spaces for the following:
  - Date the FAFSA and/or CSS/Financial Aid PROFILE information is due. (The CSS/Financial Aid PROFILE is an electronic form used by several hundred private colleges and scholarship programs.)
  - Admissions application deadline.
  - Financial aid application deadline.
  - Deadlines of college-based scholarships you've identified.
  - Deadlines for supporting documentation, such as letters of recommendation.
  - Date the folder was complete. If you sent the application by certified mail, return receipt requested, this should be the return receipt postcard date.
- Create the following files, which contain copies of materials you will use more than once, or documents you might need for future reference:
  - FAFSA (see chapter 5).
  - Student Aid Report (SAR) (when you receive it several weeks after filing the FAFSA).
  - CSS/Financial Aid PROFILE copies, if applicable.
  - Copies of tax forms: W-2, 1099, 1040.
  - Scholarship information (this is a general file; when you decide to apply, create a separate file for each, even if it only holds a copy of your essay).

Barkowitz suggests you keep copies of all the information you send to the college, so that when the college comes back later and says, "When did you mail this or what did you mean by the answer to this question?" you have all the information handy for them at your fingertips, and can resend a missing document if necessary. This might seem like a lot of record keeping, but it will save time, and maybe your financial aid prospects, if some document goes missing.

Some families are comfortable organizing this project on a personal computer or PDA. If you prefer that method, here are three tips: Make paper file folders as well, if only to store materials like catalogs, forms and handwritten notes; label the electronic and paper filing systems identically . . . and back up your computer files!

ESTIMATE THE COST OF COLLEGE

Here comes the part where the numbers get scary—but as they say, DON'T PANIC! You are going to calculate the total cost of one year of college, including as many costs as possible.[13] The worksheet below will result in a number that might seem completely unaffordable, but there's a good reason to start with a conservative number: You can find both savings and financing options for every item on the list. Because different college choices will result in different costs, create a separate worksheet for each.

This worksheet is meant to make the averages shown in the chapter 1 table (page 6) more concrete for your situation.

This estimate covers the first year, however in order to estimate total cost of two or four years of college, recalculate increasing tuition by 8% over the previous year. For line 2, multiply the yearly increase in room and board of 6%. For lines 3–5, multiply each line by an inflation factor of 4% per year.

Note that if line 5 includes the cost of a personal computer, that expense should be excluded from the figures for subsequent years, as most colleges allow an adjustment to cost of attendance for the cost of a personal computer only once every four years. (Most schools will allow a one-time adjustment to their Cost of Attendance [COA] for the purchase of a personal computer. They typically limit the total cost to $1,500 to $3,000. The adjustment will be the actual cost; they'll want to see the invoice. Also, the increase in COA will be restricted toward increasing loan eligibility, not grant eligibility.)

ONE YEAR OF COLLEGE

Line 1: Tuition and fees _____

Enter the full tuition price for the year in which you will matriculate. Over the past two decades, college tuition costs have increased by about twice the inflation rate, or an average of 6% to 8% a year. If you are calculating this before tuition is set for the matriculation year, increase today's tuition by 8% per year until the year you plan to attend.

Line 2: Living expenses _____

Enter the living expenses at the institution you'll attend, especially if you intend to live off-campus. This should be a sum of room and board, rent, gas/electric, land and/or cell phone, Internet connection, eating out, groceries, laundry, etc. If you will be living at home, estimate additional living expenses such as clothing and on-campus dining. If you will live on campus, estimate other expenses you will incur, such as phone, clothing, and medical or dental expenses. Room and board expenses tend to increase by 5% to 6% per year. If you will be staying on campus during the summer vacation, there will be additional costs, since the room and board figures are just for the academic year.

Line 3: Books and supplies _____

Enter an estimated cost of textbooks and major supplies, as well as a smaller amount for those things that tend to add up, like notebooks and paper. Textbooks are expensive. You can save on textbook prices by buying used textbooks from the campus bookstore or online.

Line 4: Transportation _____

If your target colleges are 2,000 miles from home, you're going to incur some travel expenses. If you are living at home, you will incur some commuting costs. Estimate them as completely as possible. (Are you coming home for the holidays? Will it be hard to find a cheap flight?) Most students make two trips home a year: once for the winter holidays and once for the summer. Some students also travel for Thanksgiving and many for Spring Break.

Line 5: Miscellaneous _____

A key to good budgeting is to list every kind of outlay, so use this category for one-time expenses like the purchase of a personal computer or laptop, and also all the small ways you will spend your personal "allowance," from pet food to MP3s and DVDs to an occasional night out with friends. (You are going to have some fun, aren't you?) Add an extra 10% to this figure for unanticipated expenses.

Add all five lines here: _____ .

This is a conservative estimate of the total cost of a year of college.

BOOK TO WEB

You can find an electronic version of this worksheet at www.collegegold.com.

CODE: 1004

Here's an example for a four-year private college, based on tuition of $20,000 with a tuition inflation rate of 8%, living expenses of $8,000 increasing at 6% per year, and additional expenses totaling $2,000 with an inflation rate of 4%:

1st year: $20,000 tuition + $8,000 living + $2,000 other = $30,000
2nd year: $21,600 tuition + $8,480 living + $2,080 other = $32,160
3rd year: $23,328 tuition + $8,989 living + $2,163 other = $34,480
4th year: $25,194 tuition + $9,528 living + $2,250 other = $36,972
TOTAL for four years: $133,612

(This example shows the importance of including inflationary increases. If you just multiplied the first year by 4, you'd come up $13,612 short!)

Reminder: You will pay as you go, usually with some combination of savings, current income and loans, so you don't need to have this much money available when you first arrive on campus.

ESTIMATE YOUR EFC

As mentioned in chapter 1, the Expected Family Contribution (EFC) is the amount of money that your family is expected to be able to contribute to the student's education. The amount is determined by the Federal Need Analysis Methodology formula legislated by Congress, and its purpose is to establish a basis for allocating the government money available in loans, employment opportunities and grants. It is not a perfectly accurate reflection of a family's ability to pay, since it ignores many real costs, such as credit card debt and auto loans. It is at best a rationing system. The EFC includes the parent contribution and the student contribution, and depends on the student's dependency status, family size, number of children in college, taxed and untaxed income and assets. The difference between the Cost of Attendance (COA) and the EFC is the student's financial need, and is used in determining the student's eligibility for need-based financial aid.[14]

RULE OF THUMB

In the most basic terms, the Cost of Attendance minus Expected Family Contribution equals your financial need.

Financial Need = COA – EFC

The following worksheet will help you estimate your EFC. It is a simplified formula, so your official number derived from the FAFSA form will be somewhat different, but for planning purposes, this will show roughly how much you will be required to contribute before any financial aid awards are added to the picture.

Don't be intimidated by the formula. Even with the questions and a little math, it's a lot less complicated than typical income tax forms!

The worksheets appear on pages 40 and 41, and are available online at www.collegegold.com.

TUITION FREEZE

A handful of schools have cut or frozen their tuition rates instead of increasing them. The resulting publicity generates increases in enrollment which can compensate for the lost tuition revenue. Such cuts are usually accompanied by cuts in financial aid. There are also colleges that lock in a class's tuition rate for all four years, but do increase rates for each successive incoming class.

Some colleges offer financing plans that lock in a tuition rate for the four years a student attends college, even though the plan spreads tuition payments out over ten years. In general, tuition freezes are more common among community colleges and public colleges than among private four-year colleges.

You'll find more about various forms of tuition freezes at www. collegegold.com.

EFC ESTIMATION WORKSHEET: DEPENDENT STUDENTS

This worksheet contains a simplification of the Federal Need Analysis Methodology. The Expected Family Contribution (EFC) figures it calculates are estimates and may be significantly different than the actual figures. For your actual EFC, use FinAid's EFC calculator at www.finaid.org/calculators.

PARENT INFORMATION	
A. Age of Older Parent	
B. Number in Family	
C. Number of Children in College	
D. Parent Income	
E. Parent Assets	

STUDENT INFORMATION	
F. Student Income	
G. Student Assets	

Do not count retirement funds, life insurance, and the family's primary residence as assets.

If Parent Income (D) ≤ $20,000 then set EFC to 0 and stop.
If Parent Income (D) < $50,000, then set all asset figures to $0 and continue.

ALLOWANCES AGAINST PARENT INCOME	
Parent FICA (IRS Forms W2, 1099)	
Parent Federal Income Tax (Last line of Tax & Credits in IRS Form 1040)	+
Calculate State Income Tax Allowance as 6% of Line D (above)	+
Calculate Parent Income Protection Allowance as $10,000 + Line B × $3,460 – Line C × $2,460	+
Calculate Employment Expense Allowance as 35% of income in Line D or $3,100, whichever is less	+
1. TOTAL ALLOWANCES	=

ALLOWANCES AGAINST STUDENT INCOME	
Student FICA (IRS Forms W2, 1099)	
Student Federal Income Tax (Last line of Tax & Credits IRS Form 1040)	+
Calculate State Income Tax Allowance as 3% of Line F (above)	+
Income Protection Allowance. $2,550 in 2006-07 or $3,000 in 2007-08	+
6. TOTAL ALLOWANCES	=

AVAILABLE STUDENT INCOME	
Total Student Income (Line F)	
Total Allowances (Line 6)	-
7. AVAILABLE INCOME	=

AVAILABLE PARENT INCOME	
Total Parent Income (Line D)	
Total Allowances (Line 1)	-
2. AVAILABLE INCOME	=

STUDENT CONTRIBUTION FROM ASSETS	
Total Student Assets (Line G)	
Reduction for Business/Farm Assets (50% of total Business/Farm Assets or $250,000, whichever is less)	-
8. Adjusted Net Worth	=
Asset Conversion Rate Multiply by 35% in 2006-07 Multiply by 20% in 2007-08	X
9. STUDENT CONTRIBUTION FROM ASSETS	=

PARENT CONTRIBUTION FROM ASSETS	
Total Parent Assets (Line E)	
Reduction for Business/Farm Assets (50% of total Business/Farm Assets or $250,000, whichever is less)	-
Asset Protection Allowance $1,732 × (Line A – 23) If unmarried, divided result by 2.3	-
3. Discretionary Net Worth	=
Asset Conversion Rate	X 12%
4. PARENT CONTRIBUTION FROM ASSETS	=

STUDENT CONTRIBUTION FROM INCOME	
Student Available Income (Line 7)	
Income Conversion Rate	X 50%
10. STUDENT CONTRIBUTION FROM INCOME	=

PARENT CONTRIBUTION	
Parent Contribution from Assets (Line 4)	
Available Parent Income (Line 2)	+
Adjusted Available Income (AAI)	=
Contribution from AAI 32% of the AAI amount ≤ $26,000 and 47% of the amount > $26,000	
Divide by the Number of Children in College (Line C)	÷
5. PARENT CONTRIBUTION	=

STUDENT CONTRIBUTION	
Student Contribution from Assets (Line 9)	
Student Contribution from Income (Line 10)	+
11. STUDENT CONTRIBUTION	=

EXPECTED FAMILY CONTRIBUTION (EFC)	
Parent Contribution (Line 5)	
Student Contribution (Line 11)	+
12. ESTIMATED EFC	=

Download this worksheet at www.collegegold.com, CODE: 1028

EFC ESTIMATION WORKSHEET: INDEPENDENT STUDENTS

This worksheet contains a simplification of the Federal Need Analysis Methodology. The Expected Family Contribution (EFC) figures it calculates are estimates and may be significantly different than the actual figures. For your actual EFC, use FinAid's EFC calculator at www.finaid.org/calculators.

STUDENT INFORMATION	
A. Age of Older Student/Spouse	
B. Number in Family	
C. Number in College	
D. Student & Spouse Income	
E. Student & Spouse Assets	

Do not count retirement funds, life insurance, and the family's primary residence as assets.

If Income (D) ≤ $20,000 then set EFC to 0 and stop.
If Income (D) < $50,000, then set all asset figures to $0 and continue.

ALLOWANCES AGAINST INCOME	
FICA (IRS Forms W2, 1099)	
Federal Income Tax (Last line of Tax & Credits in IRS Form 1040)	+
Calculate State Income Tax Allowance as 3% of Line D (above)	+
Income Protection Allowance *If no dependents other than spouse:* If unmarried/separated or spouse is enrolled ≥ half time, add $5,790 in 2006-07 or $6,050 in 2007-08 If spouse is enrolled < half time add $9,260 in 2006-07 or $9,700 in 2007-08 *If dependents other than spouse:* $10,000 + Line B × $3,460 – Line C × $2,460 in 2006-07 or $10,000 + Line B × $3,670 – Line C × $2,610 in 2007-08	+
Calculate Employment Expense Allowance as 35% of income in Line D or $3,100 (2006-07) or $3,200 (2007-08), whichever is less	+
1. TOTAL ALLOWANCES	=

AVAILABLE INCOME	
Total Income (Line D)	
Total Allowances (Line 1)	-
2. AVAILABLE INCOME	=

CONTRIBUTION FROM INCOME	
Available Income (Line 2)	
Income Conversion Rate *If no dependents other than spouse:* Multiply by 50% *If dependents other than spouse:* No change	X
3. CONTRIBUTION FROM INCOME	=

CONTRIBUTION FROM ASSETS	
Total Student Assets (Line E)	
Reduction for Business/Farm Assets (50% of total Business/Farm Assets or $250,000, whichever is less)	-
4. Adjusted Net Worth	=
Asset Protection Allowance $1,732 × (Line A – 23) If unmarried, divide result by 2.3	-
5. Discretionary Net Worth	=
Asset Conversion Rate *If no dependents other than spouse:* Multiply by 35% in 2006-07 Multiply by 20% in 2007-08 *If dependents other than spouse:* Multiply by 12% in 2006-07 Multiply by 7% in 2007-08	X
6. CONTRIBUTION FROM ASSETS	=

EXPECTED FAMILY CONTRIBUTION (EFC)	
Contribution from Assets (Line 6)	
Contribution from Income (Line 3)	+
Adjusted Available Income (AAI)	=
Contribution from AAI *If no dependents other than spouse:* 100% of the AAI amount *If dependents other than spouse:* 32% of the AAI amount ≤ $26,000 and 47% of the amount > $26,000	
Divide by the Number in College (Line C)	÷
8. ESTIMATED EFC	=

Download this worksheet at www.collegegold.com, CODE: 1030

A WORD ABOUT SAVINGS

If you had the foresight and means to save all the money you'll need for college during the last eighteen years, you're probably not reading this book. For the rest of you, we'll assume that your long-term savings are not enough, and so this section will discuss how to think about the role savings will play in your overall plan.

Savings are assets, and that's why they're counted in the EFC above. Savings are money in the bank, or relatively available assets like stocks, bonds, mutual funds and employer-based savings or investment assets. The money you and your family have saved for college does affect the amount of money you might receive in the form of financial aid, but only slightly, and it's almost always better from a financial perspective to have as much money as possible in the form of these assets when the time comes to pay for college. Even with the slight reduction in financial aid eligibility due to savings and the low interest rates on education loans, it is still less expensive to save for college than to borrow (see appendix).

Look at how savings are treated in the EFC worksheets above. Note how savings in the parents' names have a much lower impact on the EFC than savings in the student's name (see chapter 14).

How much you save, invest and spend over a lifetime is really a reflection of how well you manage money. For some families, education is the highest priority; for others, it takes its place beside additional important expenses. We'll talk about these family decisions in the next chapter.

You need to analyze where you are today and where you will be during the school years, using real numbers. Get the help of a good personal financial advisor if your money affairs are complicated or pose difficult choices.

Whether you have no savings at all, or substantial money set aside for college, you'll have to decide what priority paying for college takes among the many financial obligations unique to your family. That's what the next chapter is all about.

BOOK TO WEB

You can find several helpful savings calculators at www.collegegold.com.

CODE: 1018

4

Family Matters

"Our college savings alone will just barely cover tuition if you go to school right here in Mansfield," Jim said. "That means if you go anywhere else, we're going to need some financial aid, including loans, to make college afford-able."

"I understand that," said Matt, pouring dressing on his salad. He held the bottle up toward Sarah, who nodded and took the bottle. "So, what do we have to give up if I go somewhere more expensive?" he asked.

Lynn replied, "We don't have to replace the old car right away, and we can live a few more summers without a covered porch. . . ."

"Hey, that was going to be my project with Dad!" interjected Sarah. "We're going to do it ourselves."

"The materials alone will cost five thousand dollars," said Jim, adding, "but that's just one of the choices. We could also cut back on our winter vacation or maybe one of us can pick up some extra work.

"That's just this year, though," he continued. "There's also paying for a loan, and that doesn't stop when you graduate college. It won't be just Mom and me, either; you both can help a lot too."

Sarah smirked at Matt, who responded, "He means both of us. Your turn's coming soon." He stood and put his dishes in the dishwasher.

"We're in this together, kids, all of us," said Lynn. "And we're going to find a way to do it together. Are you finished?" she asked Matt.

"Yes."

"What do you say?"

"May I please be excused?" said Matt.

"No," said Lynn pleasantly. "We'd like you and Sarah to sit with us for the next half hour. It's time you learned some details about the family finances." To Sarah's apprehensive expression she added, "It's nothing to worry about, hon. Dad and I just figured it was time for everyone to know the facts."

• • •

Families should expect to pay at least half to two-thirds of their children's college costs through a combination of savings, current income, work-study and loans. Gift aid from the government, the colleges and universities, and private scholarships usually accounts for about a third of total college costs.[15]

Barbara Fritze, Vice President for Enrollment and Educational Services at Gettysburg College, advises, "The whole financing discussion can begin early in a high school career. Talk about affordability and financing right up front. Ideally, I see it as a partnership, a family decision, in which Mom and Dad and students start asking those questions earlier than ever before."

High school students, making much less money than their parents, might think they have little impact on college finance. Actually, student performance during high school makes a big difference when it comes to earning scholarships and financial aid, and students can manage large portions of the money project, even if their income is slight.

Rachael Massell, a student at Duke University who contributed by winning a number of scholarships recalls striking the right balance:

> My parents were always encouraging and supportive, rather than pushing me. When you realize that it's either going to be your parents paying $40,000 a year or you earning it in some way or paying for it in the future . . . you realize that there's a big difference between those three scenarios. If my family didn't have to go into debt to pay for college, that would be ideal.

In the 2006 *College Gold* survey, the most common helpers cited by students were parents, guidance counselors and college financial aid administrators.

You'll do better working together. Even if the conversation Barbara Fritze described is difficult—and every family has to find its own level of comfort—it can be highly beneficial. It is one more step toward maturity for students.

THE PARENT SIDE: SAVING, SPENDING, MAKING CHOICES

The investment a parent makes in a college education is best decided in the context of the family priorities. If college were the only thing that mattered, then there would be fewer choices to make; every family member could focus on that single goal. It's rarely that simple. There are other opportunities, obligations and expenditures to consider. What are all the financial goals of your family?

The purpose of this chapter is to help parents relate college financial choices to your overall family goals. We can advocate for the importance of a college education, but ultimately each family makes choices based on their circumstances, their values, their relationships and their dreams.

First, consider how many family members are going to college, and when they'll attend. Families with more than one child have to think about allocating available money among each student who will attend college (including a growing population of adults going to school for career reasons). Even though parents would like to treat each child equally from a financial point of view, children's abilities and needs call for different strategies. One child might have much better grades than her sibling, or be considering military service, or be more interested in a two-year public institution, while her sibling might be determined to graduate from an Ivy League college or earn a professional degree. Two siblings four years apart in age might strain a family's ability to pay more than twins (many of these factors are considered in the EFC calculation, described in chapter 3). Children who will be attending college later will have greater costs than children who matriculate sooner. Having multiple students in the family means planning how available money will be spent over a longer period of time than one student's two- or four-year college career.

If there's a shortfall, then the family will have to decide how to meet that shortfall. It might involve increasing borrowing or savings or decreasing non-education expenditures. Or it might involve trying to reduce net college costs below the EFC figure, such as choosing a college where total college costs will be less than the EFC.

There's often a feast-famine nature to college education costs in which things become tougher during the years children are actually enrolled in college. The goal, of course, is to try to smooth things out by saving more sooner and using loans to amortize over future income, so that a relatively constant portion of annual income is used, over an extended period, to cover college costs.

Next, decide how much of your family's assets and income you are willing to invest. Assets such as savings, investments, ownership of a business, equity in a house or other property all might contribute to college. To some extent the portion of your assets used will be dictated by the realities of college costs. If you haven't saved enough, you'll either have to make up the difference in loans or spend down your assets.

Parents should try to save at least *one-third* to *one-half* the projected costs of their child's college education. Ideally the savings plan—in the *parents'* name, not the student's—should be established when the child is born, but it is never too late to start saving. (To reach $35,000, you would need to contribute $25.12 per week for 17 years to an account that earns 5% interest. To reach $35,000 in 4 years at 5% would require $151.94 per week—more than six times as much! Part of the difference is due to interest compounding. When you save over a 17-year period, 36.6% of the savings goal comes from interest, while only 9.7% of the goal comes from interest when the savings horizon is reduced to only 4 years.)

BOOK TO WEB

You can project the total amount your current savings plan
will make available for college at www.collegegold.com.

CODE: 1032

After you assess how much savings will be available for each student, consider your ability to take on new debt. As a rule of thumb, banks will allow families to bear loan payments no higher than 37% of household income, so if you are already near that threshold, you will have to be realistic about the amount of family income that can be devoted to servicing education loans.[16] We recommend that, if possible, your educational loan payments represent no more than 10% to 15% of your income. Government loans made directly to students might exceed these limits, but they offer alternate repayment plans that can reduce the size of the monthly payments as much as 50% by extending the term of the loan; we'll revisit and expand on these rules when discussing loans in chapter 7, so for now use them as guidelines as you examine your budget.

BOOK TO WEB

You can calculate your ability to take on new debt using the
Parent Debt Calculator at www.collegegold.com.

CODE: 1020

There are a number of asset management techniques that maximize your eligibility for most forms of financial aid. Which ones you use will depend on your family's financial makeup, as you will see throughout this book.

Now in your budget considerations, go over to the expense side and consider where you'll spend your money around the time your children are in college. Will you buy a car, or invest in a business or pay major medical bills? Will you continue long-term investments, such as contributions to a retirement plan? (Most people's expenses are focused on housing, food, transportation, retirement and health care. When all the non-discretionary expenses are tabulated, most families have only about 10% flexibility in their budgets.)

Often, parents find money for college by cutting back other expenses. You might, for example, delay replacing an old car, thus freeing up $300 to $500 per month in car payments to help pay for college. On the other hand, you might need a new truck for a business that will help generate more than $500 per month in income. Another fast source of funds involves scaling back or eliminating the traditional family vacation. Other potential targets for budget cutting include eating out at restaurants, lawn and cleaning services, charitable contributions and entertainment spending (e.g., TV, movies and spectator events). Refinancing your mortgage and paying off credit card debt can help eliminate high-interest payments. You can also increase the deductible on your insurance policies and install deadbolt locks and fire alarms to reduce your insurance costs.

Savings and investments, while not expenses in the strictest sense, pose additional choices. For example, suppose you've been setting aside money in a retirement plan for a long time. Will you suspend those contributions and direct the money instead to college? It would be a bad idea, because you will lose a good tax break and grow your retirement fund more slowly, and parents in their forties have less time to save for retirement than students in their twenties have to pay back college loans.

What about private school, tutoring, test preparation, special education, athletic equipment, music lessons or other education-related expenditures for children not about to attend college? Should you shortchange younger siblings?

DOES PRIVATE SECONDARY SCHOOL PAY FOR ITSELF?

Parents often ask whether it is better to invest money in a private secondary school education or save it for college. Aside from issues of child safety, peer influence and education quality in really dismal public education school districts, the question boils down to whether a better pre-college education will pay for itself in terms of admission to a better college and more merit aid. Although a private education tends to lead to admission to more prestigious colleges, it generally does not result in enough additional merit aid to offset the cost. There are, of course, many other reasons you might consider a private school education, but a strategy that says, "Parents pay for private school so that the students can pay for college through financial aid" rarely works out.

Few families can pay for college without making tradeoffs, and fewer still enjoy making them. These tradeoffs, however, are the key to spending money in line with what you truly value.

Choices of how you'll spend your money also have an effect on the potential financial aid you'll receive. Jim Sumner, Dean of Admission and Financial Aid at Grinnell College, notes that the people at colleges and lenders who make money decisions have opinions about what a family considers important. "There's the assessed need and then there's what I would call the perceived or felt need that a lot of families have. . . . Not very many years ago, a family said they deserved more financial aid because their expenses were high: Their monthly boat payment was $5,000!"

If you really need a boat that costs $5,000 per month to be happy and fulfilled, that's your choice, but don't bother to ask for financial aid for it. Financial aid administrators distinguish between expenses that are non-discretionary necessities and expenses that are lifestyle choices.

HOW TO THINK ABOUT THE INVESTMENT

People who complete a bachelor's degree earn about twice as much money over their lifetimes as those who only complete high school, and people who go on to a professional degree earn almost four times as much in a forty-year work life.[17] That's one to three million dollars more money over the course of a career.[18]

Dr. Scott Friedhoff, Vice President for Enrollment Management at Allegheny College, puts the expenditure in perspective when he says, "Think about investing for a lifetime. This is not an investment for four years, it's not an investment for your first job and it's not an investment for a single career. It's an investment for all your careers, for your personal life, your family and . . . satisfaction and joy of living." It is difficult to find any investment that provides for a better and more reliable return on investment than a college education.

THE STUDENT SIDE—LEARNING, EARNING AND ACHIEVING

Current high school students: Although you earn less money than your parents, you have a major effect on the affordability of college, starting from the earliest days of high school. Getting good grades is an obvious contribution, because you'll be better qualified to win many forms of financial aid and scholarships. Much of your additional choices have a double payoff: Winning a major scholarship award represents a stamp of excellence that opens doors to new opportunities. The key concept for you is that the more desirable you are to schools, the better chance you'll have of finding the money.

As early as possible, talk to your guidance counselor about ways to perform at your best. (Start early because how long you've participated in activities will be important to colleges and scholarship providers.) In addition to required courses, choose classes that interest you and will stretch your abilities. The same goes for sports, clubs, arts and other extracurricular activities. Also talk about your capacity for leadership and service, which are sought by many colleges as well as scholarship providers. Are there volunteer service opportunities at your school, community or religious organization? If you are not in high school, think about work experience, community service and other activities that might apply.

When you choose activities, focus on your true strengths and interests. Colleges care less about well-rounded students than they care about a well-rounded student body. If everybody in the student body was class valedictorian, lettered in a sport and played a musical instrument, it would be a rather boring place. It is much better to pursue an activity for which you have a passion, so that you develop expertise. You will also find it easier to win scholarships if you excel in a few fields than if you are mediocre at many things. Gain exposure to several activities early on, but then pick a few that are most interesting to you and focus most of your effort over the long term.

☑ I Wish I Had Known . . .

I really wish I had known as early as middle school how important it is to get good grades and try to get as many scholarships as possible. Life would be so much easier if I had not messed up my grades.

—*Simon Bernard Ebelhar, sophomore*
Jefferson Community College

Freshman and sophomore years are a great time for exploring more interests outside of class and developing strengths in your studies. If you've really committed to activities that take practice, like AP classes, music or sports, you'll develop persistence and determination, qualities that are essential in college. In the spring of your sophomore year, you can line up a summer job, do volunteer work or internships. It's not too early to start exploring the world of work, and local business leaders are often happy to act as mentors for a young person. Relationships you establish with adults such as teachers and businesspeople will be helpful in ways you can hardly predict, from the time they nominate you for a scholarship to their recommendation for your admission to their alma mater.

Finally, don't forget the changing relationship with your parents—when you're fifteen or sixteen you should start having frank discussions with your parents about how you, as a family, will make college possible. This is not just because it is good for you to be involved, but also because college is the start of your transition from a sheltered existence to the real world.

Here's a great start: Examine your own money habits. How much do you save? What do you buy, and why? Do you know how borrowing and credit work? Do you know the difference between needs and wants? How do you tell if you are spending beyond your means? (One sign: Carrying a balance on your credit cards. Paying off credit cards in full each month is spending within your means.) What are the pros and cons of various types of investments (e.g., CDs, money market accounts, stocks, bonds, mutual funds, college savings plans, etc.)? There are lots of resources in the library and on the Web to help you control money (instead of letting money control you).

This is a good time for parents to teach their children the basics of money management.

Juniors in high school take on more adult responsibilities. Choose classes that are challenging, rather than easy, to show colleges your full range of talents instead of coasting. Meet with guidance counselors and decide which colleges you'll explore. Begin to consider possible careers, and the postsecondary schooling they require. Browse the colleges' web sites (you'll usually find the Cost of Attendance under links labeled "Admissions" or "Tuition and Fees") and course catalogs. It's a good idea to create an early list of scholarship possibilities, so if you haven't yet begun exploring scholarships at web sites like FastWeb, it's a good time to get started. Once you register, FastWeb will keep you informed by e-mail of new scholarships as they become available. Prepare for upcoming ACT and SAT tests, which influence admissions, scholarships and financial aid. Refer back to chapter 3 in the spring to start your college finance project plan, and use a couple of evenings to learn the advice in this book.

Achievement and commitment are qualities you really start to develop at this time, and they're qualities colleges examine closely. Lots of students are good at many things, but at age sixteen or seventeen, they haven't found the activities or classes where they can really excel. You don't have to be an expert as a high school junior, but those who have developed a passion for learning and depth of experience—whether in class, in performance, in a gymnasium or playing field, or in service—get a closer look than "average-average-average" students.

Senior year is crammed with the tasks described in chapter 3, so make sure you have a plan and stick to it—*and pay attention to deadlines*. College admissions and financial aid is one of the largest, longest-running and most complicated projects you will have pursued to date, so get organized. A two-week homework assignment is simple in comparison. In addition to all those tasks, seniors go to college interviews, so ask your guidance counselor for tips on making a good impression. Earn money for college with a part-time job if you can, but don't sacrifice the quality of your schoolwork.

TRADEOFFS

A final word about working through this process together as a family: Only the truly wealthy can avoid tradeoffs altogether. Some tradeoffs are obvious, such as cutting current spending to save for college. Other tradeoffs are more subtle. Guidance Counselor Lori Johnston of Hastings High School in Hastings, MI, gives this example:

> *I think of long-term investment versus making a short-term decision. A short-term decision is, "I'm going to go to the community college and live at home because I don't think I can afford any other option." Long-term thinking says, "Community college could be a good option, but I might benefit more from being out on my own, away from the family. Have I explored every way I might be able to attend a four-year college or university outside my community?"*

Be sure to confirm your tradeoffs with facts. You might think that a four-year private college is out of the question, but don't rule it out based on the official price tag. Many private schools have more resources and flexibility than public institutions in awarding financial aid. Plus, you need to also consider your future resources in addition to your current resources. The job you get after you graduate from a four-year college may have a much higher salary than the jobs available to community college graduates, making it easier to repay your loans despite the greater debt you may incur at a higher priced college.

When tradeoffs are made with all the facts in mind, greater control over finances is possible regardless of a family's assets or income. Together, students and parents can make deliberate, informed choices about paying for college as a family, and this type of shared responsibility between parent and child can carry on as students become independent adults. Knowledge is the antidote to fear.

5

Qualifying for Financial Aid

"This place is cool. Do you like it better than the University of Ohio?" asked Sarah.

Matt tossed a stone into the water. "They're just different. Ohio's so big, you can get lost," he said, "Caledonia feels pretty isolated." He picked up another stone. "But I like the people here."

"This is the most expensive one, right?"

"Pretty much tied with Oberlin, but expensive isn't what you think. It depends on how much money they have to give you, how much they have to loan you and all that stuff." Matt tossed another stone underhand into the pond.

Aiming carefully, Sarah threw a pebble exactly where Matt's had landed. She asked, "Are Mom and Dad talking to the Admissions Office?"

Matt squinted into the October sun, putting on his thoughtful look. "Nope. They went off to talk to the financial aid people about loans and stuff."

"Do you know how much money they make?" asked Sarah.

"Yeah, they told me when we filled out the pre-app."

"What's a pre-app?"

"It's a worksheet that lays out all the money you have," said Matt. "Well, actually," he continued, "it's a lot more than that. It asks questions all about your savings, and what Mom and Dad get paid, and what you and I have in our education funds and lots of other things."

"Like the house? I heard Dad say the house was worth a lot more than they paid for it," said Sarah. She hoped they wouldn't have to sell the house to pay for college.

"Nah, the house doesn't count, at least not to the feds," said Matt. "Look, it's really complicated, and when we have to file the FAFSA after New Year's I'll ask Mom and Dad if you can see it."

"What's a FARFSA?" asked Sarah.

"FAF-SA," replied Matt. He tossed a final stone and stood up. "It's another form, and it pretty much lays down the law about money for college. . . ."

• • •

Students and their families must go through a qualification process to earn financial aid. The center of this process is a form called the Free Application for Federal Student Aid (FAFSA) which, like a federal tax form, documents important facts about a family's financial situation. Colleges, federal and state governments, lenders and other sources of college money have used the FAFSA since 1992.

There is a lot of money available for college, but it's not unlimited. It comes from different sources and in different forms. This means that the people responsible for distributing financial aid are, in effect, rationing money according to specific rules. The system cannot account for every possible difference among families.[19] Still, financial aid providers need some basis for comparison.

Let's imagine a simple example: University A has $500,000 available each year in grants to students, and 1,000 students apply for those grants every year. Rather than give $500 to each student, the financial aid office decides to award much more to students who are truly needy, and much less (or nothing) to wealthier students. To do this fairly, they need to compare the students' abilities to pay. If every student completes a FAFSA, University A has at least some factual basis for that comparison.

The FAFSA is also used by others, such as scholarship providers. Steve van Buskirk, Director of Programs for the Veterans of Foreign Wars National Headquarters, tells why: "Many scholarships are dependent on that basic, foundational document because it establishes your need, your resources or lack thereof."

If you have substantial financial resources, you might assume that you won't qualify for any financial aid, but you should complete the FAFSA anyway. The financial aid need analysis formulas are complicated enough that the only way to tell whether you will qualify is to apply. For example, the number of children in college at the same time can have a big impact on aid eligibility. College costs have also risen enough that many families who think they don't qualify actually do.

There are no specific income or asset cutoffs for financial aid. Even families earning more than $100,000 a year have qualified for the Federal Pell Grant, albeit less than 1%. If the family earns more than $250,000 a year, they probably won't qualify for the Federal Pell Grant, but they can still get the unsubsidized Federal Stafford and Federal PLUS Loans (see chapter 7). Stafford and PLUS may not be grants, but they are good programs and they require a FAFSA.[20] Don't forget about the education tax benefits, which are aimed at middle- and upper-income families.

Simply put, you must complete the FAFSA if you want to take advantage of student financial aid programs. Filing the FAFSA is often a prerequisite for applying for merit aid or scholarships from colleges and other organizations. The FAFSA is required for most federal and state student aid programs. You must submit the FAFSA every year that you want aid. (In subsequent years, you will get the Renewal FAFSA, which has prefilled in some information from the previous FAFSA.)

☑ I Wish I Had Known . . .

I wish I had known not to procrastinate as much as I did, and I wish I'd followed up on the paperwork to see if it was all correct.

—anonymous college student

COMPLETING THE FAFSA

Following the timetable in chapter 3, submit the FAFSA as soon as possible after January 1 of the year you will enter college. You can complete much of the information before January, so get a head start if you can (see the calendar in chapter 3; the FAFSA pre-application worksheet is available in November).

The FAFSA is available in paper and electronic formats. You can get the paper version from your high school, the financial aid office at any college or university, the public library or by calling 1-800-4-FED-AID (1-800-433-3243).

We recommend completing the web-based version of the FAFSA at www.fafsa.ed.gov. Please note that there are other web addresses similar to this address that do not lead to the federal forms. Be sure to apply at www.fafsa.ed.gov. This site provides step-by-step instructions for completing the form. FAFSA on the Web offers several benefits, including:

- You will get your Student Aid Report (SAR) a few weeks sooner than with the paper form.
- Your FAFSA will be more accurate than a paper application, since the FAFSA on the web has built-in "edit checks" to catch simple errors and help you avoid common processing errors such as OCR errors.
- It is easier to file a Renewal FAFSA after you have completed your first FAFSA. (Remember that you have to fill out a new FAFSA every year you would like to receive aid.)
- You will save the federal government money by reducing their processing and printing costs.

To fill out the FAFSA on the Department of Education's web site, you should get a Personal Identification Number (PIN).[21] Follow the instructions at www.pin.ed.gov (it might take a day or two to get your PIN). If you have technical questions about using FAFSA on the Web, call 1-800-4-FED-AID. In addition, the National Association of Student Financial Aid Administrators holds free seminars about completing the FAFSA. Find a seminar near you at www.collegegoalsundayusa.org.

The www.fafsa.ed.gov site also offers an invaluable pre-application worksheet. The worksheet, which you can print out and fill in by hand, helps you organize all the information you will need to complete the FAFSA quickly. (Click on the link labeled "Before Beginning a FAFSA.")

BOOK TO WEB

The FAFSA calculates your official Estimated Family Contribution (EFC), which you estimated in chapter 3. In fact, a government-estimated EFC will appear on a confirmation page as soon as you complete the FAFSA on the Web. Even though this isn't the "official" number (which comes with the SAR), it will give you another bit of valuable information for your planning.

CODE: 1024

Qualifying for Financial Aid

Please note: Do not complete a paper FAFSA and try to use it to complete the online questions. FAFSA on the web not only changes the order of questions, it also changes dynamically based on the information you have already entered.

Here is a short list of information you'll need as you get started on either the pre-application worksheet or the FAFSA itself:

- The student's driver's license and Social Security card.
- The student's income tax returns, W-2 forms and 1099 forms for the previous tax year (sometimes called the base year). If the student is married, you will also need the documents for the student's spouse.
- The parent's income tax returns, W-2 forms and 1099 forms for the previous year.
- The parents' Social Security numbers, if available.
- Current bank statements.
- Records relating to stocks, bonds, mutual funds, money market accounts, prepaid tuition plans, section 529 college savings plans, Coverdell Education Savings Accounts and other investments.
- Documentation of non-taxable income, such as Social Security income, AFDC and Veterans Benefits.
- Family-owned business and farm records.

> While you're organizing your records, you can also set aside copies of any documents relating to any unusual family financial circumstances[22], such as medical and dental expenses not covered by health insurance, tuition expenses at elementary or secondary schools, unusually high child care costs, death, divorce and loss of employment. These can be used later if you request a "professional judgment" pertaining to the amount of aid for which you're eligible (see chapter 15).

Since you might need to supply some of these documents to individual colleges for verification, it's a good idea to keep copies of each in your FAFSA folder now, so you won't need to go digging for them later.

The FAFSA should require an hour or two to complete, depending on the complexity of your financial circumstances.

You must sign the completed FAFSA in one of three ways: Online, you can

BOOK TO WEB

You need the Federal School Code (also known as a Title IV Institution Code)
for each school to which you are applying in order to complete the FAFSA.
Find it at www.collegegold.com. You can get this code from the school or
1-800-4-FED-AID, or you can use the school code database at
www.fafsa.ed.gov/fotw0607/fslookup.

CODE: 1052

sign with a PIN, or you can print out a signature page online, sign and mail it to the address provided. Offline, you can sign your Student Aid Report (SAR) when it arrives (see below). Signing online with a PIN is quickest, and your PIN can be used to file Renewal FAFSA forms for all the years you're in school. Also note that if you are a dependent student (by the federal government's definition) both the parents and the students will need their own PIN. Each individual who would sign the paper form needs an individual PIN.

If you prefer to fill in a paper copy of the FAFSA, we recommend you send it in via certified mail, so you have proof of the date of mailing.

Whether you file electronically or by mail, make or print a copy of the completed FAFSA, including the worksheets, before mailing it. Keep it in a safe place with copies of all the records you used to complete the form. Not only will this be useful as a reference for subsequent years, but it might also be required for verification.

You should submit the FAFSA as soon as possible after January 1. You cannot submit the form before January 1, because the FAFSA uses your financial information from the prior tax year when calculating eligibility for the upcoming award year.[23] You *can* complete the pre-application worksheet before January 1, which will give you a head start.

For example, if it is now November 1, 2006, and you are applying for financial aid for the academic year running from September 2007 through June 2008, you must wait until January 1, 2007 to submit the FAFSA. To meet the deadlines for most states you should submit the form no later than March 1, with February 15 being ideal. (State deadlines are listed at www.fafsa.ed.gov/before003a.htm.) Some states and colleges require the FAFSA to be filed as early as February 1—some even earlier!

Do not wait until you've filed your income tax returns with the IRS. You

AVOID THESE COMMON ERRORS

Errors in filling out the FAFSA form can result in processing delays, an inaccurate EFC or even an erroneous denial of aid, so double-check the information you submit, and avoid these eleven common errors:

- The number one mistake students make is leaving a field blank. All questions must be completed. If the answer is zero or the question does not apply to you, write in a 0.
- Use your legal name as it appears on your Social Security card. Be careful to write your Social Security number (SSN) and date of birth accurately and clearly.
- Read the questions carefully. The words "you" and "your" on the FAFSA always refer to the student, not the parents.
- In the question that asks about your interest in different types of aid (e.g., work-study and student loans), answer "yes" to each question. Answering "yes" does not obligate you to accept a loan. Answering "no" will not get you more grant aid. By 2007–2008, this question might be changed to assume simply that all students are applying for all forms of aid.
- Another common error is to confuse "total income tax" with the Adjusted Gross Income (AGI), taxes withheld or taxes due. Be sure you are reporting the total income tax and not just the withholdings or the additional taxes due.
- The Earned Income Credit, retirement plan contributions, combat pay and military food and housing allowances are considered "untaxed income" on the FAFSA.
- Do not skip the questions about the educational attainment of your parents. The purpose of these questions is to qualify you for state scholarships for first-generation college students.
- Remember to count yourself, the student, as one of the people who will be college students during the award year.
- Some families forget to complete Worksheets A, B and C, perhaps because they appear at the end of the application. Although

continued

the worksheets are not submitted with the application, the totals for each worksheet are included on the FAFSA form. Failing to complete the worksheets may result in an EFC that is higher or lower than the correct value.

- The question concerning the type of income tax return you filed or will file—a 1040, 1040A or 1040EZ—should be completed based on the type of return you were eligible to file, not the return actually filed. Many paid tax preparers routinely complete the 1040, even when the taxpayer was eligible to file a 1040A or 1040EZ. (Note that if you opt to itemize deductions, you are considered as being required to complete the 1040. See www.finaid.org/educators/needs.phtml for tips on how to determine whether an IRS Form 1040 was required.) The type of income tax return you were eligible to file can have a big impact on aid eligibility.

- The instructions on the FAFSA concerning the questions about income earned from work are confusing, and not entirely correct. They incorrectly handle partnership income, negative income, retirement plan contributions, and the employer portion of FICA taxes, all to the detriment of the financial aid applicant. Instead of using lines 7 + 12 + 18 from IRS Form 1040, add Box 5 from your W-2 statements to line A.4 or B.6 of Schedule SE.

Finally, sign the form (if submitted electronically, your PIN does this) and make sure everybody who is supposed to sign the form signs it. An unsigned form will not be processed. Even though the rest of the form should be completed in black ink, you should sign the form in blue ink (this will distinguish the original copy from most photocopies).

Make a copy or print the online copy of the form before mailing/submitting it.

Note to veterans: See the list of veteran-specific errors in chapter 9.

BOOK TO WEB

For a list of additional common errors, see www.collegegold.com.

CODE: 1054

should either estimate your income—you'll have a chance to correct it with exact figures later—or complete your tax returns early. (Your December pay stubs and bank account statements should contain information about your total income for the year. You'll find this helpful in estimating your income.)

MAXIMIZING ELIGIBILITY FOR STUDENT AID

You can maximize your eligibility for financial aid with a few strategies that take advantage of the way the federal methodology works. As with the tax code, it's up to individual families to work within the current law to maximize their family's eligibility for financial aid.

This is a cause of some controversy among financial aid professionals, who fear that these strategies are, in effect, advising people to rearrange their finances to unfairly qualify for more aid. However, financial aid administrators are themselves in the business of helping people afford college in the best way possible, and until Congress comes up with a "perfect" methodology, we think the fairest situation is one in which all families learn as much as possible and take the actions that seem most sensible in the context of their entire financial lives, their values and the importance they put on education. Plus, many of the strategies for maximizing aid eligibility also make sense as good financial planning tips.

A word about honesty: We strongly discourage any family from trying to break the rules. The penalties for lying on financial aid applications are severe and can include a fine of up to $20,000 and up to five years in jail. The federal government requires that every school verify the FAFSA applications of at least 30% of its students, and many verify 100%. Verification is a process where students are required to provide supporting documentation to prove that the information they have provided the financial aid office is accurate. (One reason the government bases FAFSA data on the prior tax year is that it's verifiable.)

Remember, too, that if you succeed in making yourself look less affluent than you really are, you're making it harder for the financial aid administrators to distribute limited financial aid funds fairly. Do you really want to be reducing the amount of aid available to lower income families? A good rule of thumb to follow is: *If a reasonable person would feel uncomfortable telling a financial aid administrator about using a strategy, don't use it.* Ask your school's financial aid administrator if you have questions about the appropriateness of using any strategy. Remember that their job is to help people attend college and they are not your enemy.

The following tactics are intended mostly to help you avoid unintended mistakes. For example, a parent who conscientiously saves for her children's college education in her child's name qualifies for less aid than a parent who saves the money in her own name, all other factors being equal.

As in good financial planning, one piece of advice doesn't fit all. For example, it's common advice to reduce parent assets by paying off the mortgage early. Too often, however, families focus all their attention on that strategy even though only 10% of families have any contribution from parent assets, and those that do, often have a very small contribution resulting from those assets.

A more successful method than pursuing one or two tactics is to test strategies against your unique financial situation. Before you try to minimize parent assets, for example, first compare your qualifying assets (by adding up your non-retirement; non-home-equity assets, such as savings and investments) against the "asset protection allowance." (The typical family has an asset protection allowance of $40,000–$50,000, so the family savings and investments might not be counted at all.) You might have little reason or no reason to reduce your assets.[24]

Furthermore, some financial moves which appear sensible for one reason, such as raising money for college by selling stock, can negatively impact eligibility for financial aid in other ways . . . all depending on when the action is taken.

Many of the following strategies are just good, sound financial practices. For example, using cash in the bank to pay off credit card debt will benefit the family financially by reducing the amount of interest they are paying, in addition to improving the family's eligibility for student financial aid.

Overall, it's a good approach to focus on those strategies that have the biggest impact. Below you will find the basic principles of maximizing eligibility, followed by the ten strategies that have the biggest impact on the greatest number of families.

The basic principles for maximizing eligibility are:

1. Reducing income during the year(s) upon which the financial aid need analysis is based. (This can be a tricky choice, because the natural assumption is that you need more income, not less, during college years. However, there are cases in which this makes sense. For example, if a parent decides to take a sabbatical from work or accept a severance package from an employer, moving the unemployment period to the year upon which the income is based can result in a larger aid package.)

2. Reducing "included" assets. There are two types of assets, those that are included in the need analysis formulas and those that aren't. Converting included assets into non-included assets will increase eligibility by sheltering them from the need analysis process. However, most financial planners recommend that parents maintain a contingency fund equal to six months' salary in relatively liquid form for emergencies and other unforeseeable circumstances.

3. Increasing the number of children enrolled in college and pursuing a degree or certificate at the same time. The parent contribution is split among all children who will be simultaneously enrolled in college.[25]

4. Taking advantage of the differences in the way the need analysis process assesses the assets and income of the student and his or her parents.

With these principles in mind, here are our top ten tactics for maximizing your family's eligibility for student aid:

1. Save money in the parent's names, not the child's name.

2. Pay off consumer debt, such as credit card and auto loan balances (and resist the temptation to run up a new balance).

3. Spend down the student's assets first, before touching the parents' money—it's counted at a higher rate when calculating the EFC.

4. Accelerate *necessary* expenses to reduce available cash. For example, if you need a new car or computer, buy it before you file the FAFSA. If the parents intend to give their student a computer or car as a graduation present, they should buy it before they file the FAFSA, using the student's money.

5. Minimize capital gains.

6. Maximize contributions to your retirement fund. (Note: The current year's contributions get added back in as untaxed income on the worksheets, but are not counted as assets.)

7. Do not withdraw money from your retirement fund to pay for school, as distributions count as taxable income, reducing next year's financial aid eligibility. If you must use money from your retirement funds, borrow the money from the retirement fund instead of getting a distribution.

8. Prepay your mortgage.

9. Use section 529 College Savings Plans, Prepaid Tuition Plans or

CODE: 1010

Coverdell Education Savings Accounts. A plan owned by a parent has minimal impact on financial aid[26], and one owned by a grandparent has no impact at all.

10. Choose the date to submit the FAFSA carefully, as assets and marital status are specified as of the application date. Applicant marital status cannot be updated.

Keep in mind that the federal regulations governing financial aid change frequently. There is no guarantee that any of these strategies will work in the long run, since the federal need analysis methodology is amended annually by Congress and undergoes a major overhaul every four to six years (see "Book to Web" note above).

THE STUDENT AID REPORT (SAR)—THE NEXT STEP

Four to six weeks after you file the FAFSA (two to four weeks if you file electronically), you should receive a copy of your Student Aid Report (SAR) from the U.S. Department of Education. The SAR summarizes the information you submitted on the FAFSA and presents the Expected Family Contribution (EFC) which tells you the amount your family is expected to contribute to your education for the next academic year. Review the SAR carefully for errors of fact. Corrections must relate to the accuracy of the information as of the date the original FAFSA was submitted, not subsequent updates.[27] If necessary, make any corrections on Part 2 of the SAR and return it promptly to the address listed on the SAR. You will then receive a new SAR. Your timing may affect the aid packages that you are of-

FEELING INDEPENDENT?

Many families have heard that "independent" students receive more financial aid. The question of who is an independent student is the source of much confusion and some questionable FAFSA filings. Independent students might qualify for more financial aid (sometimes they qualify for less aid), but you can't just declare yourself to be independent. For the FAFSA, the federal government says you're an independent student if you meet at least one of the following criteria:

- You will be twenty-four years old by December 31 of the financial aid award year.
- You are a graduate student or attending a professional school.
- You are married as of the date you submitted the FAFSA.
- You are a U.S. armed forces veteran (or on active duty as of July 1, 2006).
- You have one more more legal dependents other than a spouse, such as children who receive more than half their support from you and will continue receiving more than half their support from you during the award year. Other people may also qualify as dependents, provided that they live with you in addition to satisfying the 50% support test.
- You are an orphan or ward of the court, or were a ward of the court until age eighteen.

Financial aid professionals might declare you independent under additional criteria, such as both parents being incarcerated, hospitalized or institutionalized. Note that parent refusal to contribute to the student's education or to complete the FAFSA or provide verification documents are insufficient grounds for a dependency status override.

fered. Remember that this is not an "appeals" process asking for a smaller EFC—just a confirmation of facts.

If you do not receive the SAR within a reasonable amount of time, call the federal processor at 1-319-337-5665 (or 1-800-4-FED-AID). You can also write to

Federal Student Aid Programs
PO Box 4038
Washington, DC 52243-4038

The SAR report is eight pages long, including instructions and correction forms. Your government-calculated EFC is found at the bottom of page two of the (current) form, and looks like the information below. We've highlighted the place on the form where you'll find the EFC (note that this government sample uses zeros in place of real numbers, and is expressed in monthly amounts).

Study your SAR carefully; it will recap all the information you supplied. If ANY of your information is inaccurate, immediately correct the mistake. You can do this online at www.fafsa.ed.gov (click the link labeled "Make Corrections to a Processed FAFSA") or report the correct information in writing to the address above.

Your Expected Family Contribution is determined by a complex federal needs analysis formula. Financial aid administrators cannot directly change the EFC or the amount of financial aid. But the financial aid administrator may use "professional judgment" to adjust the inputs to the need analysis formula, when justified by documented unusual circumstances. The federal need analysis methodology then calculates a new EFC using the same formula based on the new information. This usually results in a different financial aid package. If you believe that you cannot meet the EFC, tell the financial aid administrators at colleges you plan to attend, and ask for a "professional judgment review." It helps if

For Financial Aid Office Use Only

This information will be used by your Financial Aid Administrator to determine your eligibility for student aid.

SAR C Flag: Y
Application Source: 2A
Transaction Source: 4C
Processed Record Type: X
Duplicate SSN Flag: X

Dependency Status: I
Dependency Override: X
FAA Adjustment: X
Reprocessing Code: X

Rejects Met: 01 02 03 04 05 07
Application Receipt Date: 06/19/2005
Transaction Receipt Date: 06/20/2005
Verification Flag: X

MONTHS:	1	2	3	4	5	6	7	8	9	10	11	12
PRIMARY EFC:	00000	00000	00000	00000	00000	00000	00000	00000	00000	00000	00000	00000
SECONDARY EFC:	00000	00000	00000	00000	00000	00000	00000	00000	00000	00000	00000	00000

PC: 99999
SIC: 99999

Auto Zero EFC Flag: Y   SNT Flag: N   Pell Eligible Flag: Y

MATCH FLAGS:

SSN Match Flag: 4
DHS Match Flag: X
DHS Sec. Conf. Flag: X
NSLDS Match Flag: 2

Selective Service Registration Flag: 4
DHS Verification #: 123456789012345
VA Match Flag: 1
NSLDS Database Results Flag: 1
NSLDS Transaction Number: 01

Selective Service Match: X
SSA Citizenship Code: X
FSSN Match Flag: 4
MSSN Match Flag: 4

COMMENTS: 001 002 003 004 005 006 007 008 009 010 011 012 013 014 015 016 017 018 019 020

THE CSS/FINANCIAL AID PROFILE

Another form called the CSS/Financial Aid PROFILE is required by a few hundred private colleges for financial aid applications. The form is administered by the College Board and differs somewhat from the FAFSA in that it contains questions specific to the school or program you're applying to, whereas the FAFSA asks the same questions of everyone.

The CSS/Financial Aid PROFILE asks for more detailed financial information than the FAFSA. For example, it takes into account such factors as whether your family owns a home. It tracks three years of income data, not one. It makes allowances for certain expenses not covered on the FAFSA, as well as elementary/secondary school tuition payments. With a more in-depth picture of the family's finances the CSS/Financial Aid PROFILE allows the colleges to fine-tune their financial aid packages.

The PROFILE can also require a fee to complete, and can be completed earlier than the FAFSA. Ask the colleges that interest you if they use the CSS/Financial Aid PROFILE and, if so, go to profileonline. collegeboard.com to complete the form.

you supply them with independent third-party documentation of the unusual circumstances and their financial impact on your family.

Changes in your EFC will not necessarily result in more gift aid. As a general rule, unless the family has a very low income, a decrease in the EFC will yield an increase in eligibility for student loans and work-study, not grants. Just because you demonstrate increased financial need doesn't mean that the school and government will throw more grants and scholarships your way.

DO YOU NEED HELP?

The FAFSA is a lengthy form, and somewhat complicated . . . but as we've mentioned, if you can do your taxes, you can complete the FAFSA. Most questions can be answered just by reading the instructions carefully.

Some families use paid preparers to help them complete the form. They want the assurance of someone saying, "Yes, you've done it right; you're not making any mistakes." In general, we don't believe this benefit is worth the $75 or more charged for this service. One of the most labor intensive parts of the process is gathering all of the necessary information. In order for the paid preparer to complete the FAFSA for you, you're going to have to provide him with the same information you'd provide on the form—income, assets and all the rest. In some cases, paid FAFSA preparers take a question-and-answer approach to getting that information, but it amounts to the same thing. Using a paid preparer won't save you any time, and may introduce additional sources of error and delay into the process.

Unless you are mortally afraid of filling in forms, we recommend you put your time into completing the FAFSA carefully, and seek specific advice from free resources—the government, guidance counselors, college financial aid administrators and on reliable web sites. If you have any questions about completing the FAFSA or federal student assistance programs, call the Federal Student Aid Information Center at **1-800-4-FED-AID** (1-800-433-3243, TDD 1-800-730-8913) from 9:00 a.m. to 8:00 p.m. Eastern Standard Time, Monday through Friday. The Federal Student Aid Information Center toll-free hotline often has extended hours during the peak application season.[28]

Some preparers will provide tips on how to maximize aid eligibility, but these are not complicated strategies and the most effective legitimate ones are in this book. Beware of potentially deceptive strategies. If someone other than you, your spouse or your parents complete the FAFSA, or told you what to write, that person must complete the "Preparer's Use Only" section of the form. Preparers must complete this section even if they are not paid for their services. If the preparer refuses to sign the form, it's a sign that they encouraged you to provide false or misleading information. The penalties for doing so are severe.

BOOK TO WEB

The U.S. Department of Education publishes a collection of answers to frequently asked questions about the FAFSA form at www.studentaid.ed.gov/students/publications/completing_fafsa/index.html.

CODE: 1064

WHAT HAPPENS NEXT?

When you submitted your FAFSA, you were able to specify the names and school codes of up to six colleges. These colleges will automatically receive a copy of your Student Aid Report. If you decide to attend a college that was not listed, you should either go online to add the college[29] or provide the college with a copy of your SAR. You may also need to provide a copy of your SAR to other institutions that require it, such as some scholarship providers. Do this as soon as you confirm its accuracy, and before their deadlines.

Send all financial aid forms to the financial aid office together, as early as you can. When all your paperwork is received at a financial aid office, financial aid administrators combine the SAR data with other information they requested of you. Their goal is to create a package of financial aid grants, loans, tuition discounts, work-study and other opportunities that, combined with your family's contribution, meets the cost of attending their school. The next four chapters will examine the components of that package in detail.

6

Government Grant Programs

Whic Matt and Sarah toured the Caledonia College campus, Lynn and Jim Gordon met with Rachel Piedmont, Caledonia's Director of Financial Aid.

"We worked out an expected family contribution," said Lynn, holding up the EFC worksheet. "It's not official because we'll file a FAFSA in January, but it comes to about $3,000."

"May I see that?" asked Rachel. Lynn handed her the page, and she studied it. After a moment, she made several notes on her yellow pad and handed the worksheet back to Lynn.

"Yes, Matt would definitely be eligible for a number of programs we administer through this office," she said. "We administer both need- and merit-based programs here. Shall we talk about the standard federal government grant programs first?" She added with a smile, "We like to start with the financial aid you don't have to pay back. . . ."

• • •

Let's start by admitting that government grant programs are created by, well, *governments*, and not surprisingly, they are numerous, complicated and lack transparency. Many factors affect who gets how much, and families don't walk into the process knowing how much aid they'll get. It is also difficult to determine how specific changes in your family's situation, such as an inheritance or a divorce, will affect eligibility for aid, since these situations are treated as exceptions to the standard need analysis process. If you transfer from one college to another, you have to reapply. Because government programs change frequently, it's also hard to predict if you'll be eligible for the same aid year after year—for example, changes made in 2004 dropped about 80,000 families from eligibility for the largest federal grant program, the Federal Pell Grants. In 2006, more than 300,000 families became eligible for the new Academic Competitiveness Grants and SMART grants.

That said, the government is a primary source of college money for American families—tens of billions of dollars each year.

First, let's define the term: An educational **grant** is a gift of money for your education that doesn't need to be repaid. You cannot use it for any purpose other than the cost of attending college. Federal and state education grants are typically based on demonstrated financial need.

Educational **loans** do have to be repaid, whether they're coming from government or private sources, and we'll talk about them in chapters 7 and 8.

👍 MERIT AID, NEED-BASED AID

Colleges offer **merit aid** to talented students they want to attract. They also offer **need-based aid**, in the form of scholarships, grants, employment and low-interest loans, to low-income students with the least resources.

When you complete a FAFSA, the U.S. Department of Education sends a Student Aid Report (SAR) to you, and an Institutional Student Information Report (ISIR) to your state department of education and the schools you've listed on the form.

The colleges who receive your ISIR use it to put together a financial aid package that can include government grants along with other forms of student aid.

The fact is, you won't know how much grant aid you can get until you're deep into the process. Fortunately, you already are: the FAFSA you completed in chapter 5 is the key, because the resulting Expected Family Contribution (EFC) will drive eligibility for federal and state aid.

If your EFC is below a certain threshold, and you fulfill certain other requirements, you'll be eligible to receive federal and state grant money. How much grant money you receive is also affected by the cost of attendance and whether you're enrolled full time (vs. less than full time—this includes attending college for less than a full school year).

☑ **I Wish I Had Known . . .**

More about the whole process, and the stresses it brings on. Especially more about government grants.

—C.O., freshman
Salem State College

FEDERAL GRANTS

About a quarter of all undergraduate students in recent years have received federal grant money, and the median values for awards come in at approximately $3,300 for full-time students and $2,200 for part-time students.[30] You must reapply for federal grant money every year, based on the submission of a new FAFSA. You do not receive a check directly from the government; instead, college financial aid offices receive the money and credit your school account. Because grant money can be used for the total cost of attendance, you are permitted to use it for living expenses, books and materials, etc., after it is applied to institutional charges like tuition. If there is any money left over after the government and institutional aid is applied to school charges, the balance is paid to the student to cover non-institutional expenses.

To receive federal grants, a student must satisfy all the requirements for filing a FAFSA and:

- Be a U.S. citizen (or an eligible non-citizen as defined by the Higher Education Act of 1965).[31]
- Complete high school before entering college (GED certificates and home schooling do satisfy this requirement, as well as those allowed early entry in a degree-granting program at a college).
- Use the money only for educational purposes in a degree or certificate program.
- Certify that he or she is not currently in default on a federal student loan or owe a refund of a federal student grant.

- Have not been convicted of selling/possessing illegal drugs.
- Maintain satisfactory academic progress once in school (to continue qualifying for grants in subsequent years).
- Complete a Selective Service registration (men only).[32]

Two programs for undergraduates make up most of the grant money available from the U.S. government (excluding military/veterans benefits—see chapter 9):

Federal Pell Grants provide more than 90% of federal student aid grant money (not counting education benefits for military personnel and veterans); in 2005 that amounted to about $13 billion. Schools receive as much Federal Pell Grant money as is needed to provide for qualifying students. Federal Pell Grants can be prorated for students who attend school less than full time, and even accelerated for students who attend beyond the traditional school year.

Who qualifies: Undergraduates with an EFC of $3,850 or less, based on a maximum Federal Pell Grant of $4,050 in 2006–07. In 2003–04, 97% of recipients came from households with an income under $50,000.

How much: Awards range from $400 to $4,050 depending on financial need. The average grant currently is about $2,500.

Federal Pell Grant money is widespread, but not automatic. According to Lena C. Terry, Director of Financial Aid at the Bellin College of Nursing, not all schools participate in federal student aid programs, and a few degree or certificate programs are ineligible. Check with the financial aid offices of the colleges you want to attend.

Federal Supplemental Educational Opportunity Grants (SEOG) are awarded to students with exceptional financial need. They totaled $771 million in 2005. Schools receive a set amount of money each year; their financial aid offices decide who gets how much (another reason to talk to the financial aid office early—before all the money is committed to others).

Who qualifies: Undergraduate students with the lowest EFC figures. Federal Pell Grant recipients receive priority.

How much: Awards range from $100 to $4,000 per year depending on need, availability of funds to a particular school and a school's financial aid policies.

In 2006, Congress established two new smaller programs. The new Academic Competitiveness Grants and National SMART grants will provide additional grants to between 300,000 and 510,000 students (less than 10% of Federal Pell Grant recipients). Key requirements include:

1. You must be a Federal Pell Grant recipient.
2. You must major in math, science, engineering, computer science, technology or "national security" foreign languages.
3. You must have a 3.0 GPA.
4. You must be enrolled full-time in a degree program.
5. You must be a U.S. citizen.

The grant is $750 for freshmen, $1,300 for sophomores, $4,000 for juniors and $4,000 for seniors. (This is a new budget item. If there's a funding shortfall, award amounts will be reduced proportionately.)

In addition, there is a federal grant program available to undergraduate students called the **Leveraging Educational Assistance Partnership (LEAP)** program. LEAP provides both outright grants and payment for community service work-study. Although it's federal money, the program is administered through the states and colleges, so a LEAP grant is also available on a school-by-school basis, and can be part of a school's financial aid package. The LEAP program grants a smaller amount nationally as compared to the others, providing only $64 million in 2005. However the amount per student varies greatly by state. Ask the financial aid office for more information.

BOOK TO WEB

You can search for additional grants (for graduate and undergraduate students) from many U.S. federal agencies at the government's web site www.grants.gov. One example: the well-known Fulbright Educational Exchange Program pays for college study in a foreign country. It covers the costs of round trip transportation, tuition, books, maintenance for one academic year and health and accident insurance. It is administered by the U.S. Department of State.

STATE GRANT PROGRAMS

State grant averages are close to federal figures: $3,300 for full-time and $3,000 for part-time students.[33] The FAFSA is also a prerequisite for state grant eligibility. State programs differ, however, depending on state priorities. Pennsylvania, for example, wants to develop technology students, and offers grants for those studying new technologies. California offers the State Graduate Fellowship program for specific courses of study, such as teacher training. Ohio offers up to $3,000 per year to students enrolled in nursing programs through a program called The Nurse Education Assistance Loan Program (NEALP). Georgia's HOPE Scholarship program provides full tuition at public colleges and $3,000 at qualifying private colleges. Total state grants came to $6.3 billion in 2005.

Some states offer assistance to students attending only their public universities; some offer grants to students with particular circumstances. For example, Massachusetts offers a $2,500 grant to undergraduates attending its state university who have experienced "the loss of a parent and or spouse who is killed or missing in the line of public service duty in the Commonwealth of Massachusetts." The grant is not dependent on demonstrated financial need.

CLOSE TO HOME

It can help to go to school in your home state. State programs are often re-served for residents. Melissa Ibanez, Director of Financial Aid at the University of Pittsburgh, Bradford Campus, in Pennsylvania, says, "As a financial aid person, I have to mention this to out-of-state students, 'Hey, look, you're from New York State. Yeah, I know you're only twenty miles across the border from us. But, you know, you're not going to get a state grant here. You're looking at four years as an out-of-state nursing student— you're probably looking at $80,000 worth of debt. Is that realistic? Are there schools in New York that might work for you?' "

Generally, one must be a state resident to qualify for state grant programs. Residency requirements vary from state to state, but typically involve a durational component and documentation of intent to establish residency. The durational component generally requires at least one parent to be a state resident for at least a year before the child matriculated in college. In some states a year is defined as a full calendar year, and not just the previous twelve consecutive months. For independent students two years' residency may be required, and there may also be a minimum age.

Demonstrating intent to establish residency isn't well defined, but can include registering to vote in the state, filing a declaration of domicile form, filing state and federal income tax returns listing an in-state residential address and attending secondary school in the state. It also helps to register a vehicle in the state, obtain a state driver's license, open a local bank account and get a local library card.

BOOK TO WEB

You can find links to individual state requirements at www.collegegold.com.

CODE: 1058

Because each state has different grants available, we recommend you take a two-track strategy for learning more, both discussing available state money with your financial aid administrator and visiting the relevant web page of your state's department of education.

7

Government Loans

"**F**inancial aid here—and at most colleges—usually includes some loans," said Rachel. "That's usually the last thing parents want to hear, but it's not as bad as you might think."

Lynn and Jim looked at each other, but did not reply.

Rachel smiled. "Nobody sensible wants to pile on more debt than they can handle, and the good news is that the federal government makes a lot of money available for borrowing at terms most families can afford."

"How much do most families end up paying?" asked Jim.

"The answer to that is, it depends," Rachel replied. "I'm not trying to be flippant. It really does depend on which programs you qualify for, how much you've saved and so forth. That's why we make an individual plan for every student who comes to Caledonia needing financial aid. It's not limited to government programs, but let's start there. Do you have a few more minutes?"

Lynn and Jim both nodded.

"Okay, great," said Rachel. "Judging from that EFC worksheet you showed me, here are the programs I think you'll end up using. . . ."

• • •

Loans make up the largest amount of student aid: The federal government will loan more than $60 billion to students in the coming year to pay for college. The money is loaned either directly from the U.S. Department of Education to fami-

BOOK TO WEB

Think you understand how interest affects a loan? Answer this multiple choice question:

The total amount paid back (both principal and interest) for a $10,000 loan with a 10-year term at 10% interest is:

A. $1,000
B. $11,000
C. $15,858
D. $18,100
E. $20,000
F. $32,479

Find the correct answer and see how you did against other students at www.collegegold.com.

CODE: 1072

lies (the Federal Direct Student Loan Program (FDSLP), also known as Direct Lending or DL), or from financial institutions or colleges through the Federal Family Education Loan Program (FFELP). The terms of the two programs are similar; the primary difference is the source of funds. The interest rates on DL/FFELP loans are lower than private education loans because the government subsidizes the interest students pay on the government-guaranteed loans.

Roughly half of undergraduate students use federal loans as part of their college financial plan. Loans are debts, not gifts or grants, and must be paid back over time (with interest). The government has established rules for repayment of loans, and also a mechanism for consolidating many loans into one.

You'll find a breakdown of financial aid on pp. 90–92, showing how various forms of aid are distributed by income.

Government education loans come in two major categories: Student loans, such as the Federal Perkins and Stafford Loans, where the student is the borrower; and parent loans, such as the parent Federal PLUS loan, where the parent is the borrower.

Leo Kornfeld, an expert in national issues of financing education, puts the borrowing choice directly: "The way you improve your lifestyle is by getting a college education. And if the only way you can get it is by getting yourself into debt with student loans, then it's still a very good investment. I'd like to think some day the government will increase the grant program so that people shouldn't have to start off life with a large indebtedness. . . . But when you examine the options, if the choice is between not going to college and getting a degree with a debt, I vote for getting a degree with a debt."

☑ I Wish I Had Known . . .

I wish I had considered the costs of my books when I was applying for my loan.

—*anonymous college student*

THE FEDERAL PERKINS LOAN

The Federal Perkins loan is meant for students who have the greatest financial need. It is the best student loan available for undergraduate and graduate students. It is a subsidized loan, with the interest being paid by the federal government while the student is in school and during the nine-month grace period after graduation before repayment begins. Part-time as well as full-time students are eligible.

Federal Perkins funding comes from a limited pool available to each school. When all the money budgeted for the year has been allocated, the college can make no more Federal Perkins loans until the next year. That is one reason why it is better to apply for aid as early as possible. If a school has given out all their Perkins funding, there is no more Perkins money to distribute no matter how needy a student may be.

Who qualifies: Students who demonstrate the greatest financial need. Federal Pell grant recipients get priority.

Who makes the loan: The college attended.

How much: College financial aid offices determine the actual amount of the loan as part of the overall aid package. Undergraduates can borrow up to $4,000 per year with a cumulative limit of $20,000. Graduate students can borrow up to $6,000 per year with a cumulative limit of $40,000.

Loan terms: Interest rate is set by law at 5%. Students have up to ten years to repay the loan, depending on amount borrowed. Interest is subsidized (paid by the government) while the student is enrolled in college.

FEDERAL STAFFORD LOANS

Federal Stafford loans have two variations: **Federal Direct Student Loan (FDSL)** program loans, administered by "Direct Lending Schools," are provided by the U.S. government directly to students and their parents. **Federal Family Education Loan (FFEL)** program loans are provided by financial institutions, such as banks, credit unions and savings & loan associations. (Some colleges participate in the FFEL program through a "School as Lender" program.) Which loan you choose depends on the school you attend (a few schools participate in both programs, about two-fifths participate in Direct Lending, and about three-fifths participate in FFEL). You may qualify for both types of loan, but they may not be used for the same period of enrollment at the same school.

Schools might also publish a "preferred lender list" of lenders they recommend (often because they have a good track record with the school, or lower costs). You are not required to pick a lender from the school's preferred lender list and can choose any lender. The school's preferred lender list is simply a list of lenders the school recommends. Schools are required to certify loans from any participating lender, not just those on their preferred list.

All Federal Stafford Loans are either **subsidized** (the government pays the interest while you're in school and during the grace period) or **unsubsidized** (you are responsible for paying all the interest). To receive a subsidized Federal Stafford Loan, you must be able to demonstrate financial need.

With the unsubsidized Federal Stafford loan, you can defer the payments until six months after graduation by "capitalizing the interest." This delays paying the interest while you are in school by adding the interest payments to the loan balance. The result increases the size and cost of the loan. Most lenders capitalize the interest once, when the loan enters repayment, although they could capitalize the interest as frequently as once a quarter. The best loans capitalize only once, when the loan enters repayment, thereby avoiding compounding of interest (paying interest on the interest).

Who qualifies: All students, regardless of need, are eligible for the unsubsidized Federal Stafford Loan. Subsidized loans are available only to students with demonstrated financial need (determined by the FAFSA process).

Who makes the loan: Either a financial institution (for the FFEL) or the government (FDSL). Both loans are administered through the college you attend.

Loan Limits		
Year	Current Limit	Limit as of 7/1/07
Freshman	$2,625	$3,500
Sophomore	$3,500	$4,500
Junior	$5,500	$4,500 (unchanged)
Senior	$5,500	$5,500 (unchanged)
Unsubsidized Graduate	$10,000	$12,000
Total Graduate	$18,500	$20,500
Medical	$38,500	$40,500

How much: Dependent undergraduate students can borrow as much as $23,000 before graduation, with yearly limits as shown in the table above (new loan limits go into effect on July 1, 2007). Independent undergraduate students and dependent students whose parents were denied a Federal PLUS loan can borrow an extra $4,000 during the freshman and sophomore years, and an extra $5,000 beyond that, with a cumulative Federal Stafford Loan limit of $46,000. No more than $23,000 of this may be subsidized.

Loan terms: Starting in 2006–07, the interest rate is fixed at 6.8%. Repayment periods range between ten and thirty years[34], depending on amount owed and type of repayment plan selected. Federal Stafford Loans charge origination and guarantee fees. Starting in 2006–07 the Federal Stafford loan fees will drop to 3%, and gradually get reduced to 1% by 2010–11. The loan fees are deducted from the disbursement check. Beware of advance fee loan scams that ask you to pay the fees in advance.

Graduate students are also eligible to borrow Federal Stafford Loans, but with a maximum Stafford debt of $18,500 ($20,500 starting July 1, 2007) for each year of study (no more than $8,500 subsidized). The total Stafford debt cannot exceed $138,500 by the completion of the degree (no more than $65,500 subsidized). There are higher loan limits for medical school students.

RULE OF THUMB

The interest rate on the Federal Stafford Loan starting July 1, 2006, is a fixed rate of 6.8%. The interest rate on the Federal PLUS loan is 8.5%.

FEDERAL PLUS LOANS

The Federal Parent Loan for Undergraduate Students (PLUS) helps parents borrow money to cover any costs not already covered by the student's financial aid package, up to the full cost of attendance. Federal PLUS money is considered to be part of the Expected Family Contribution and not part of the financial aid package. It is thus an alternative or supplement to private education loans, which generally have higher interest rates.

Starting on July 1, 2006, graduate and professional students are eligible to borrow under the Federal PLUS loan program to pay for their own education.

Federal PLUS loans are a financial obligation of the parents (or graduate student for the graduate Federal PLUS), not the undergraduate student. If the student agrees to make payments on the Federal PLUS loan, but fails to make the payments on time, the parents will be held responsible.

Like the Federal Stafford loan, parents may take out the loan directly from the government or through a lending institution, depending on school participation. For a Federal Direct PLUS loan (Federal PLUS Loans borrowed directly from the federal government) parents must complete a Direct Federal PLUS Loan application and master promissory note, contained in a single form that you get from your school's financial aid office. Benefits of the program include a faster turn-around time and generally less bureaucracy than the bank-based loan program. For a FFEL PLUS Loan (Federal PLUS Loans borrowed through a source other than the federal government) parents must complete and submit a Federal PLUS loan application, available from the school, lender or your state guaranty agency. After the school completes its portion of the application (certifies the loan), it must be sent to a lender for approval.

Parents can be denied a Federal PLUS loan if they have an adverse credit history, including having had education debts discharged in bankruptcy within the past five years or being more than ninety days late on any debt. If this is the case, the parents may still be eligible for a Federal PLUS loan if they secure an endorser without an adverse credit history, such as a relative or friend who is able to pass the credit check. An endorser promises to repay the loan if the parents fail to do so.

Colleges are not in the business of compensating for an adverse credit history with greater aid, says Melissa Ibanez of the University of Pittsburgh at Bradford: "Financial aid offices just cannot make up the difference—in most cases—for those individuals who aren't able to secure the necessary loans." Parents might qualify for a loan without passing the credit check if they can demonstrate that extenuating circumstances exist, but this is rare.

If one or both parents are denied a Federal PLUS loan because of an adverse credit history, or the college financial aid office determines that a student's parents are likely to be denied a Federal PLUS Loan, the student becomes eligible for increased unsubsidized Federal Stafford Loan limits.[35]

Who qualifies: Parents of dependent undergraduate students (enrolled at least half time) and graduate and professional students.

Who makes the loan: Like the Federal Stafford, Federal PLUS Loans may be made through financial institutions or directly from the federal government.

How much: The maximum amount of the loan is determined by subtracting all available student aid (including grants and scholarships) from the student's cost of attendance.

Loan terms: Starting in 2006–07, the interest rate is fixed at 8.5%. Repayment begins sixty days after the funds are fully disbursed, and the repayment term is ten years.

Federal PLUS loans charge a fee of up to 4% of the loan, deducted proportionately each time a loan disbursement is made. For a FFEL PLUS loan, a portion of this fee goes to the federal government, and a portion goes to the guaranty agency (which administers the Federal PLUS Loan Program in your state). For a Federal Direct PLUS loan, the entire fee goes to the government.

If the parents don't like the Federal PLUS loan because it is a parent obligation and not a student obligation, but otherwise like the fixed interest rate, they could make a private agreement with their child to have the child make the payments after they graduate and get a job.

PAYING BACK THE GOVERNMENT

You are responsible for repaying federal student loans even if you do not graduate. If you do not make any payments on your student loans for 270 days and do not make special arrangements with your lender to get a deferment or forbearance, your loans will be **in default.** Defaulting on your student loans has serious consequences. (See chapter 14, "Danger Zones," for more on default.)[36] For both Federal Stafford and PLUS loans, borrowers may be charged collection costs of up to 18.5%, and late fees as well, if they don't make their loan payments when scheduled.

FAFSA OR NOT?

Families who believe they are too wealthy to qualify for government loans might miss out on options for which they are in fact eligible. Too many times, we've heard families say, "We didn't fill out the FAFSA because we make [or have] too much money."

It's true that you don't have to complete the FAFSA to qualify for the Federal PLUS loan. You do, however, have to complete it for the unsubsidized Federal Stafford loan, and we would encourage families to do so even if that's all they expect. It just makes sense to find out if there's even a chance that you qualify for other government aid.

As far as practical advice for wealthy families, the main focus should be on loans (federal and private) and education tax benefits (see chapter 15), 529 college savings plans and prepaid tuition plans. They can also take advantage of the lower tax bracket for children . . . [37] a move often referred to as "tax scholarships"—essentially using the tax code to save money.

A **deferment** occurs when a borrower is allowed to postpone repaying the loan. If you have a subsidized loan, the federal government pays the interest charges during the deferment period. If you have an unsubsidized loan, you are responsible for the interest that accrues during the deferment period. You can still postpone paying the interest charges by capitalizing the interest, which increases the size of the loan. Most federal loan programs allow students to defer their loans while they are in school at least half time.

A **forbearance** allows the borrower to temporarily postpone repaying the principal, but the interest charges continue to accrue, even on subsidized loans. The borrower must continue paying the interest charges during the forbearance period. Forbearances are granted at the lender's discretion, usually in cases of extreme financial hardship or other unusual circumstances when the borrower does not qualify for a deferment.

You can't receive a deferment or forbearance if your loan is in default.

Although many families do not consider federal education loans to be a form of financial aid, these loans provide cash flow assistance and have features that reduce their costs, such as low interest rates and subsidized interest. The Federal Perkins Loan and the subsidized Federal Stafford Loan are part of the financial aid package because the government pays the interest on these loans while the student is enrolled at least half time and during the grace period. The unsubsidized Federal Stafford and the Federal PLUS Loan are intended to help meet the family's expected family contribution, and thus are not considered part of the college's financial aid package. They do, however, help the family pay its share of the cost by spreading out repayment over multiple years—again, this is the essence of any loan.

As a general observation, students with packages combining federal grants and federal loans borrow about twice as much as they receive in grants, averaging $4,200 per year in the first half of this decade.[38]

The availability of debt says little about your ability to manage that debt later. Director of Student Aid and Family Finance Bob Shorb of Skidmore College asks students to think ahead, offering a simple starting point: "For students to come out with a bachelor's degree in liberal arts, and starting work with an entry-level salary, a $17,000 student loan debt is something they can manage. We have not seen that to be problematic."

Coming out of college with an entry-level salary and $46,000 student loan debt, however, might be problematic, which is why financial aid administrators like Bob Shorb also end up providing families with basic financial advice as well.

As a general rule, don't borrow more for your education than the expected starting salary in your field. If you borrow too much, you will find it difficult to handle the monthly payments. You might be able to reduce the size of the monthly payments by consolidating your loans and using one of the alternate repayment plans, but do you really want to still be paying off your student loans when your children enter college? Consider that an extra $20,000 in education debt will add about $250 a month to your loan payments (that's about the difference in lease payments between a Chevy and a Lexus). If you borrow too much while you are in school, you may not be able to afford a new car after you graduate.

REPAYMENT PLANS

A consolidation loan allows you to combine all of your student or parent loans into one loan from a single lender for simplified repayment.

The consolidation loan is like a refinance, with the proceeds from the consolidation loan being used to pay off the balances on the other loans. The interest rate on the consolidation loan is the weighted average of the interest rates on the loans being consolidated (using the loan balances as the weights), rounded up to the nearest ⅛th of a percent and capped at 8.25%. The use of the weighted average preserves the cost structure of the underlying loans. (For additional information about consolidation loans, see Government Loan Consolidation on page 253.)

A key benefit of consolidation is the ability to reduce the size of the monthly payment by using one of several alternate repayment plans. The available repayment plans include Standard Repayment, Extended Repayment, Graduated Repayment, Income Contingent Repayment, and Income Sensitive Repayment.

Although these repayment plans reduce the size of the monthly payment, they extend the term of the loan and increase the total interest paid over the lifetime of the loan. Education lenders like the alternate repayment plans because a loan with a longer term and higher average balance is more profitable to the lender. Accordingly, you should resort to these plans only if absolutely necessary. You can continue using Standard Repayment with a consolidation loan if you are able to afford the monthly payments.

Extended repayment is like standard repayment, but with a longer term based on the loan balance of the consolidation loan. As demonstrated in the following chart, the term of the loan can be extended from 12 to 30 years.

Loan Balance	Extended Repayment Term
Less than $7,500	10 years
$7,500 to $10,000	12 years
$10,000 to $20,000	15 years
$20,000 to $40,000	20 years
$40,000 to $60,000	25 years
$60,000 or more	30 years

Graduated repayment starts off with lower monthly payments, and gradually increases the monthly payments every two years until the balance is paid in full.

The Income Contingent Repayment (ICR) plan is designed to make repaying education loans easier for students who intend to pursue jobs with lower salaries, such as careers in public service. It does this by pegging the monthly payments to the borrower's income, family size and total amount borrowed. The monthly payment amount is adjusted annually, based on changes in annual income and family size. Income Contingent Repayment (ICR) is currently available only from the U.S. Department of Education, not from banks or other

REPAYMENT PLANS

Interest rates are just one factor in calculating whether a loan is affordable. Another key consideration is the repayment plan (that is, how much you'll pay each month, and for how long, in order to pay off the loan).

Many student loans offer a choice of repayment different from the standard ten-year term. This table shows the effect of terms longer than ten years for a 6.8% loan.

Note that while the longer term reduces the monthly payment, it also increases the total amount of money paid out over the life of the loan. For example, if you choose a fifteen-year term instead of the standard ten-year term, your monthly payment will go down 23%, but you will end up paying 57% more in interest over those fifteen years than you'd pay for the ten-year loan.

Loan terms	Reduction in Monthly Payment	Increase in Total Interest Paid
12 years	12%	22%
15 years	23%	57%
20 years	34%	118%
25 years	40%	184%
30 years	43%	254%
Graduated Repayment	50% (initial payment), 38% average reduction	89%
ICR: Salary = initial debt, 4% annual raise	41% declining to 33%, 37% average reduction	178%

Also note that the maximum reduction in the monthly payment is 50% in any of these plans, while the increase in total interest ranges from 22% to 254%.

financial institutions making government-guaranteed loans through the Federal Family Education Loan (FFEL) Program.

FFEL lenders offer Income Sensitive Repayment (ISR), which pegs the monthly payments to the greater of the interest that accrues and a percentage of your gross monthly income. The percentage is chosen by the borrower and is between 4% and 25%.

FINANCIAL AID BREAKDOWN

The following charts show the distribution of financial aid according to income of the recipient.

Note that these charts weight the amounts by the percentages receiving aid to yield the percentage of the aid package coming from each source or type of aid. As income increases, the percentage receiving aid generally decreases. Seventy-two percent of families earning under $40,000 receive financial aid, while only 51% of families earning more than $80,000 receive financial aid. The average amount received increases from $7,200 to $8,200. The percentage receiving grants drops from 64% to 34%, and the average grant amount increases from $3,900 to $4,600. Essentially, this means that wealthier students are less likely to get aid, but when they do get aid, they tend to get more. This is partly because wealthier students tend to attend more expensive colleges as is illustrated by the chart that shows average cost of attendance by family income.

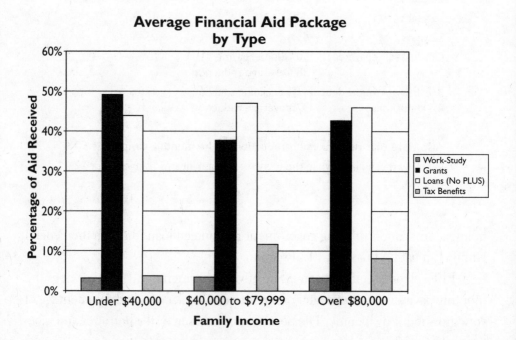

Average Financial Aid Package by Type

Average Financial Aid Package by Source

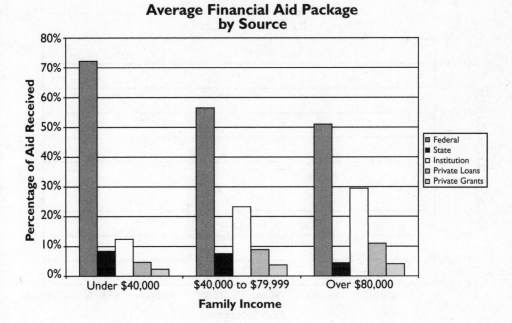

Relationship Between Aid Received and Cost of Attendance by Family Income

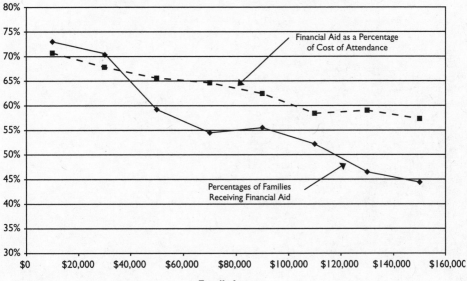

Average Cost of Attendance
by Family Income

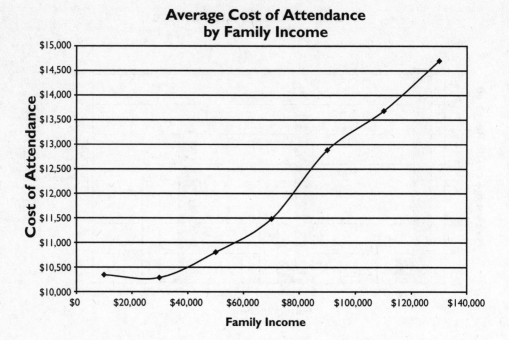

8

Private Loans

Matt positioned the overstuffed library chair to face a window, sat and emptied the contents of a folder onto the windowsill. He studied the quad lawn below, where students walked in the autumn sunshine, and for the hundredth time that day, imagined what it would be like to live among the stone buildings and landscaped courtyards of Caledonia College.

"What's that stuff?" asked Sarah, seated on the sill of the next window. She rummaged through her backpack.

"Loan literature," said Matt, sorting through a dozen colorful envelopes and postcards. "I've been getting them for a while now, mostly from banks."

"Aren't Mom and Dad supposed to get those?"

"I don't know. We've got twenty minutes before we're supposed to meet. I thought I'd check these out," said Matt. He opened an envelope.

"You got a dollar? I'm hungry," said Sarah. "There're snacks and stuff in the hallway downstairs."

Matt opened his wallet and gave her two dollars. "Get me a granola bar or something, okay?"

"Thanks," said Sarah, and, shouldering her bag, walked to the door.

Matt studied the letter he'd just opened. "Dear Student," it began. "It's never been harder to pay for college . . ." Matt skipped to the colorful graphic on the second page and read the unfamiliar phrases: "10- 15- or 20-year term,"

"PRIME + 0% interest" (how can anything be 0% interest? he wondered), "APR . . ."

Maybe Mom or Dad could explain all this stuff.

•   •   •

Private Education Loans, also known as Alternative Education Loans, might help bridge the gap between the actual cost of your education and the amount the government allows you to borrow in its programs. Private loans are based on your credit history, not financial need, so there are no long government need analysis forms to complete. These loans are offered by private lenders, with terms that are set by the lender, not the government. As such, the terms do vary from lender to lender. Some families turn to private education loans when the federal loans or other programs don't provide enough money, or when they need more flexible repayment options.

Many banks, credit unions, specialized education lenders and other financial institutions want to lend you money for college because it is a highly profitable and low-risk business. The total private student loan volume exceeded $13 billion in 2005, and is growing at about 25% a year. Millions of students each year get private student loans.

Depending on your needs, private education loans can be a good addition or alternative to government-funded loans. There are several reasons to explore private loans:

- **Variable interest rates.** The interest rates on private education loans are variable, changing at least once a year. This contrasts with the interest rates on federal student loans, which are fixed rates. If you expect interest rates to drop, a variable rate loan can be better than a fixed rate loan. If you expect interest rates to rise, a fixed rate loan may be better. The interest rates on private education loans are typically pegged to standard indexes called the Prime Lending Rate or the London Interbank Offered Rate (LIBOR).[39]

- **Cost.** Private education loans are less expensive than most credit cards, but are usually more expensive[40] than most government education loans. Private education loans are also somewhat less expensive than unsecured private loans from your local bank. Some home equity loans and lines of credit may be less expensive than private student loans.

- **Credit based.** Eligibility for private education loans is based on your credit history usually expressed in a credit rating called a FICO score (see www.myfico.com).[41] Borrowers with a FICO score of 650 or lower will find it difficult to obtain a private education loan. If you don't have a good credit history, you can still get a private education loan if you have a creditworthy cosigner. The interest rates and fees charged by private education loans will also depend on your credit score and the credit score of your cosigner. Even students with good credit scores might want to have their loans cosigned by a creditworthy cosigner because this can reduce the interest rates and fees. Most private student loans include a cosigner release option that absolves the cosigner from responsibility after the borrower has made 48 on-time monthly payments. If you have an excellent credit history (i.e., a FICO score of 750 or higher), the interest rates on private student loans may even be competitive with the interest rates on Federal PLUS loans. On the other hand, government education loans (excepting Federal PLUS loans) are available largely without regard to credit history.[42]

- **Student obligation.** Some parents do not like the Federal PLUS loan because only the parent is obligated to repay the loan, unlike the Federal Stafford loan which is a student obligation. (Some parents enter into an informal or formal agreement with the student to have the student take responsibility for making payments on the Federal PLUS loan after they graduate and get a job.) Most private education loans are student loans, in which the student has the primary obligation to repay the loan. Although the parent is still on the hook as a cosigner of the loan, at least the student shares the responsibility. The activity on the loan will be reported on the credit history of both the borrower and cosigner.

- **In-school deferment.** Repayment on a Federal Stafford loan is generally deferred until after the student graduates.[43] Repayment on a Federal PLUS loan begins sixty-days after full disbursement.[44] Many private education loans allow the repayment obligation to be deferred until after the student graduates by capitalizing the interest. This adds the interest to the principal balance of the loan, increasing the size of the loan.

- **Generous loan limits.** Most private education loans offer higher loan limits than the Federal Stafford and Perkins loans. Although the Federal PLUS loan is limited by the difference between the cost of attendance and financial need, and so should be sufficient to handle most costs, many families prefer a blend between the terms of the Federal Stafford and Federal PLUS loans, such as a student obligation with higher loan

limits. The private education loans address this preference. From a lender perspective, bigger education loans are more profitable than and no more risky than smaller education loans. The federal loans have lower limits because the cost to the government increases with the amount borrowed due to the student and lender interest subsidies.

- **Eligible expenses.** Federal loans may be used to pay for only qualified higher education expenses, such as tuition and fees, books and supplies, and room and board, as defined in the college's "student budget." Private education loans allow other expenses to be included, such as the purchase of a personal computer or laptop, study abroad and previous school charges. Some private education loans do not require school certification, and so may be used for any purpose, such as continuing education or certain living expenses.

- **Deductible interest.** Up to $2,500 in interest paid on education loans, including both government and private education loans, is deductible as an adjustment to income on your federal income tax return. This means you can take the deduction even if you don't itemize. Only private education loans that are borrowed solely to pay for qualified higher education expenses are eligible; mixed-use loans, such as home equity loans and credit card debt, are not eligible. While one can deduct the interest paid on a home equity loan or line of credit without limit, one must itemize to take advantage of this deduction.

- **Privacy.** One can apply for a private education loan without completing a FAFSA. Although the information submitted on financial aid applications is protected by the Family Educational Rights and Privacy Act of 1974 (FERPA), some families may be concerned about too many people having access to their asset information via the FAFSA. Although one must submit a FAFSA to obtain a Federal Stafford Loan, one does not need to submit a FAFSA to obtain a Federal PLUS loan.

Private loans also present significant differences in structure, costs and risks, compared to government-funded loans:

Private loans tend to be more expensive. Federal and state education loans generally have lower interest rates and fees than private lenders can offer. In addition, private loan borrowers are more exposed to increased costs from rising interest rates, since private education loans offer variable rates and the government loans offer fixed rates. The fees charged by some private loans can significantly increase the cost of the loan. A loan with a relatively low interest rate but high fees can potentially cost more than a loan with a slightly higher interest rate and no fees. (The lenders that do not charge fees often roll the difference into the interest rate.) For example, 6.8% with 4% fees on a ten-year term is the same as 7.72% with no fees.

Bad credit adds up to 4% on interest rates and up to 9% on fees.

👍 **RULE OF THUMB**

An extra 1% in the interest rate costs
more than a one-point increase in the fees.

Private loans generally offer less forgiving terms. Government loans offer a variety of deferments and forbearances, such as the ability to avoid making payments until the student graduates. While private education loans may also defer the repayment obligation, interest continues to accrue and is added to the balance of the loan, significantly increasing the size of the loan. With the subsidized Federal Stafford and Perkins loans, the federal government pays the interest during periods of deferment. The federal loans can also be discharged in several situations, such as total and permanent disability, death and closed schools, and provide generous loan forgiveness provisions for teachers, first responders and others who work in national need areas.

Private loans are difficult to compare. Most private education loans do not tell you exactly what interest rate you will get and the fees you will pay until you've already invested a lot of effort in completing a preliminary paper or online application. Even then, it is hard to compare costs. A twenty-year loan may have a lower Annual Percentage Rate (APR) than a fifteen-year loan despite being a more expensive loan, since increasing the loan term tends to decrease the APR. It is also not immediately apparent whether a 7% interest loan with 4% fees is more or less expensive than a 6% interest loan with 6% fees. (It turns out that the former is slightly more expensive.) So even if you want to use the least expensive loan, you may have trouble figuring out which loan costs less.

Here's an example:

To obtain $10,000 after 4% fees, one would have to borrow $10,416.67 (the fees get rolled into the loan). Using a 7% interest rate and ten-year term, the monthly payment would be $120.95 and the total payments would be $14,513.37. To obtain $10,000 net after 6% fees, one would have to borrow $10,638.30. Using a 6% interest rate and ten-year term, the monthly payment would be $118.11 and the total payments would be $14,172.70.

Thus 7% interest + 4% fees is MORE expensive than 6% interest + 6% fees.

The tables below (called "Factors Affecting Loan Cost") show the effect of different fees, interest rates and terms on loans. You can use these tables to compare loan offers with different fees and rates. There's also a ranking of which factors affect the ultimate cost of a loan most and least.

FACTORS AFFECTING LOAN COST

Table A below will help you calculate the cost of a loan. Table B shows how fees and interest rates interact to create the overall cost of a loan.

You'll also find a number of calculators designed to help you make the best decisions on loan costs at www.collegegold.com.

As a broader review of loan terms, here's a general ranking of factors affecting loan cost. We've ranked them on a scale of 1 to 10, with 10 increasing loan cost the most, and 1 the least.

Interest Rate – 10
Capitalization of Interest – 8
Loan Term in Years – 5.5
Fees – 2
Discounts on Rates or Fees – 1

TABLE A

The following table shows the cost per $1,000 borrowed for a ten-, fifteen- or twenty-year term at interest rates of 1% to 15% with fees of 0% to 10%. This is the cost in addition to repaying the amount borrowed. It assumes that the amount borrowed is increased to cover the cost of the fees, so that the net disbursement is the same. This table can be useful for comparing the costs of different loans, and seeing how much that money is going to cost you.

Private Loans

Total Cost to Borrow $1,000

Rate	Loan Term	0%	1%	2%	3%	Fees 4%	5%	6%	7%	8%	9%	10%
1%	10	$51	$62	$73	$84	$95	$107	$118	$130	$143	$155	$168
	15	$77	$88	$99	$111	$122	$134	$146	$158	$171	$184	$197
	20	$104	$115	$126	$138	$150	$162	$174	$187	$200	$213	$226
2%	10	$104	$115	$127	$138	$150	$162	$175	$187	$200	$213	$227
	15	$158	$170	$182	$194	$207	$219	$232	$246	$259	$273	$287
	20	$214	$226	$239	$252	$265	$278	$292	$306	$320	$334	$349
3%	10	$159	$170	$182	$195	$207	$220	$233	$246	$259	$273	$287
	15	$243	$256	$268	$281	$295	$308	$322	$337	$351	$366	$381
	20	$331	$344	$358	$372	$386	$401	$416	$431	$447	$463	$479
4%	10	$215	$227	$240	$253	$266	$279	$292	$306	$321	$335	$350
	15	$331	$345	$359	$373	$387	$402	$416	$432	$447	$463	$479
	20	$454	$469	$484	$499	$515	$531	$547	$564	$581	$598	$616
5%	10	$273	$286	$299	$312	$326	$340	$354	$369	$383	$399	$414
	15	$423	$438	$452	$467	$483	$498	$514	$531	$547	$564	$582
	20	$584	$600	$616	$633	$650	$667	$685	$703	$722	$741	$760
6%	10	$332	$346	$359	$373	$388	$402	$417	$433	$448	$464	$480
	15	$519	$534	$550	$566	$582	$599	$616	$633	$651	$669	$688
	20	$719	$737	$755	$773	$791	$810	$829	$849	$869	$889	$910
7%	10	$393	$407	$422	$436	$451	$467	$482	$498	$514	$531	$548
	15	$618	$634	$651	$668	$685	$703	$721	$740	$759	$778	$798
	20	$861	$880	$899	$918	$938	$959	$979	$1,001	$1,023	$1,045	$1,067
8%	10	$456	$471	$486	$501	$517	$533	$549	$566	$583	$600	$618
	15	$720	$738	$755	$773	$792	$811	$830	$850	$870	$890	$911
	20	$1,007	$1,028	$1,048	$1,070	$1,091	$1,113	$1,136	$1,159	$1,182	$1,206	$1,231
9%	10	$520	$535	$551	$567	$583	$600	$617	$635	$652	$670	$689
	15	$826	$844	$863	$882	$902	$922	$942	$963	$984	$1,006	$1,029
	20	$1,159	$1,181	$1,203	$1,226	$1,249	$1,273	$1,297	$1,322	$1,347	$1,373	$1,399
10%	10	$586	$602	$618	$635	$652	$669	$687	$705	$724	$743	$762
	15	$934	$954	$974	$994	$1,015	$1,036	$1,058	$1,080	$1,102	$1,126	$1,149
	20	$1,316	$1,339	$1,363	$1,388	$1,413	$1,438	$1,464	$1,490	$1,517	$1,545	$1,573
11%	10	$653	$670	$687	$704	$722	$740	$759	$777	$797	$816	$837
	15	$1,046	$1,067	$1,088	$1,109	$1,131	$1,154	$1,176	$1,200	$1,224	$1,248	$1,273
	20	$1,477	$1,502	$1,528	$1,554	$1,580	$1,608	$1,635	$1,664	$1,693	$1,722	$1,753
12%	10	$722	$739	$757	$775	$793	$812	$832	$851	$871	$892	$913
	15	$1,160	$1,182	$1,204	$1,227	$1,250	$1,274	$1,298	$1,323	$1,348	$1,374	$1,400
	20	$1,643	$1,669	$1,697	$1,724	$1,753	$1,782	$1,811	$1,842	$1,872	$1,904	$1,936

(continued)

Total Cost to Borrow $1,000 (continued)

Rate	Loan Term	0%	1%	2%	3%	Fees 4%	5%	6%	7%	8%	9%	10%
13%	10	$792	$810	$828	$847	$866	$886	$906	$927	$948	$969	$991
	15	$1,277	$1,300	$1,324	$1,348	$1,372	$1,397	$1,423	$1,449	$1,475	$1,503	$1,530
	20	$1,812	$1,840	$1,869	$1,899	$1,929	$1,960	$1,991	$2,023	$2,056	$2,090	$2,124
14%	10	$863	$882	$901	$921	$941	$961	$982	$1,003	$1,025	$1,047	$1,070
	15	1,397	$1,421	$1,446	$1,471	$1,497	$1,523	$1,550	$1,578	$1,606	$1,634	$1,663
	20	$1,984	$2,015	$2,045	$2,077	$2,109	$2,142	$2,175	$2,209	$2,244	$2,280	$2,316
15%	10	$936	$956	$976	$996	$1,017	$1,038	$1,060	$1,082	$1,104	$1,127	$1,151
	15	$1,519	$1,545	$1,571	$1,597	$1,624	$1,652	$1,680	$1,709	$1,738	$1,768	$1,799
	20	$2,160	$2,192	$2,225	$2,258	$2,292	$2,327	$2,362	$2,398	$2,435	$2,473	$2,511

TABLE B

The following table shows the relationship between interest rates and fees on a ten-year repayment term. For example, a 7% interest loan with 4% fees is slightly more expensive than a 6% interest loan with 6% fees.

How Fees Affect the Cost of Borrowing

Rates	0%	1%	2%	3%	Fees 4%	5%	6%	7%	8%	9%	10%
1%	1.0%	1.2%	1.4%	1.6%	1.8%	2.0%	2.3%	2.5%	2.7%	2.9%	3.2%
2%	2.0%	2.2%	2.4%	2.6%	2.8%	3.1%	3.3%	3.5%	3.7%	4.0%	4.2%
3%	3.0%	3.2%	3.4%	3.6%	3.9%	4.1%	4.3%	4.5%	4.8%	5.0%	5.2%
4%	4.0%	4.2%	4.4%	4.7%	4.9%	5.1%	5.3%	5.6%	5.8%	6.0%	6.3%
5%	5.0%	5.2%	5.4%	5.7%	5.9%	6.1%	6.4%	6.6%	6.8%	7.1%	7.3%
6%	6.0%	6.2%	6.4%	6.7%	6.9%	7.1%	7.4%	7.6%	7.7.9%	8.1%	8.4%
7%	7.0%	7.2%	7.5%	7.7%	7.9%	8.2%	8.4%	8.7%	8.9%	9.2%	9.4%
8%	8.0%	8.2%	8.5%	8.7%	8.9%	9.2%	9.4%	9.7%	10.0%	10.2%	10.5%
9%	9.0%	9.2%	9.5%	9.7%	10.0%	10.2%	10.5%	10.7%	11.0%	11.3%	11.5%
10%	10.0%	10.2%	10.5%	10.7%	11.0%	11.2%	11.5%	11.8%	12.0%	12.3%	12.6%
11%	11.0%	11.2%	11.5%	11.7%	12.0%	12.3%	12.5%	12.8%	13.1%	13.3%	13.6%
12%	12.0%	12.3%	12.5%	12.8%	13.0%	13.3%	13.6%	13.8%	14.1%	14.4%	14.7%
13%	13.0%	13.3%	13.5%	13.8%	14.0%	14.3%	14.6%	14.9	15.2%	15.4%	15.7%
14%	14.0%	14.3%	14.5%	14.8%	15.1%	15.3%	15.6%	15.9%	16.2%	16.5%	16.8%
15%	15.0%	15.3%	15.5%	15.8%	16.1%	16.4%	16.7%	16.9%	17.2%	17.5%	17.9%

Private Loans

Private loans are limited to creditworthy borrowers or borrowers with creditworthy cosigners. If you and your parents both have bad credit, you may not be eligible for private education loans or will pay much higher rates and fees. The published interest rates are usually just the lowest rate they charge for good credit customers during the in-school period. Borrowers with bad credit can expect interest rates that are as much as 4% higher, loan fees that are as much as 9% higher, and may be subjected to loan limits that are as much as two-thirds lower than the advertised figures.

We feel that private education loans should be used only after you've exhausted all other types of student aid. That said, with the current fixed rates for federal education loans (Perkins 5.0%, Stafford 6.8%, PLUS 8.5%), some private education loans may be temporarily competitive with Federal PLUS loans for customers with excellent credit.

For undergraduate students, going with private loans is currently a matter of choice, not necessity, since Federal PLUS loans are available up to the cost of attendance. For graduate students, on the other hand, private loans are often a necessity, though the higher Federal Stafford loan limits and new graduate Federal PLUS loans help hold down the amount of private loans needed.

It's not the business of this book to recommend specific lenders, but if you decide that private loans will be best in your situation, there are a few common-sense rules you should follow.

Focus on actual costs. With a few exceptions, most private education loans are in the same ballpark for actual costs, although the loans might be structured differently. Costs do vary among loans, given the combination of interest rates and fees, and capitalization of interest. For example, some loans are tied to the "Prime Lending Rate" and some tied to the "LIBOR," which are different lending benchmarks. Prime is higher than LIBOR, so an offer of Prime + 0% can be about the same as LIBOR + 2.8%, even though at first glance it might look like a better deal.

Keep in mind that private loans can be set with variable rates, so if interest rates go up, families will be paying more. If they go down, families will pay less.

The current trend among lenders is to offer private education loans with no fees for their best credit customers. A lender that advertises a lower interest rate may charge higher fees to make up the difference. If you intend to pay off the loan early, a loan with lower fees will cost you less, assuming that the equivalent no-fee interest rates are about the same.

Private education loans are a growing business, and you will see many of them advertised. College financial aid offices differ on whether they will actually recommend specific lenders, but they can help you understand the detailed differences in the loan terms—as can good financial advisors.

Also remember that the rates advertised by lenders might not be apples-to-apples comparisons, so compare loan offers based on the actual costs of the loan setup you require. This is a problem familiar to anyone who has explored payment options for a house or other large loan.

☑ **I Wish I Had Known . . .**

That I couldn't qualify for any private student loans without a cosigner.

—anonymous college student

Watch your cash flow. It's a good idea to know your monthly uncommitted cash flow—the total amount of money income you can devote to paying for college, as well as the assets that are available for paying for college. This will help determine how much you can afford to pay for debt repayments and how much as direct payments of college bills. It helps to first look at the extremes—the shortfall if you take on no debt, and the maximum debt you can afford to repay given your average monthly discretionary income. The actual split will be somewhere in between. A good rule of thumb is you should borrow about 125% of the difference between annual college costs and the amount of income and savings you can devote to paying for college bills, rounded up to the nearest $1,000. For example, if college costs after financial aid are $10,000 and you have $6,000 available to pay this bill, that would suggest that you borrow $5,000 to pay the bill. That would leave you with $1,000 for the loan payments, which would total about $744 a year at 8.5% interest. Next year the amount available to pay the bill would be $5,250, so this rule of thumb will suggest that you borrow $6,000.

ALTERNATIVES TO PRIVATE LOANS

Home equity loans and lines of credit: Private education loans tend to have interest rates that are in the same ballpark as home equity loans. If your private education loan has a variable interest rate and interest rates are low, you might consider using a fixed rate home equity loan to pay off the private education loan, effectively locking in the interest rate. A home equity line of credit might also be used to help pay for college. A home equity line of credit is usually offered as a variable rate loan but you only pay interest when you've actually drawn down the line of credit. If you're an independent student or a parent with a student who qualifies for need-based student aid, you should be careful about using a home equity loan (as opposed to a line of credit), as any excess funds will be treated as an asset on the FAFSA. Keep in mind that both home equity loans and home equity lines of credit decrease the net worth of your assets.

Borrowing from retirement funds: You can borrow money from your 401(k) to help pay for your children's education. For many plans, you can borrow up to 50% of your vested savings, to be paid back within five years. It is not, however, necessarily a good idea. You lose the tax shelter that a 401(k) provides, and delay the growth of a retirement fund. If you lose your job, you might have to pay the money back right away. This strategy should be employed only with a complete understanding of the consequences.

Although borrowing from your retirement plan has the benefit of paying the interest to yourself, this is merely a substitute for the money it would have earned from being invested. There are also significant restrictions on borrowing from your retirement plan. If you don't repay the money on time, it can lead to severe tax penalties. Interest paid on the loan is not tax deductible. Generally speaking, borrowing from your retirement plan is one of the worst options available.

You cannot borrow money from your IRA to help pay for your children's education, but you can take an early distribution to pay for qualified higher education expenses without paying the 10% tax penalty. You still pay regular income tax on the distribution, if applicable. This is a bad idea, however. Not only are you cutting into your retirement savings, but the distribution will count as income on next year's FAFSA, increasing your EFC and reducing your aid eligibility. Between the taxes and the lost aid eligibility, you may be netting as little as 16 cents on the dollar and no more than 50 cents on the dollar. Plus remember that a student probably has more time to pay off a loan than you might have to save for your retirement.

Alternative financing strategies also come with tradeoffs.

- **Interest tax deduction.** Home equity loans and lines of credit are tax deductible, if the taxpayer itemizes deductions[45] on Schedule A of the

1040. On the other hand, the taxpayer can deduct up to $2,500 a year in student loan interest even if he or she doesn't itemize.[46]

- **Responsible party.** The parent or graduate student Federal PLUS borrower is responsible for repaying the Federal PLUS loan. The student is not responsible for repaying the Federal PLUS loan, although many parents enter into agreements with their children to have them make the payments on the loan. In contrast, many alternative loans make the student responsible for repaying. However, those loans often require the parent to cosign the loan, making the parent responsible for repaying if the student defaults on the loan. Since the parent is on the hook either way, it is often better to focus on which loan costs less.

- **In-school deferments.** Many alternative loans allow the parent to defer payments while the student is in school. However, several Federal PLUS loan providers are now allowing the family to defer payments as well. In both cases deferring payments substantially increases the size of the loan by adding the interest that accrues to the principal.

PRIVATE LOAN CONSOLIDATION

As with government loans, private loans can be consolidated. Again, this would happen later in the student's college career or after college (we're including it here to make you aware of the possibility). Private student loans cannot, in general, be consolidated with federal student loans, and the low interest rates on federal consolidation loans are not available to private education loans. Some private education lenders offer private consolidation loans that can consolidate federal loans with private education loans, but these aren't consolidating the private education loans into the federal consolidation program. Often the lender is consolidating the federal loans into the federal consolidation program and the private education loans into the private consolidation loan "behind the scenes," presenting the borrower with a single monthly payment. In some cases the lender is using the proceeds of the private consolidation loan to pay off the federal loans, increasing the cost.

Even if a lender is willing to "consolidate" your federal loans with your private education loans, you should consolidate them separately, as the federal consolidation loans offer superior benefits and lower interest rates for consolidating those debts.

The interest rates on private loan consolidation programs are dictated by the lender, not the government. There may be additional fees charged for originating these loans. Most private consolidation loans are variable interest rate loans, not fixed rate loans. There is rarely much of an advantage to consolidating your private education loans.

When evaluating a private consolidation loan, ask whether the interest rate is fixed or variable, whether there are any fees and whether there are prepayment penalties.

A FINAL WORD ABOUT BORROWING

Just because money is available doesn't mean students and parents should borrow it, regardless of whether the borrowing program originates with the federal government or private lenders. Skidmore's Bob Shorb has seen plenty of families get into trouble even during the low-interest days of the early '90s:

"What is scary is these mega supplemental loans that students are taking out," says Bob. "Let's say it's a situation where the EFC is $20,000 per year and the parents only want to pay $5,000. So now you've got that student taking out a $15,000 loan to replace what their parents aren't paying. If they do that each year, they graduate with a liberal arts degree and $60,000 of debt. . . . We don't encourage students to do that."

A ten-year $60,000 loan borrowed at 9% interest requires a monthly payment of $760 to repay. If you allow 10% of your gross (pre-tax) monthly income to pay student debts, that requires a salary of $91,206 per year—quite a stretch for a new graduate—and remember, we're talking about loans *in addition to federal programs like the Federal Stafford loans*. Even at 15% of gross income, you'd need a salary of more than $60,804 just to meet the payment.

A good rule of thumb is that you should borrow no more than your anticipated starting salary to pay for your education. For example, if you expect to get a job paying $48,000 a year after you graduate from a four-year college, you should borrow less than $12,000 a year and $48,000 in total to pay for your education from all sources.

Regardless of which loan options the family chooses, they should always consider using up any remaining unsubsidized Federal Stafford loan eligibility before tapping into the other types of loans. If a Federal PLUS loan is unavailable for one of several reasons (for example adverse credit, the parent receives only public assistance or disability benefits), higher Federal Stafford loan limits might apply.

As we said in chapter 7, we think it's a good idea to limit borrowing to what you truly need. Remember: "Live like a student while you are in school, so you don't have to live like a student after you graduate."

BOOK TO WEB

Use the loan calculators on www.collegegold.com throughout this book to determine payments and other critical data as you judge which loans might be right for your situation. There are also calculators to help you analyze the differences among loans.

CODE: 1022

Financial Aid for Work and Service

"**Y**ou must be Matt," said Rachel Piedmont, "and you must be Sarah. Please come in."

"I don't want to interrupt," said Matt. "We were told to meet Mom and Dad downstairs at two, but they weren't there."

Rachel motioned for Matt and Sarah to sit, saying, "Well, these meetings can run long." She gestured to Jim and Lynn. "Usually, I just give families a lot of homework, but your parents already know a lot, so we were digging down into the kind of financial aid package a family like yours might get here."

"Okay," said Matt. Sitting in a financial aid office made him feel self-conscious. He thought, this is where we find out if I can really go to a school this expensive.

Rachel continued, "We've covered a lot of ground, including grants and loans. Before you go, I'd like to mention the ways in which you can help your parents."

"You mean scholarships?" asked Matt. "I'm already applying for those . . ."

"That's great," said Rachel, "but before we get into that, I want to tell you that many students work during the school year to help pay for college. There are many options, from military programs and other national service to local jobs. The biggest program I have here is work-study, where students work part-time for the college. Do you think you could work for fifteen hours a week and still keep up your grades?"

Matt brightened. "No problem. I do that now," he said.

• • •

You can earn additional money for college—sometimes a lot of money—by working. This financial aid might be made in direct payments to you while you are in college, or it might take the form of loan forgiveness later. The work can take place before, during or after your college education. The four major sources of earned financial aid are work-study programs (including co-op and internship programs), employer-based aid, national service and aid based on military service. Many students also work during the summer vacation to earn money for school.

FEDERAL WORK-STUDY

The idea behind work-study is simple: Students earn part of the cost of their education by working part-time. The federal government pays a portion of the student's salary, making it cheaper for colleges and businesses to hire the student. For this reason, work-study students often find it easier to get a part-time job. State governments or colleges may also finance their own work-study programs, and work-study money is frequently a component of an overall financial aid package. Work-study is available for both undergraduate and graduate students.

The work-study arrangement has much in common with a regular job: The college is a student's employer, and pays the student directly, but there are some important differences. A student's work schedule is arranged to make study possible, and the job is contingent on remaining a student in good standing. The total hours worked and money paid are based in part on financial need, in part on the availability of funds (federal funding for work-study is awarded annually to colleges, and once a college commits the money, no more is available) and in part on meeting your obligations to academic progress.

Often, students work directly for the school in positions as varied as administrative staff, grounds crews, security personnel or food service. Off-campus, the Federal Work-Study program includes a community service component. Schools are required to use 7% of their Federal Work-Study program funds to pay for students employed in community service jobs. In addition, schools can request supplemental funding for community service jobs. If you are eligible for a Federal Work-Study job, the school will be delighted if you are interested in a

Financial Aid for Work and Service

community service job, especially if it involves working as a reading tutor for children or performing family literacy activities.

Some colleges place students in Federal Work-Study jobs with private, for-profit employers; these jobs must be relevant to the student's course of study.

You must indicate on the FAFSA form that you are interested in work-study, and since the funds are limited, you have one more incentive to get that form filed as soon as possible after January 1 of the year you'll attend college! If you file late, all the college's work-study money might have been awarded by the time your FAFSA information is received.

The money you earn from Federal Work-Study is generally subject to federal and state income tax, but exempt from FICA (Social Security) taxes, provided you are enrolled full-time and work less than half-time. Money earned from a Federal Work-Study job is not counted as income for the subsequent year's need analysis process. Financial aid administrators arrange students' work-study programs with care not to overwhelm college work. Although students might imagine completing both full-time work and full-time study, in reality both will usually be shortchanged. Tom Mortensen, a senior scholar at the Pell Institute for the Study of Opportunity in Higher Education in Washington, DC, has seen this too often: "I hear that story constantly on campus," says Mortensen. "Kids are sleeping through their classes, or not doing as well as they could have because of the hours they're working."

David Levy, Assistant Dean and Director of Financial Aid at Caltech, tells of a recurring conversation: "Students applying for financial aid say, 'Well, yeah, I knew school was expensive, but I thought . . . I could just work my way through school.' Sorry, but it isn't likely."

Studies have found that a small amount of term-time work, no more than ten to fifteen hours a week, can help improve academic performance. Working a modest amount while in school teaches you valuable time management skills; it is often worth listing on your resume when you graduate. Working more than twenty hours a week, however, will likely negatively impact academic performance. According to the 2003–04 National Postsecondary Student Aid Study, 7.5% of undergraduate students had work-study jobs, working 13.9 hours a week on average, with a median of 11 hours per week.

Working on campus is generally encouraged because it works out well for the balance between work and studies. Off-campus work in internships or co-op programs relevant to one's career goals and major have their own payoff, such as developing a deeper understanding of the field of work that attracts you.

LaNice Hagen, a student at Florida State University, shares this advice for students considering work: "At career expos, where people come to hire, they want you to have experience already. The only way for you to do that would be through an internship while you're in college. You don't have time to work full-time and go to school. I would also definitely make a list of all the occupations that I'm interested in and then interview people that currently hold those occupations. Find out about jobs from the people doing them, and not something that I just read on the computer!"

EMPLOYER-BASED AID

Some employers provide tuition assistance as a benefit, both to employees and their children. The more common form of the benefit is tuition assistance for current employees, offered because companies believe a more educated workforce makes them more competitive in today's economy. Approximately 85% of employers (mostly large and mid-size companies) offer some form of this benefit. In practice, about 8.7% of undergraduate students received some form of employer-based tuition assistance, and the average award amount was $2,088.

The first $5,250 in employer tuition assistance is excluded from gross income and not subjected to federal income tax. Payments above $5,250 may also be tax-free, if they represent a "working condition fringe benefit" as defined by the Internal Revenue Service. This means that if you had paid for the expenses yourself, you would have been able to deduct them as an employee business expense. (For example, this would be allowed for college study that improved your ability to do your job.)

Full-time employees make up a small minority of undergraduates, however. For most families, the truly relevant employer tuition program is aimed at helping the children of employees attend college. These have different restrictions under the tax code and are less common. As of 2005, approximately 27% of employers offered some form of college scholarship benefit to employees for their children's college attendance.[47]

Not surprisingly, colleges are among the most generous with this benefit. The Massachusetts Institute of Technology (MIT) and the California Institute of Technology (Caltech), to cite two examples, offer 100% tuition to those children of employees who attend the college.

Many large companies provide scholarships for the children of their employees and tuition reimbursement because it helps them retain talented staff. For example, the insurance company Aflac awards thirteen scholarships a year to children and grandchildren of employees for their first year of college, for any major at any college. Aflac also provides tuition reimbursement on a sliding scale to employees seeking an undergraduate degree, and a similar program to those pursuing a Masters degree. Federal Express offers permanent part-time and full-time employees tuition reimbursement for both undergraduate and graduate school, in programs ranging from $1,500 to $5,000 per year. Seattle-based Starbucks Corporation awards two $25,000 scholarships to the University of Washington for children of its employees.

It's not just large companies. Bullen Ultrasonics in Eaton, Ohio, reimburses 100% of tuition for current employees, not just to improve their current job skills but to enable them to move up. If a machine operator wants to earn a degree in order to move into management, Bullen will reimburse 100% of tuition, books, lab fees and other expenses.

Ask your family's (parents, spouse and grandparents) employer(s) if they have financial aid programs, and take advantage if you can. The HR department will know. In addition, some labor unions offer benefits such as tuition assistance and scholarships to their members and their members' children.

Co-op programs combine your studies with paid work experience in a field related to your major or career goals. Companies like Pfizer and General Electric have large co-op programs as do many smaller firms. Typically, co-op programs are arranged between a college financial aid office and a local employer. There are three different types of cooperative education:

- Parallel: part-time work and part-time study
- Extended day: full-time study and part-time work or full-time work and part-time study
- Alternating: a quarter, semester or year of full-time work alternated with a session of full-time study

Co-op programs usually begin with an initial period of full-time study, which eventually becomes an integrated program of class time and relevant work experience. It's a great way to help pay for tuition. Salaries range from $2,500 to $14,000 a year and vary depending on your field of study, prior experience and your level of education.

Internships typically take place over a shorter period of time, and are paid less than co-op programs. Like co-op programs, internships provide valuable work experience, which builds your resume and helps you understand a business or profession. An internship might be arranged through the financial aid office, but you should also be in touch with your college's career center, which can connect you with internships throughout your school year. (Many schools use www.monstertrak.com to match students with internship opportunities.)

AMERICORPS

You can earn money for college attendance, or to pay back student loans after graduation, by performing community service in one of the programs under an umbrella organization called AmeriCorps.

AmeriCorps is not a single program, but a clearinghouse and network of many service programs at the national and state levels. It was created in 1994 to bring together service-minded citizens with organizations that needed them, in fields such as education, environmental work, health and public safety. For example, following Hurricane Katrina, AmeriCorps funded programs run by national organizations as big as the American Red Cross, and groups as local as the Youth Bureau in West Seneca, NY, whose members traveled to Slidell, LA, to repair roofs of homes damaged by Hurricane Katrina in 2005.

The AmeriCorps award for a year of full-time service—at least 1,700 hours of work—is currently $4,725. It can be prorated for less than full-time work and participants can receive two awards. Note that this money is earned in addition to what the job pays, and like most earned income, it's taxable.

Members of AmeriCorps can also receive a forbearance on their federal student loans, meaning they do not have to make loan payments during their service. Interest continues to accrue while you work, but if you successfully complete a term of service, the National Service Trust (parent organization of AmeriCorps) will pay all or part of the accrued interest. Other types of student loans might also be eligible for forbearance; check with your lender.

AmeriCorps*VISTA is focused on helping low-income individuals and communities with the problems endemic to poverty. VISTA (Volunteers in Service to America) dates back to the "War on Poverty" of the mid-'60s and, in its own words, works "to fight illiteracy, improve health services, create businesses, increase housing opportunities, bridge the digital divide and strengthen the capacity of community organizations." Somewhat different benefits are available to

AmeriCorps*VISTA members. Detailed information is available at 1-800-942-2677 or on the web page at www.americorps.gov/about/programs/vista.asp.

When you do the math, it's clear that people don't join AmeriCorps-funded and other service organizations just to earn an education benefit. AmeriCorps work is national service; it's generally low paid and hard work, but for the more than 70,000 Americans who participate in AmeriCorps each year, the real reward is their satisfaction in giving back to their country.

The Peace Corps (not part of AmeriCorps) also offers two forms of education benefit. Volunteers engaged in Peace Corps work may defer repayment of Federal Stafford, Perkins and consolidation loans. Volunteers may receive loan forgiveness for 15% of Federal Perkins loan debt for each year of Peace Corps service, up to a total of 70%.

☑ **I Wish I Had Known . . .**

That community service was a key component of the application acceptance process . . . I can't complete many scholarship applications because I don't have any community service experience!

—*Beth Taylor, sophomore*
Purdue University

FEDERAL LOAN FORGIVENESS PROGRAMS

The federal government offers to cancel its college loans for graduates who agree to teach in underserved school systems. Working with the states, the Department of Education will forgive up to 100% of Federal Perkins Loan debt in return for five years of employment (the percentage varies by year) in one of three positions:

- Teaching in a school serving students from low-income families.
- Teaching special education (including teachers of infants, toddlers, children or youth with disabilities).
- Teaching in the fields of mathematics, science, foreign languages or bilingual education, or in any other field of expertise determined by a state education agency to have a shortage of qualified teachers in that state.

During the time that you are employed by the school system and earning loan forgiveness, you might also qualify for deferment of any loan payments. You must notify the college that administers the loan to arrange deferment and cancellation of your debt; the school determines whether you qualify.

This program is not restricted to public schools. The U.S. Department of Education states that "you may receive teacher cancellation for services performed in a private academy if the private academy has established its nonprofit status with the Internal Revenue Service (IRS), and if the academy is providing elementary and/or secondary education according to state law."

A similar program can cancel Federal Stafford loan debt incurred after October 1, 1998. If you teach full-time for five consecutive years in a low-income school, a portion of the loan may be forgiven.[48] This applies to the various forms of Federal Stafford loans described in chapter 7, both subsidized and unsubsidized.

The need for teachers in low-income school districts is great. Just to cite two examples from 2005, California had 6,392 schools officially designated as low-income; even the small, wealthy state of Connecticut had 429 schools with the designation.

A similar program exists to provide loan forgiveness and forbearance for graduates who work as full-time child care workers in child care facilities serving low-income families.[49] The eligibility and forgiveness terms are somewhat different from the teacher program, and participation is subject to the availability of funds year by year.

Beyond teaching, federal loan forgiveness is available for graduates who serve in the following professions:

- Nurse or medical technician providing health care services.
- Employee of an eligible public or private nonprofit child or family service agency who is providing or supervising the provision of services to both high-risk children who are from low-income communities, and the families of such children.
- Qualified professional provider of early intervention services in a public or other nonprofit program under public supervision.
- Staff member in the educational part of a preschool program carried out under the Head Start Act.
- Qualifying law enforcement or corrections officer.[50]

For a student with an interest in teaching, child care or other service

BOOK TO WEB

The U.S. Department of Education keeps a database of low-income school districts that qualify for the loan forgiveness programs. Go to https://www.tcli.ed.gov/ and click on "search" to access the database.

jobs, who also feels inspired to help America's less fortunate communities, the government's loan forgiveness programs can add an extra reward for those who serve.

AID FOR MILITARY SERVICE

Education benefits have been part of military service for more than sixty years. Service members and veterans can qualify for as much as $80,000 in educational funding. Five programs make up the bulk of military education assistance: The Montgomery G.I. Bill, Military Tuition Assistance, College Fund Programs, Loan Repayment Programs and Reserve Officers Training Corps (ROTC) Scholarships.

BOOK TO WEB

This section was written with the help of Christopher Michel, Founder and Chairman of Military.com. You can find more about military service and benefits for military personnel and their families at www.military.com and in Chris's book, *The Military Advantage.*

The Montgomery G.I. Bill (MGIB): The program named after Congressman "Sonny" Montgomery is the centerpiece of military education benefits. It is run by the Veteran's Administration. Active-duty service members contribute $100 of military pay per month for their first year of service while "on duty" (total contribution of $1,200). After two years of active duty, service members are eligible to begin using the MGIB for tuition and other required college fees. As of October 2005, the G.I. Bill benefit was valued at over $37,000. Service members can contribute an additional $600 per service year as a "buy-up" and reap as much as $5,400 in additional aid.

The Department of Veterans Affairs (VA) pays only the actual cost of tuition and fees if you use the regular G.I. Bill while you're on active duty. However if you're a veteran, you can get up to $1,034 a month for full-time attendance, or less depending on your level of attendance. This money goes directly to the student, not the school, so if your cost of full-time enrollment is less than $1,034 per month, you pocket the difference.

The federal government also has an educational assistance program for survivors and dependents of service members who have been killed, permanently disabled (or died while disabled), captured, detained or missing in action.

Veterans are eligible for MGIB benefits for ten years after discharge. Any active-duty service resets the discharge date and extends benefits for ten years after the new discharge date.

The **Reserve G.I. Bill (RGIB)** offers similar education benefits to those who undertake a six-year obligation to the Armed Forces Reserve or National Guard. The RGIB benefits are currently $10,692 for 36 months of school.

👍 Veterans and the FAFSA

Earning military service aid does not disqualify you from the full range of government grants and loans available to non-service members, but it does reduce your financial need. Veterans' education benefits are treated as a resource, reducing financial aid need dollar for dollar. Veterans should exercise care when completing the FAFSA, as there are a variety of common errors that can have a severe negative impact on aid eligibility: (1) In the question about veterans education benefits, report the monthly amount, not the annual figure; (2) Veterans education benefits are not reported on Worksheet B, but Veterans non-education benefits and VASWSAP are; (3) Combat pay, housing allowance (BAQ), and subsistence allowance (BAS) are reported as untaxed income on Worksheet B and in the income earned from work figures[51]; (4) Social Security Administration Wages (code W of the W-2 statement) should be ignored; (5) Don't include on Worksheet B any amounts that were included in AGI, to prevent them from being double-counted.

If you are on active duty or are a veteran, and have questions about the MGIB and your particular situation, call your local VA office or 1-888-GIBILL-1 (1-888-442-4551). You can also find a local VA office by going to www.va.gov and click on "Facilities Locator" at the bottom.

U.S. MILITARY SERVICE ACADEMIES

Each branch of the service operates its own Service Academy as a four-year institution of higher education. All students receive a full scholarship with a small monthly stipend. Upon graduation, you're commissioned as a second lieutenant in the Army, Air Force, or Marine Corps or as an ensign in the Navy or Coast Guard. The United States Merchant Marine Academy operates in a similar fashion—graduates serve in paid positions in the transportation or maritime industries, and as U.S. Naval Reserve officers or active duty officers in any of the Armed Services. Appointment to a service academy is extremely competitive. For more information, call 1-800-822-8762 (Army Academy), 1-800-638-9156 (Naval Academy, including Marines), 1-800-443-9266 (Air Force), 1-800-883-8724 (Coast Guard Academy) or 1-866-546-4778 (United States Merchant Marine Academy).

ROTC SCHOLARSHIPS

The Reserve Officer Training Corps (ROTC) is an on-campus program designed to augment the military service academies. In exchange for your commitment to serve, the ROTC program provides you with money for college while you're in school. You must study military science along with your other college courses and, upon graduation, members of the ROTC are commissioned to serve as officers in the active, reserve or guard components of each branch.

Each branch of the service has a specific set of courses and training that potential officers must complete prior to joining the service, and ROTC programs allow students to do this while completing their college education. (There is no military commitment for the first year in ROTC, allowing you to pursue ROTC on a trial basis to see if ROTC is for you.)

The Coast Guard has a similar program called College Student Pre-Commissioning Initiative (CSPI). For more information, call 1-877-NOW-USCG.

Full ROTC scholarships pay for almost all tuition, fees and books charges for four years of college, and the service branch also provides a monthly living allowance. (The Army, for example, currently provides a monthly allowance of $300 in the first year, $350 in the second year, $450 in the third year, and $500 in the fourth year of college.) ROTC scholarships also come in one, two and three-year lengths.

This chart, from Military.com, compares differences among the ROTC programs of the Army, Air Force and Navy/Marines:

Branch	Can I choose my school?	Can I choose my major?	Minimum Test Requirements
Army	Students that apply for Army ROTC scholarships can choose up to three schools. Scholarships are awarded based upon availability at the school of your choice. The Army does try to match the needs of the student in most cases, but the Army does have final say as to which school you attend.	Yes, within limits.	920 SAT/19 ACT
Navy & Marines	Navy ROTC grants the student the most flexibility in selecting schools. Students can attend any one of 67 host NROTC universities once they obtain a scholarship.	Yes, but you must complete 1 year of calculus and 1 year of calculus-based physics.	520 M 530 V SAT 22 ACT (Navy) 1000 SAT or combined 45 ACT (USMC)
Air Force	Air Force ROTC scholarships are distributed by major. You are free to choose any school as long as the school you want to attend offers AFROTC and has an approved scholarship major.	Must be approved by the USAF.	520 M 530 V SAT 24 ACT

Military Tuition Assistance (TA): The TA programs are run separately by the five branches of the U.S. Armed Forces. Each service will pay up to $4,500 per year of tuition expenses. Benefits differ among the Army, Navy, Marine Corps, Air Force and Coast Guard—for example, benefits may be extended to civilian employees of the Coast Guard but not the other branches, and the Navy pays a lower total benefit per fiscal year.

Tuition Assistance is reset each fiscal year—if it's not used, it's lost. TA is generally paid directly to the college, not to individuals.

If you plan to use Tuition Assistance (TA), and your tuition and fees exceed your service's limit, you can use the "MGIB Top-up" to pay the balance. The amount you use is charged against your MGIB benefits, making it in effect an advance against future benefits. Top-up gives you a way to combine your education benefits and get the most value from your benefits. Find more information about top-up at www.gibill.va.gov/education/pamphlets/tatu.htm.

If you qualify for and learn an occupational specialty that the military considers critical (for example, the Navy nuclear field) your service branch might provide a "kicker" in addition to what you earn through the regular MGIB. Each service controls the amount of extra money it provides, and the extra funds can increase the amount of your MGIB benefit up to $71,000 as of 2006. Different service branches offer different dollar amounts of this benefit. These College Funds are awarded on a competitive basis according to academic merit (i.e., scoring in the top half of the Armed Services Vocational Aptitude Battery).

In general, each service's recruiters sign up individuals for the College Fund.

Student Loan Repayment Program: The military offers a benefit for those who have acquired federal education loans prior to enlistment, called the Student Loan Repayment Program (SLRP). In exchange for serving full-time duty (and scoring at least 50 on the Armed Forces Qualification Test), service members can qualify to have their loans repaid by the branch in which they serve. The benefit amount varies by service,[52] and is only available for the Army, Navy and Air Force. The benefit is available for new recruits and re-enlistees.

Military education benefits are also available for non-degree programs (which are outside the subject matter of this book). Benefits also depend on the

BOOK TO WEB

Most states also offer education benefits for service members and veterans. To find benefits available from your home state, visit www.military.com/education/statebenefits.

CODE: 1066

many variables of military service, the different branches and changing needs. If you have questions about veterans' benefits, call the national VA answer service at 1-888-GIBILL-1 (1-888-442-4551). You can also find a local VA office at www.va.gov (click on "Facilities Locator" at the bottom). If you are thinking of enlisting, a recruiting office or the information available at www.military.com can explain the benefits in more detail.

Financial Aid Administrators

"It's been a pleasure talking with you," said Rachel Piedmont. "Do you have any final questions today?"

"No, I think we can get most of this information to you just after Matt finishes his application to Caledonia," said Jim.

Rachel turned to Matt and Sarah. "Do you have any concerns?" she asked.

Matt looked at his parents, then to Sarah, and then said, "How do you decide how much our family will get?"

Rachel nodded, as if she'd expected the question. "We have a formula we use based on the information you give us. It's called an 'institutional methodology,' which is really a way to make sure the awards are fair. We work hard to make sure you receive all the forms of aid that you're eligible to receive, and we bring in every resource we have, from federal grants to loans the government guarantees, to on-campus employment, to scholarships based here at the college."

She continued, "And since your parents tell me you are very interested in music, I think you should talk to the music department here about the Caledonia Performance Scholarship. Let me write down the director's name, and I'll tell her she might be hearing from you."

She wrote the name Dolores Vicente and a phone number on the back of her own business card, and then handed it to Matt.

Jim rose and shook Rachel's hand. "We've taken a lot of your time, Rachel. Thanks very much for your help."

"Thank you for coming to this meeting prepared. It makes my job easier," Rachel replied. To Matt, she said, "What do you think of Caledonia?"

"He loves it," Sarah interjected. "So do I."

"Maybe we'll get both of you someday," said Rachel, shaking Sarah's hand, then Lynn's. She took Matt's hand last, saying, "Feel free to call me if you have any more questions. I mean it."

● ● ●

All the steps we've shown so far in *College Gold*, from filling out the FAFSA to exploring different sources of money for college, come together in one place at every college: the financial aid office. It's essential that you develop a solid working relationship with the financial aid administrators[53]; not only because they are experts in financial aid, but because the financial aid administrator is your family's active partner in creating the best possible plan for you. You've heard their voices throughout this book, and in this chapter you will hear more about their mission—how they work, how to work with them and how they can help.

WHAT IT'S ALL ABOUT

The financial aid office serves families differently according to their financial situations, says Daniel Barkowitz, Director of Financial Aid at MIT. Daniel explains that the families he advises fall into three broad groups: "Those who are fairly well-off need assistance simply in making choices about financing strategy. Do I borrow or not borrow money, how much should I borrow, should I use a payment plan? Those in middle-income families might need some resources [a mix of grants and loans] to afford the difference between, say, a state college and a private college. And then there are those who are in the neediest situations, who really require [financial] support. When even the concept of college is just a dream, the financial aid office can help make that dream a reality."

Carla Bender, Associate Director of Financial Aid at Hope College, puts the work of the financial aid office in practical terms when she says, "First, we assist families to understand the availability of funds as well as the *context* in which funds are available—what are the qualifying criteria, and what are the restrictions? Families need both the good news and the bad news. Second, [we] help them find all the resources we've identified."

For example, if a family knows nothing about federally guaranteed loans, she urges them to file the FAFSA form quickly, guides them toward the loans for which they might qualify and helps them determine which loans are right for them.

Carla continues with two imperatives for her financial aid decisions: "We try our best to make sure that everybody is assessed based on the same guidelines, so we are as fair as we can be. In those situations where the formulas don't reflect an accurate understanding of the family's financial situation, we want to apply reasonable professional judgment to improve the financial aid package when possible."

Financial aid administrators work right at the heart of two emotionally charged territories—family finances and the desire of parents to give their children the best possible chance. When it comes to money and education, people can be excited, engaged and forward-looking, but they can also quickly become frustrated, upset or even angry. Financial aid administrators deal with hundreds of families each year, and each family has a personal stake in the outcome. Their most important skill might just be the ability to listen carefully.

Financial aid administrators must not promise help that they cannot deliver, and so they have to be realistic. While families might imagine them sitting atop a pile of cash, arbitrarily choosing those who will or won't get help, the actual forces that shape their decisions are much more complex and policy driven.

To help you understand the work of financial aid administrators a little better, here are six truths about their work lives:

They are there to help. It's natural to be apprehensive about the outcome of your work with the financial aid office, but remember that their entire reason for being in the job is to do their best to make college more affordable or even possible for you.

They have to say "no" a lot. Years ago, a sign appeared on the door of a financial aid office that said, "NO is also an answer." Ouch. There is a limit to the amount and composition of financial aid at each college; eventually every financial aid administrator has to say, "No, there's no more." Their job involves distributing limited funds fairly.

They are pressed for time. With few exceptions, financial aid offices feel frustrated by lack of time and staff; at times they feel hampered and bogged down in federal regulations and paperwork. They work long hours. Every family is anxious and wants to discuss financial aid packages ASAP, but there are only so many phone calls you can make in a day.

MARY'S STORY

Daniel Barkowitz of MIT tells this story of why his job, for all its frustrations, can be so satisfying:

"Mary[54] was going to be the first person in her family to attend college. Nobody she knew was familiar with the process, and when she was accepted to a school far from home, she unfortunately never replied to say she was planning on coming. In September, Mary packed all her belongings, got on a bus from Florida to Massachusetts and arrived a week before classes were scheduled to begin. The dormitories were closed. She had no family or friends locally, no place to stay. The financial aid office bent over backward to find a place for her. They hired her as a work-study student in the fall, in part to make sure that everything worked out well.

"Mary graduated in four years as one of the top members of her class. It was a case where our investment—from both a financial as well as a time perspective—paid off in a big way.

"For all the students like Mary who actually leap into the unknown, there are many who don't even think of themselves as able to attend college. Reaching them, helping them go so much further in life than they expected, is the great reward of this work."

P.S. Don't let this happen to you! Notify the college that you'll be attending in the fall, and contact the financial aid office before you arrive on campus to make sure you've completed all the paperwork and the financial aid arrangements are all in order.

They have to work a seasonal schedule. College admissions schedules and aid decision deadlines mean much of their work comes in a concentrated period from February to May. Want to help a financial aid administrator? Get your paperwork in early!

They usually earn less money than the families they serve. It's easy to think of the financial aid administrator as a banker—because they are the "face" of college money, you might think of them as not having money worries of their own. They actually make average salaries, and have kids of their own to send to college! (We know a financial aid administrator at an expensive women's college who considers herself lucky that she only has sons. "How could I afford to send them here?" she asks with irony.)

They want the families to be their partners. Financial aid administrators repeat the basics of financial aid advice hundreds or even thousands of times a year, and welcome a family who arrives already knowing the basics. The more you know about where and how you'll find money for college, the more productive your brief time with each college's financial aid office can be. That's one of the reasons we wrote this book.

✓ I Wish I Had Known . . .

That the process is not as stressful as I first thought. I had a financial aid administrator that helped me out a lot!!

—*Marjo L. Martinez, freshman*
Colorado Technical University

HOW TO WORK WITH A FINANCIAL AID ADMINISTRATOR

Alison Rabil, Director of Financial Aid at Barnard, believes the most important thing to know about working with her is: "The more we know, the better off you're going to be. Unfortunately, financial information is very sensitive; it's difficult to divulge [to a stranger] and the forms can be onerous."

The Family Educational Rights and Privacy Act of 1974 (FERPA) protects the privacy of educational records, including all the information students and their families provide to the financial aid office. In general, only staff in the financial aid office will see the information you provide. Some examples of FERPA protections: Social Security numbers of students may not be revealed or appear on mailing labels; parent financial information may not be released to the student without written consent; student financial information cannot be released to a student's ex-spouse without written consent.

If you can give the financial aid administrator all the information they need, there's a good chance they'll discover the relevance of information you might not have realized was important. They might be able to make adjustments to provide more aid. If you have any concerns about the privacy of your information, discuss them with the financial aid administrator.

Vince Pecora, Director of Financial Aid at Towson University, points out that families are, in a sense, consumers of the financial aid administrator's services, and as such should both insist on getting good communication (which he says colleges are getting better at providing) and on playing their role responsibly. "Consumers have to be receptive, reading their mail (from the college and financial aid administrator), [and] responding in a timely fashion."

The right composition of a family's contribution varies depending on its unique financial picture, and more and more, financial aid administrators are moving into the role of financial advisor. Once all information is known and an EFC is established, a skilled advisor will ask how much the family can afford on a monthly basis. There is much to consider here as well, and even though the financial aid administrator is not the family's personal financial advisor, he or she can ask the right questions, for example:

- Which savings earmarked for education should be spent; how much, which first and when? (Assets in the child's name should generally be spent first.)
- Should the family pay tuition and fees once at the start of the semester or on a payment plan? (Most colleges have these.)
- Are there other family assets, such as stock or property, which would be advantageous to sell to finance college? (There are tax and need analysis implications for these. See chapter 5, "Maximizing Eligibility for Student Aid.")
- How much can the family afford to borrow to pay for their children's education?

If you can come to this conversation with a clear idea of what you might be able to afford on a monthly basis, the financial aid administrator can help you construct the right package for your circumstances. (Remember that you and the Financial Aid Administrator might differ on what you can afford, or what you consider the right amount of financial aid. They are working with regulated aid programs and formulas, and trying to award aid fairly to a large number of students subject to many constraints. You are focused on just one family situation: yours. Differences are almost inevitable. See the section on "Professional Judgment" in chapter 15.)

Financial Aid Administrators

Understand that a college financial aid administrator might not be a certified financial planner or accountant and should not try to persuade you to invest or sell assets. It is his or her job to lay out the choices and ask the right questions. They are the experts in the ways families pay for college, and have seen it done in many ways, so whether you work with a family financial advisor or make your own plan, incorporate as much of their knowledge as you can. They can help you avoid decisions that will negatively impact your aid eligibility, such as taking an early distribution from your retirement plan. Their job (and yours) is to construct the best package for your family.

They have a perspective specific to their field. For example, borrowing all you need to meet your EFC might seem manageable for a year of school. You can handle the cash flow at $400 per month. But you'll still be paying off that first year when the second comes due, so the monthly payment increases. Then the third and fourth years' bills come in, and perhaps a younger sibling enters school, and the monthly payment grows and grows. . . .

When the time comes to plan your payment, choices without clear right or wrong answers often appear. Here are some examples:

A couple in their mid-thirties, with two young children, manages to save $6,000 a year. Do they put it into a college fund or into retirement accounts?

A family owns a business. As the first of three children approaches college age, the family has an opportunity to expand the business, but must take a large loan to do so. Should they borrow money for college at the same time?

An independent student is faced with the choice of working two jobs during college to make ends meet, or postponing college in a plan to work full-time now and study full-time later.

Another family, strapped monthly for cash but convinced a certain school will benefit their child enormously, considers whether to ask grandparents for financial help on favorable terms, but risks feelings of unfairness between siblings, or taking on debt and cutting back expenses in ways they think will really hurt.

Not easy decisions! In these situations the financial aid administrator can offer an independent and objective source of information and possible solutions.

In addition to answering questions, you must ask plenty of them. Even if you've supplied all required information, questions create the dialogue that financial aid administrators want, and they can alleviate anxieties.

You must be clear about the processes colleges use. Know their deadlines, the documentation they require and how they like to receive information (more and more "paperwork" is moving online). Ask when you will know their decision. Ask how private scholarships or grants might affect a financial award package.

Questions to consider asking

Jim Sumner, Dean of Admission and Financial Aid at Grinnell College, suggests everyone, regardless of their financial situation, ask, "Do you do merit-based aid and/or scholarships as well as need-based aid? And how do I apply for both?" Merit-based aid, which is awarded to students the college desires regardless of need (because they've demonstrated academic, athletic or artistic talents, or qualities like leadership), varies tremendously between colleges.

Ask about state financial aid programs, their awards, deadlines and restrictions. Ask open-ended questions like, "Given what you know about me (or my child) as a student as well as my financial situation, what am I missing? Where else might I look for help in paying for college?"

Make sure you have a clear understanding of the financial aid office's "Institutional Methodology," by which it calculates the amount of the college's own aid each family qualifies for. (Note: The institution's methodology for determining your family's contribution might yield a different EFC than the federal need analysis methodology. It might, for example, take into account some portion of the value of your home, which the federal formula does not. The details differ from college to college. Ask for details.)

Question your own assumptions with the help of the financial aid administrator. In Jim Sumner's experience, he says, "Too many families who have financial need assume they don't. Too many families who have little or no need think they are needy.

"There are so many factors just in the FAFSA," adds Jim. "I worry that too many people put themselves in or take themselves out based on two or three things rather than the full financial picture."

Barbara Fritze of Gettysburg College comments that families sometimes worry that asking too many questions might jeopardize their chance for admission. She says, "Even my best friends and neighbors are afraid of asking questions like, 'Is it going to make a difference if, from an admissions standpoint, I say on my application that I need financial aid?' Or, 'Should I mention that I've received an award offer from another school? Would that make a school reconsider its award?' "

Barbara responds, "Ask them! Ask direct questions like, 'Do you have a financial aid packaging strategy? If so, can you tell me a little bit about that, and how would that pertain to my son or daughter?' "

Here are ten questions to ask the financial aid administrator:

1. What is your policy on outside scholarships? If a student earns a private scholarship, will you reduce the overall aid package? If so, what types of aid will be adjusted and in what order?
2. Tell me about your "professional judgment" policy (see chapter 15). How do you treat our family's unusual financial circumstances? (Tell the college about your unusual circumstances!)
3. How much of the aid package will be grants and work-study, and how much is loans? Do you practice front-loading of grants?
4. What is your school's mix of merit-based vs. need-based aid?
5. Am I overlooking any sources of aid?
6. Please discuss the privacy of student aid information. (Discuss any specific concerns you might have, such as release of parent information to the student, financial aid application information to an ex-spouse and income/asset information outside of the financial aid office.)
7. What can I do to minimize the amount I need to borrow?
8. What percentage of students get aid? What does the typical aid package look like? (Average amount of aid of each type.)
9. Do I make too much money to qualify for financial aid?
10. What is the average indebtedness of those who most recently graduated from your college?

Other common questions include questions about divorce, parent refusal to help, independent student status, appeals process, defaulting on student loans, verification and requirements for retaining aid (Satisfactory Academic Progress).

You have a right to ask questions—be polite and get the answers you need.

HOW A FINANCIAL AID PACKAGE COMES TOGETHER

After all the family's relevant information is known, all the forms completed and all the questions answered, the financial aid office constructs your individual financial aid package. The first thing that they do is determine the appropriate cost of attendance (commuter or residential status makes a difference), then subtract

PARENTS, CHILDREN AND FINANCIAL AID ADMINISTRATORS

David Levy of Caltech points out that partnership includes parents. Whether or not a student's parents join conversations with the financial aid administrator, or help with all the forms and such, they are assumed by necessity to be helping with financial support. "One of the most frustrating things we find is when a student shows up in our office after they've been admitted and says their parents refuse to help pay for college. We will work with you and your family, but we can't just assume the role of your parents in paying for college."

Financial aid formulas can only measure a family's ability to pay, not its willingness to pay, and thus a parent's unwillingness to help has no bearing in the formulas.

the EFC, then look to how much federal and state student aid you're eligible for. Then that leaves a remainder which is where the school's funds come in.

Let's introduce a new term: After your EFC, federal grant and other aid is added up, your financial aid package is designed to cover your **remaining financial need (RFN).** The RFN drives the subsidized Federal Stafford loan amount, and also plays into Federal Perkins loan eligibility. Here's how they come to that figure:

Starting with the Cost of Attendance **(COA)** for one year,

Subtract your Expected Family Contribution **(EFC)**

Subtract your Federal Pell Grant (if you're eligible)

Subtract aid from sources outside the school (grants, scholarships, etc.) and . . .

the remainder is your Remaining Financial Need **(RFN).**

Here's a simplified look at the RFN calculation for a student applying to a private college with a cost of attendance of $25,000:

$25,000	COA
−1,550	EFC
−2,500	PELL
−3,000	Scholarship
$17,950	**RFN**

Colleges usually set an institutional goal of packaging a set dollar level of "self-help" when putting together aid packages. Self-help is the contribution of the student and/or family above the EFC. Usually it is in the form of subsidized loans and work-study (as described in chapters 7–9). Any financial need above that level is typically given in the form of grants where that money is available. The idea is that all students, regardless of need, should have a similar self-help level.[55]

The self-help level is set yearly, as part of the college's budget. It can vary from school to school. That means that you might have more loans in your package from one school than from another. At budget time, when schools are debating things like increasing tuition and other expenses and how much financial aid to offer, they look very closely at the self-help level. Obviously, loans cost the schools a lot less than grants. But they realize that the self-help level has a greater impact on families than increases in tuition rates.

Because self-help has the greatest impact on families, colleges often place a greater priority on limiting increases in the self-help level than on limiting increases in the cost of tuition. So when you hear that college costs are rising faster than inflation, keep in mind that colleges are trying to focus on limiting the most important factor to students, self-help and not the total cost of tuition. The Massachusetts Institute of Technology, to cite one example, cut their self-help level significantly in recent years.

Carla Bender notes that funds are limited for school-administered programs like Federal Perkins loans, Federal Supplementary Educational Opportunity Grants and Federal Work-Study. "If we're given a pot of $300,000," says Carla, "we try to determine the highest award that we give to any one student and still spread out aid among enough students." Often there is also a minimum award amount, so that the funds aren't diluted by making tiny awards.

It is at this point that financial aid becomes as much of an art as a science, as the financial aid office staff try to configure the components to suit each family's situation best. Even within the constraints of federal and school formulas, they can offer different amounts of aid in different configurations, and so they try to weigh the many factors we've mentioned above. In other words, financial aid administrators look at a student's *eligibility* for aid, their *need* for aid and whether they *merit* aid.

Eligibility is the most straightforward—you either meet the criteria for certain forms of aid, or you don't. For example, do you qualify for a subsidized Federal Stafford loan? If you do, you get it, up to the annual and cumulative loan limits. The Federal Pell Grant also functions like an entitlement.

Need is based on hard numbers—how much you can afford to pay or borrow—but also introduces more subjective criteria for meeting the need. Given two students with equal financial need, can one handle more work-study responsibility than the other? Does a college give a little grant aid to a lot of students, or concentrate its dollars so that more grant aid goes to the needier students?[56]

Merit is the most subjective of the categories, because it reflects the values of the school as well as the achievements of the students. Merit aid is under the control of the school (federal aid is predominantly need-based), and the school gets to judge which achievements in academic, athletic, artistic, social or other areas matter most to it. Many schools do not offer merit-based aid at all, believing that all financial support should be based on need alone. The more selective the institution, the less likely it is to offer merit aid. The less-competitive colleges are more likely to offer merit aid in order to attract talented students to the school.

Incidentally, this is a topic of hot discussion in American colleges today. Tom Mortensen, Senior Scholar at the Pell Institute for the Study of Opportunity in Higher Education, poses the critical point of view when he says, "Many four-year institutions are practicing 'enrollment management' with the objective of maximizing institutional profits and prestige. Basically, they want more full-pay students that are more likely to contribute to the endowment of the institution." Others believe this is changing, based on the percentage of schools offering merit aid.

Eligibility, need, and merit, and the limited amount of resources available permeate lengthy discussions in which students' financial aid packages are hammered out.

"Sometimes people don't realize how much care is taken with their aid applications," says Brian Lindeman of Macalester College. "We spend a lot of time around the table running a fine-tooth comb through each aid application, discussing special circumstances and asking not just what's possible but what's fair."

"How should we deal with a kid who's got divorced parents or parents who have remarried?" Brian continues. "How should we deal with 'paper losses' such as depreciation, with student assets, with home equity? How should we deal with another sibling or family member in college elsewhere? We'll take a good look at all of these and more."

Keep in mind that your aid package can be a combination of loans, grants, work-study and scholarships in varying amounts.

At Grinnell, says Jim Sumner, merit aid matters:

Let's say we have admitted two students from Newton, MA, who both need $20,000. One of them is a National Merit scholar and the valedictorian and the best violinist the Boston Youth Symphony ever produced and runs 100 meters in eleven seconds — she gets $20,000 in cash assistance. The other one is seventeenth in the class and very active, has scored at our median 1400 on the SAT and is otherwise great, but she doesn't have a huge distinction like six patents on unique inventions. Well, we're going to give her $20,000, too, but it's probably going to be something like $15,000 in grants, $3,000 in student loans and $2,000 in campus work.

Those "full ride" students with $20,000 cash grants are as rare as Jim's example indicates, however. Most families have to face the fact that loans will be part of the picture.

It's not always what you expect: Bob Shorb of Skidmore notes that this can be hard for families who had not anticipated additional debt, and this includes those who pride themselves on financial prudence. "Some parents aren't ready for this," he says. "They're in their forties and saving for retirement. Sometimes they say, 'I just can't do that' or, 'I just *won't* do that. We work up the numbers as best we can, and if the family feels they can't borrow as much as the package says, it doesn't mean we give them more aid — it means they have to consider borrowing."

WHEN YOU GET YOUR AWARD PACKAGE

You will receive notice of your financial aid package in an award letter. It should arrive in the mail at the same time or shortly after you are accepted to the college and can be a key factor in deciding whether to attend a school or in making a decision between schools. The award letter lists your expected family contribution and each component of the aid package — grants, loans, work-study and the rest. When you receive your award, do the following:

Check your award letter to confirm that the information is correct. Are the dollar amounts from the FAFSA and SAR accurate? Does the award include every financial aid program you expected — Federal Pell Grant, Federal SEOG, Federal Perkins loan, Federal Stafford loan (subsidized and/or unsubsidized), Federal PLUS loan, work-study, college grants/scholarships, state money and any other sources of money you anticipated? If not, ask the financial aid administrator why?

Understand all the information supplied—and see if anything's missing. Is the cost of attendance fully spelled out? Some award letters list direct costs (like tuition and fees) but ignore indirect costs (like transportation and personal expenses). If items you expected to see are missing, call the financial aid office and clarify why they are not in the letter. If the indirect costs are excluded and the school will not adjust the cost of attendance to include them, you'll have to add them to your overall budget for school . . . and find additional money to pay for them.

Compare awards. When you receive award packages from two or more colleges, you should compare them carefully. We'll show you how in chapter 15.

The award letter represents the financial aid office's best award, given your individual circumstances and all the factors we've discussed above. It is not necessarily the *final* word however. There is usually an appeals process if you feel you should receive a different financial aid package. In chapter 15, we'll discuss how changing circumstances and unusual financial circumstances might result in more or less aid being available when the time comes for you to accept the award and join the school. Financial aid administrators can exercise their "professional judgment" to make adjustments to the inputs in the need analysis formula when there are documented unusual circumstances. This results in a new documented EFC, which in turn results in a new aid package.

Before we go to the final steps in the process of comparing and accepting financial aid packages, however, it's time to dive into the third big source of money for college: scholarships. One positive reason your financial aid package might change is that you have, in the time since applying for financial aid, won scholarship money on your own. In the next chapters of *College Gold* we'll show you how to do just that.

The World of Scholarships

"Y ou've done a good job so far with your applications," said Sally Becker, Matt's guidance counselor. "And it looks like you and your parents are doing the right things when it comes to applying for financial aid."

"Thanks for your help," said Matt. "The workshop last month really taught us a lot."

Sally studied the checklist on the folder Matt had given her. "You've filled out an early FAFSA . . . that's good . . . talked to your college's aid offices . . ." She looked at Matt and asked, "What have you done about scholarships?"

"Well, I got applications for the three you mentioned here in town, and I've been looking online since the summer," replied Matt. "I've been getting pretty regular e-mails about scholarships I might go for. Some of them are in that folder. Do you think my grades are good enough to even try to win some of those?"

"Yes, I do."

"I'm not exactly first in my class," Matt continued, sounding uncertain.

"You have a 3.6 GPA, Matt, and a lot of other things going on. You do well in English, which means you'll probably be able to write good essays," said Sally. "You know, scholarships get awarded for all sorts of reasons, not just grades." She sifted through the papers in the folder. "Let's talk about this one, for instance. Last year a student like you won $1,500 from this organization."

• • •

When it comes to paying for college, scholarships are the stuff of dreams. Students dream of winning a "full ride," in which all expenses are covered by a college or scholarship-granting institution. Parents dream of children who earn their tickets to college purely on their exceptional talents and hard work. These dreams do come true for some. For the rest of us, scholarship money can become one of several components of a full college financing plan. And in that role, there is very good news for students: A lot of money is available, new scholarships are created all the time and with some research and hard work, you can earn those awards.

In this and the next two chapters, we'll tell you the facts about scholarships—why they exist, how to find them and how to win them.

At the simplest level, scholarships are awards of money to pay for college. The awards are granted to students who 1) fit the initial criteria required by the scholarship, 2) apply for the scholarship and 3) earn the award when their applications are compared to those of other applicants. Students earn the award by writing essays, demonstrating academic excellence, entering competitions or any number of other ways that we'll detail below.

Many, many scholarships are awarded by colleges to their students. Less than 10% of colleges offer full-ride academic scholarships, but many more offer academic scholarships for lesser amounts. In addition, private institutions, corporations and other organizations offer scholarships in an incredible diversity of subjects, as we'll see later in this chapter. As of this writing, FastWeb's database includes 1.3 million scholarship awards totaling approximately $3 billion.

Scholarship programs often offer benefits beyond the money. Winning an award is a mark of distinction. It confirms your talents and hard work. It is a stamp of excellence that can open doors to new educational opportunities.

When you get to college, the financial support of a scholarship is a relief. "I know I don't have to worry about paying off loans," says Rachael Massell, a student at Duke University and winner of enough scholarships to pay for her entire cost of attendance. "For many students, those worries are as much a part of college as doing their homework."

Rachael continues: "Some scholarships are much, much more than a way to pay the bills. Until I was interviewed for the Robertson Scholarship Program [a prestigious, four-year award at Duke University and the University of North Carolina], I still did not really have a focus in terms of what I wanted to do with my life. . . . They saw something in me that I had not really seen in myself before that point, that I had the potential to act toward social change."

For many students, the scholarship-granting institution becomes a source of long-term relationships. Tom Holcombe of the Holland & Knight Charitable Foundation, sponsors of The Holocaust Remembrance Project says, "We have found that, despite being a significant dollar amount, the scholarships become a secondary prize for these students and the real and significant prize is the opportunity to visit Washington, D.C., with Holocaust survivors and with other like-minded students from all across the nation. The students, teachers, and Holocaust survivors spend an intensive week learning from each other. We visit the U.S. Holocaust Memorial Museum, participate in a special day of human rights training, and visit many popular monuments and historic sites in Washington, D.C. It is truly a life-changing experience."

There's a great benefit for families in scholarships, too, because they are a significant source of money that the student can earn, taking his or her place as a young adult partner with the parents. Remember thinking in chapter 4 about parents and students working together? Earning scholarships is a unique contribution students can make to this shared project.

Scholarship money is awarded for excellence in a number of categories, for example:

Academic scholarships are a broad category, generally awarded to students with high achievement in academic subjects. Some rely solely on GPA, test scores and field of study. Others are awarded to students who demonstrate leadership, artistic creativity, active community service or other noteworthy skills and accomplishments in addition to academic talent. Academic scholarships inspire the familiar image of a student getting a "full ride" because she's a genius, but they're not always awarded in so straightforward a manner. Sometimes a student is offered an academic scholarship because of a combination of factors, says David Gelinas, Director of Financial Aid at Sewanee: The University of the South. "For us, there's no formula that says, 'if you have X score and Y grades, you automatically get the scholarship.' We look at the entire candidate."

Some scholarship organizations start with test scores and grades, and then go further. National Merit Scholarships® are awarded according to several criteria in addition to high PSAT/NMSQT scores: the student's academic record, information about the school's curricula and grading system, two sets of test scores, written recommendations from school officials, information about the student's activities and leadership, and the student's own essay.[57]

Another example: the All-USA College Academic Team,* a group of

---

* allstars.usatoday.com

twenty scholarships awarded by *USA Today* to high school and undergraduate students who, in the sponsor's words, "not only excel in scholarship but extend their intellectual abilities beyond the classroom to benefit society."

At some colleges and universities, academic scholarships are offered by different departments. Although the financial aid office may serve as a clearinghouse for these awards, we recommend that you contact the specific departments that interest you to ask what scholarship opportunities are available.

A STORY ABOUT THE REAL YOU

I came from a family with two married parents with a reasonable (not in need of financial aid) income. So I applied like crazy—for local, national, public and private scholarships and aid. On a whim I also applied to USC and for USC financial aid. I was surprised when I was called for an interview, and even more surprised to speak with the Dean of the School of Architecture. As we spoke, he told me the main reason my application stood out was because I wrote about my aspiration to become a shepherd and live in the mountains, which is true. It was this aspect of my true self—not my SAT scores, not my GPA, not clubs or activities or any of that—that had made me stand out. Regardless of the outcome of the interview, I was so happy I nearly cried, just to realize that my best quality was me. It turns out I received a Trustee Scholarship—a full ride—to USC (and I did cry when I found out!).

—*anonymous student*

Essay contests require applicants to write an essay about a specific topic. This is not always a case of writing "why I deserve a scholarship." The student's essay should demonstrate a real passion for learning about a topic, an ability to research it or both. The topic might be very specific; for example, the **Ayn Rand Institute** sponsors essay contests answering questions about Rand's books. The **JFK Profiles in Courage Essay Contest** requires applicants to write an essay of less than 1,000 words about an elected public official who acted courageously to address a political issue at a local, state, national or international level.

Science and math competitions are a competitive path to scholarship money for students with real talent in the scientific or mathematical disciplines. These are sometimes won through research and other science or technology projects, and sometimes in direct competition solving difficult problems. Examples include competitions run by corporations like **Apple**, **Intel** and **Siemens**.

Other knowledge-based contests. Some contests, like the **Common Knowledge Scholarships**, have minimal eligibility requirements, because they are awarded strictly on the basis of winning a competition.

Scholarships for volunteering and community service reward individuals who help others through service. The **Comcast Leaders and Achievers Scholarship Program** awards more than one thousand $1,000 scholarships for community service and leadership to high school seniors in communities served by Comcast. The **Heart of America Christopher Reeve Award** is awarded annually to just one extraordinary student "who has demonstrated tremendous courage and compassion in serving his or her community."

NEHA'S STORY—SERVICE

Neha Chauhan, of Staten Island, NY, found that her road to scholarship money began in a high school science class:

"I conducted a comprehensive science research project on Alzheimer's disease. While the scientific implications of my research were important, I wanted to go beyond academia, take off my latex gloves and lab coat, and address an issue often overlooked—educating society, in particular, youngsters about Alzheimer's disease. I decided to take action, and was soon introduced to the Alzheimer's Foundation of America (AFA), an organization so incredibly dedicated to helping those affected by Alzheimer's disease. With the help and guidance of AFA, I founded Teens for Alzheimer's Awareness (www.afa teens.org), a web-based organization that shows teens how to raise awareness of Alzheimer's in their communities."

The organization was the center of Neha's many scholarship applications. "I did all of them myself. They were easy after a while, because there's so much standardization in the applications. The first five were difficult; the forty-fifth took about half an hour," she says. Neha earned $80,000 in awards and is now majoring in Economics at Harvard.

Fellowships, research grants and assistantships are usually awarded to graduate students, often in return for help in research or teaching work (which, in turn, helps fulfill the educational or research mission of the college, and teaches graduate students how to teach and do research). They might include tuition breaks and even living stipends. Fellowships might bridge the gap between college-based and private scholarship money. For example, the **Consortium for Graduate Study in Management** (www.cgsm.org) is an umbrella organization that, with money from corporate sources, awards scholarships at well-known graduate business schools to further its mission of bringing underrepresented and diverse populations into the world of MBAs. According to Lena C. Goodman, Director of Financial Aid at Bellin College of Nursing, "Fellowships are usually funded through grants either from the government or other foundations (or even the college itself) to help support a particular aspect of the educational process or a specific category of student, such as graduate nursing students or minority students."

Fine arts, performing arts and craft arts scholarships are awarded to students with outstanding achievement in the arts. These scholarships may require an audition or recording of student performances, or a portfolio of the student's work, in addition to an application and essay. Sometimes artists and performers compete for the award, for example in musical recitals. Like academic and athletic scholarships, they are typically based in colleges that the student will attend. Some, like the **Donna Reed Foundation Scholarships** (for acting and musical theater) are awarded by private institutions.

Athletic scholarships are offered by colleges to promising athletes in the form of tuition discounts or stipends for living expenses. Colleges want winning teams. Not every school is looking for male football players, however. Tennessee and Connecticut want great female basketball players. You might think of UCLA and Duke as great basketball schools; for years both have also produced some of the country's best golfers, both male and female.

The process to get most athletic scholarships is different from that for the other categories. Many Division I schools will scout outstanding high school athletes. If your high school is not on the scouting circuit, there is usually a process to contact the coach or athletic department to be considered. The coach for each team generally decides which students receive scholarships. Formal athletic scholarships are only available at Division I and Division II schools. Division III colleges may not award financial aid based on athletic ability, though they can award need-based and/or academically related financial aid. As a result, a talented athlete may receive a need-based (or academic) scholarship at a Division III school and participate in the sport of his or her choice. It is up to each individual college to decide how to award such aid.

Athletic scholarships are awarded not only by colleges, but also by other organizations, and not always for star talent. For example, the **United States Tennis**

Association (www.usta.com) awards a scholarship for academically accomplished students who also participate extensively in a community tennis program.

Pageants are among the largest scholarship competitions specifically for women. The best known pageants are the **Miss America** and **America's Junior Miss** competitions. These are not just limited to one national event; they operate on local and state levels, with the final competitors selected on the state level. Participants can win scholarships and prizes at every level and these many levels mean opportunities to be a scholarship winner many times over.

Finally, there are numerous scholarships based on specific life circumstances or experiences, such as religious affiliation, disability, illness (such as cancer), minority status, interest in a particular major or career, or hard-to-measure qualities like leadership and dedication to a cultural or political set of values. These diverse scholarships are offered by institutions and organizations based on their specific mission.

UNUSUAL SCHOLARSHIPS

Paying for college is not all forms and checklists. Sometimes you just have to lighten up. Find a quirky corner of the scholarships world and you'll have a chance to show your creative side.

Yes, there is a scholarship for left-handed students: the Frederick and Mary F. Beckley Scholarship of up to $1,000, awarded only to left-handed students who will be attending Juniata College in Huntingdon, Pennsylvania. The Duck® Brand Duct Tape Stuck at Prom Scholarship Contest awards up to $2,500 each to a couple who appear at their prom wearing clothing and accessories made of duct tape. The Kor Memorial Scholarship is awarded by the Klingon Language Institute to recognize and encourage scholarship in the field of language study. Familiarity with Klingon or other constructed languages is not required, but creativity is preferred.

There are even scholarships for duck calling, beef eaters, vegetarians, twins, singing the national anthem, welding, knitting, bowling, surfing, playing marbles, golf caddying, apple pie, papermaking and people with a last name of Zolp.

Knowing who gives scholarships, and why, is helpful in seeing just how many opportunities exist to find and earn this money for college.

BOOK TO WEB

You can find more unusual scholarships listed at www.collegegold.com.

CODE: 1040

WHO GIVES SCHOLARSHIPS—AND WHY?

Scholarships are as individual as the institutions that offer them. There is no single common application form that lies at the heart of every scholarship program, and there is no single "trick" to winning a scholarship. Even the way they are disbursed differs. Some are one-time payments, some pay out over all the years a student is in school. Some scholarship-granting organizations require winners to maintain a certain grade level, or even to "requalify" by pursuing the interest that brought them the scholarship in the first place. Understanding the sponsor's goals in offering the scholarship can help you tailor your application to improve your chances of winning the scholarship.

Colleges want to attract certain kinds of students. *What* kind of student they want depends on each college's particular vision for its student body. A small liberal arts college like Colgate wants academic whizzes . . . and really wants to include a few great hockey players as well. From Texas University, USC, Oklahoma and too many other colleges to list here, scouts search the country for great football players. Colleges understand that most students have a choice of which college to attend.

James Sumner, Dean of Admission and Financial Aid at Grinnell, points out that "merit aid is used to craft and build each entering class of freshmen, so we pay attention to grades and scores, of course, but also participation in sports or the debate team, and all the other things that build an interesting and talented class."

Scott Friedhoff, Vice President for Enrollment Management at Allegheny College in Pennsylvania, describes a kind of student he is likely to consider for a scholarship: "We're known best for attracting students with unusual combinations of interests and skills and talents. So, it would be very common for example to see a student who wanted to major in biology, minor in English or art and also liked to swim, play rugby, do yoga and ballroom dancing.

"Traditionally colleges have looked very closely at standardized test scores, SATs, class rank, GPA—very quantifiable criteria. Now, more of us are digging a little deeper and really asking the next questions, 'How will this student fit?' and 'How will this student contribute?' "

For example, they might offer scholarships in specific majors to encourage students to enroll in underrepresented majors (e.g., scholarships for women and underrepresented minorities in science and engineering). When you consider the unique identity of each college—whether it's about science, or focused on the arts, or athletics, or a great state institution, or a place where students get the best business education—it makes sense that the college would put its resources into finding students who fit that identity.

Private organizations offer scholarships as all or part of their mission. Scholarship-granting institutions might pay awards to schools directly on behalf of the student, or award money to the student with the understanding that it will be used for education. A few even take a "no strings attached" attitude; once the money is won, the student is free to spend it as he or she chooses.

A STUDENT'S STORY

A student sent us this story in response to the 2006 *College Gold* survey. We have withheld the student's name for privacy:

I decided to go to a small private college because I knew I would get the attention I needed. I come from a single-parent household and my mother comes from a different country, so I knew it would be very hard for her to pay for college by herself. I applied for financial aid and also decided to apply for athletic scholarships for cross country. After the whole process I was able to come to Saint Mary's College of California and receive much needed financial aid, a scholarship on the cross-country team and aid in books. I stay active through sports, programs on campus, community service and clubs. You cannot just expect everything and not give back in return.

Private organizations include:

Scholarship-focused organizations, whose main reason for being is to offer scholarships to reward certain types of students. An example: the <u>Jack Kent Cooke Foundation</u>, which focuses on scholarships for outstanding individuals with financial need. The foundation makes awards each year to undergraduate transfer students (moving from community colleges to four-year institutions), graduate students and even scholars as early as seventh grade.

Corporations. Many large corporations have scholarship programs for students. The programs burnish the image of the corporation, and help identify promising students who might one day become leaders within the company. Examples of well-known corporate scholarships include those sponsored by <u>Best Buy</u>, <u>Target</u>, <u>Discover Card</u>, <u>Prudential</u> and <u>Xerox</u>.

Foundations large and small. Some, like the <u>Bill and Melinda Gates Foundation</u>, see scholarships as part of a larger mission to lower the barriers to education. Others, like the <u>Davidson Institute for Talent Development</u> and the <u>Intel Science Talent Search</u>, are focused on identifying and rewarding students who show the greatest promise for future contributions to society.

Employment-based providers award scholarships to students based on their company or occupation, or that of their parents. For example, the <u>Walton Foundation Scholarship</u> is open to the sons and daughters of Wal-Mart employees. The <u>Humana Foundation Scholarship</u> is offered to children of parents who work for Humana, a large national health insurance firm based in Louisville, KY. <u>Bound Tree Medical Corporation</u>, a distributor of emergency medical products based in Dublin, OH, sponsors a scholarship for the children of career or volunteer firefighters, emergency medical technicians and paramedics. There are also countless employee tuition assistance programs across the country.

Unions sponsor scholarships as well. The <u>Union Plus Scholarship</u> is available to members of an AFL-CIO union or their children. Like others, union scholarships can be quite specific; for example, the <u>JNS College Scholarship</u> is available to members of the American Federation of Government Employees (AFGE) to attend a college degree program at the George Meany Center for Labor Studies, Inc.

Service organizations, both national and local. The <u>Elks</u>, <u>Kiwanis</u>, <u>Lions</u>, <u>Rotary</u>, <u>Veterans of Foreign Wars</u> and many others have widespread scholarship programs, many of which identify students who have been active in service to their communities.

Political and advocacy organizations working to promote their beliefs seek to identify like-minded students, and help them attain a college education. One example we'll hear from in the next chapter: the **Phillips Foundation**.

Business and professional associations. There's one for just about every profession. Associations seek to promote their field of work, educate customers and influence government and public opinion. They provide scholarships to encourage talented students to pursue careers in their fields.

Religious and social organizations support the students among their members with scholarships. Churches grant scholarships (and many, of course, have affiliated colleges), as do synagogues and mosques, and their associated organizations. Social organizations of every kind, from minority organizations to political parties to local clubs, likewise help students with college gold.

BOOK TO WEB

It's impossible to list all the scholarship-granting organizations in a book this size. Scholarship databases like the one at www.fastweb.com can help you find scholarship-granting organizations and specific scholarships based on your individual profile. The typical high school senior matches about one hundred awards on FastWeb, so there are many opportunities to try to win an award.

It's worth considering why these organizations offer scholarships as you think about where to look for college money (and how to win it). As previously mentioned, sometimes offering a scholarship is just good public relations for corporations, foundations and service groups. Most of these private organizations, in addition, see giving money for college as part of a larger mission. Some want to promote their ideas and values. Some see this as part of "giving back" to communities that have supported them. Some believe that good corporate citizenship means helping more American students go as far as they can. Some will tell you that building a more educated workforce is critical to keeping the American economy strong. Some want to help ensure a steady supply of future talent in fields that are essential to their business. They want to touch the future.

Tom Holcombe of the Holland & Knight Charitable Foundation notes that the deeper mission goes beyond the college years. "Why do we do this?" he asks, answering, "These young people are one day going to be our leaders. They're going to be the lawyers, the mayors, and the governors and bank presidents and dot.com executives. They're going to be in positions to make decisions. What an honor it would be for us to have some small part in shaping the way they would make decisions in the future for good."

According to Patti Ross, Vice President of the Coca-Cola Scholars Foundation, the mission is sometimes to overcome hidden barriers, like a family's assumption that, even if a student goes to college, they can't go to the best possible college. "The whole notion of national scholarship providers is not only access but choice," says Patti. "We want people to have access to college, but we also want them to be able to make a choice in the schools that they attend."

Generally you can find out what motivates a scholarship provider by reading the information they provide. Visit the web site and read about the mission of that award provider. This can go a long way in letting you know what the award provider may be looking to accomplish, and possibly what you should highlight in your application.

✓ I Wish I Had Known . . .

Apply for as much as you possibly can because the more you apply for, the more likely you are to receive SOMETHING. Be yourself on the applications—that's what everyone wants to see.

—*Margaret Boulton, freshman*
University of Southern California

HOW TO THINK ABOUT SCHOLARSHIPS

Students might be concerned that earning private scholarship money will decrease the total amount of financial aid offered by a college. But even if you're on a full aid package, scholarship money is good in the long run. Sometimes scholarships can help meet the need that a college was unable to meet. This may give you a chance to consider a college with a lesser aid package. Also, outside scholarships will probably reduce the "self-help" aid (loans and work-study), meaning you might have more time for your studies and less debt when you graduate. Ask the college's financial aid office about their outside scholarship policy. The best situation is when the scholarship money replaces loans and work-study before affecting grants, since loans have to be repaid and grants don't. Scholarship money can sometimes be deferred to fill in financial gaps later in your academic career. Also don't forget to consider that the additional benefits we mentioned earlier in the chapter, such as making important connections and showing distinction, come from receiving an academic scholarship, not need-based financial aid.

Paul Peter Linden-Retek, a Coca-Cola Scholar currently at Harvard University, says that "outside scholarships become most important when you fall into that financial middle ground. Many of my friends weren't eligible for much grant assistance, and so they have a large number of loans. Even the small outside scholarships really do add up to reducing the loans."

The bottom line: A scholarship is aid you have already earned. Whether it affects your aid package or not, you still won't have to pay it back later.

With the high cost of college, is it realistic to think that you can win enough money in scholarships to get that "free ride"?

We think that's the wrong question to ask. A few people do earn enough in scholarships, competitions and the like to pay for all of college and even graduate school. But for most students, scholarships are one piece of the larger plan.

David Levy, Assistant Dean and Director of Financial Aid at Caltech, sums up the myth and the right way to think about scholarships. "Students or parents think that they are so bright and talented that they're going to get a scholarship and it's going to cover all their costs. Only about 4% to 6% of all financial aid is in the form of merit or talent-based scholarships. It's not as prevalent as people might think it is. But there are scholarships available . . . and we encourage students to look for scholarships because it can help reduce their loan obligations or their work obligations while they're students. It's essentially a sound investment against having to borrow an extraordinary amount of money."

Another way to think about scholarships is to look at the effort you put into earning scholarships: If you put in 50 hours of work applying to 25 different scholarships, and win 6 scholarships worth a total of $9,000, your "wage" for that time comes to $180 per hour. Not too bad a payoff, especially for a high school student. Perhaps you *will* be one of those students who earn more than that; scholarships are earned through hard and dedicated work. Like most good things, the more time and effort you put into pursuing scholarships, the more likely you are to win college gold.

One thing is for sure, if you don't apply for scholarships, you will not earn this money.

Let's go on to see just how to earn that reward.

12

Finding Scholarships

Matt talked to Dolores Vicente at Caledonia, and she encouraged him to audition for the music scholarship sponsored by Caledonia's music department. By mid-October, Matt's classical guitar teacher had helped him record two Spanish dance pieces, and then they recorded two tracks of a G.P. Telemann duet, combining the tracks so Matt appeared to be playing both parts. It was so good Matt included it with all his college applications.

Now it was November 1. With two months to go before the Gordons could submit a final FAFSA and the rest of the financial aid paperwork, Matt turned his attention back to the scholarships he had found online. Some had to do with music, of course. As Matt searched, however, he found more and more sources of scholarship money. Some scholarships were extraordinary—tens of thousands of dollars—and Matt could see that they were highly competitive. Most, however, were smaller awards of one or two thousand dollars, and there were many more of those. One of the awards had an October 15 deadline, so it was too late to apply for it for this year. Matt decided that many small awards, if he could earn them, were just as good as one large award. Although winning a big scholarship sounded like a dream ticket to college, he didn't want to bet everything on just one or two competitions.

· · ·

Getting scholarships begins with *finding* scholarships. In this chapter, we'll show you how to locate scholarships large and small for which you are eligible; in the next chapter we'll show you how to apply for—and win—those awards.

FIRST, TALK BACK TO YOUR OBJECTIONS

The first obstacle to finding scholarships is the belief that the search is futile. In the back of many students' minds lurk a dozen excuses to give up before they even get started, such as:

"Applying for scholarships takes too long."

"I'm not smart enough to win a scholarship."

"There's no real money in scholarships."

"I don't have the time to apply to scholarships."

"I hate writing essays."

. . . and so on. The problem is, these objections take you out of the running. They prevent even the possibility of earning scholarship money. You can't win if you don't apply.

Getting into college and paying for it is a huge step into adulthood . . . but with a clear plan and a little work, you can do it.

THE STEP-BY-STEP APPROACH

Steve van Buskirk runs a large scholarship program for the Veterans of Foreign Wars and notes, "It takes a lot of work, and it takes a lot of research, and a diligent approach, but there's a lot of money out there."

Rachael Massell, a student from Glassboro, NJ, who now attends Duke University, summarizes the "diligent approach" this way:

The summer between my junior and senior year of high school, I sat down and made a list of all the scholarships that I could apply for. . . . I was really organized about it, and everything I read had told me to apply for as many as possible because the more you apply for, the better your chances are of actually getting one. I was going to be thrilled if I got one or two. . . .

Rachael's hard work resulted in eighteen scholarships that completely paid for college, demonstrating how persistence and being thorough can pay off. You might not win as much as Rachael, but you can't win any scholarships if you don't apply.

WHAT IF YOU'RE "AVERAGE"?

Lou Fraulo, Supervisor of Counseling and Guidance Services at Clifton (NJ) High School, says that the "average college prep kid" might not be a shoo-in for scholarship money, but points out that there are unexplored resources. "We don't try and discourage them," says Lou. "We tell them there's money out there if you look. It might be something surprising . . . maybe your father served in Vietnam, for example. You don't have to be the sharpest tool in the shed. There is at least some money for you out there."

Every scholarship sponsor has a set of criteria and is seeking the most qualified candidate for their award. So while you don't need to have good grades, you might need to be good at art or sports, service or some other distinguishing characteristic. Here are three examples:

The **David Letterman Telecommunications Scholarship** at Ball State University is intended for average students who nevertheless have a creative mind. Winners are selected primarily based on creativity.

The **Horatio Alger Association** provides scholarships for students who have demonstrated integrity and perseverance in overcoming adversity; it looks for character, not a 4.0 GPA.

The **Prudential Spirit of Community Awards** recognize children in grades 5 to 12 who have engaged in volunteer activities and have demonstrated exceptional community service.

ORGANIZE YOUR SEARCH

As we've seen, different scholarships emphasize different qualities to win, but the process of applying is similar for most. And if you're going to apply for more than one or two scholarships, the first step is to organize a process you can repeat many times. You might be able to adapt the same essay for several applications, reducing the effort required for each subsequent scholarship. If you start off organized, you are also less likely to miss an application deadline or forget to ask for a letter of recommendation.

During your senior year in high school you will be undertaking several large projects, perhaps the most complicated projects you've tackled to date. Applying for college admission, financial aid and scholarships are not like term papers you can finish over a weekend. They require sustained effort over an extended period of time and often involve many tasks. Whether this is your first experience with a big project or your five hundredth, it is best to get as organized as possible. One of the benefits of applying for scholarships is the opportunity to learn or practice your time management and organizational skills.

Just as you created a set of file folders for colleges in chapter 3, now create a separate file folder (either paper or computer-based) for each scholarship. Create a checklist for each folder listing all the required materials (both the application materials and your completed applications). The checklist should contain all deadlines and the dates you requested and sent the materials. Highlight any unusual or especially time-consuming prerequisites on the folder.

When you apply for a scholarship, keep a copy of the entire application—if it gets lost, you can quickly resend it. (You will also find it helpful to refer to old applications when applying for additional scholarships.)

Keep one list, separate from all the folders, of each scholarship you're applying for and its deadline, so you can see at a glance which applications are most urgent. A spreadsheet can be a useful tool for listing and organizing deadlines and checklists. But don't get bogged down in creating a tool to organize the application process. It doesn't matter how you get organized, so long as you review the checklist regularly. You don't want to get distracted from your primary focus, which is applying to all the awards for which you qualify.

START SEARCHING AS EARLY AS POSSIBLE

It is best to start searching for scholarships as soon as possible. Note that some scholarships accept applications as early as the summer before your senior year. Don't wait until you submit your college admissions and financial aid applications in the fall, or you will miss many deadlines. Many scholarships have prerequisites—a science fair project or an art portfolio—and it takes time to build your qualifications.

AWARDS FOR YOUNGER STUDENTS

You don't have to be a high school senior to win a scholarship. For example, the **Davidson Fellowships** are awarded by the Davidson Institute for Talent Development to U.S. students under age eighteen who have completed a significant piece of work in the fields of Mathematics, Science, Technology, Music, Literature, Philosophy or Outside the Box (a great category). The **Kohl's Kids Who Care Program** honors students ages six to eighteen who are involved in community service. The **National Geography Bee** is a three-stage competition sponsored by the National Geographic Society. It is open to U.S. students in grades 4 to 8 who are age fifteen or younger by the date of the national competition.

If you are a student who is not entering college directly after high school, don't worry. There are plenty of scholarships for you as well. In fact, most awards are not specific about your current year in school as they are specific about which year you are going into. Whether you're entering as an undergraduate freshman, or returning to get an advanced degree, the process to find and apply for scholarships is largely the same. For the purposes of simplicity in this book, we referred to the senior year. If you are not entering college directly from high school, you can assume the senior year is the year before heading off college.

When should you start applying for scholarships? Daniel Barkowitz, Director of Financial Aid at MIT, urges students to start applying no later than September of the senior year. Scholarship organizations do not accept late applications.

Organizing your time is another key to success. There's a repeating pattern when pursuing scholarships: locate/apply; locate/apply; locate/apply. New scholarships come into view as you learn how to research them. As you apply for one, the application itself makes you think you might qualify for another. Online scholarship searches like FastWeb send e-mail reminders of new scholarships and approaching deadlines. The more you make this part of your senior year routine, the easier it will be to keep organized . . . and you won't be rushing to find scarce scholarship money in June.

There is also some flexibility in your schedule; since you can apply throughout the year, you can fill openings in your schedule with scholarship applications. For example, many successful scholarship applicants do research and writing in the summer before their senior year, before classes, activities and the admissions/financial aid tasks start to pile up.

Some students believe that only large scholarships are worth their time, but for most this is a mistake. The competition for truly large scholarships is intense. (You'll find a list of some of the most prestigious and lucrative scholarships at the end of this chapter.) Don't ignore the small awards—they add up and tend to be less competitive. Winning several small awards can impress the judges for the bigger scholarships.

ELIGIBILITY

The first task in finding scholarships is deciding which ones you might win. In chapter 11 we described the different categories of scholarships, and you should look into the categories that might be right, such as academic, artistic or athletic scholarships. In addition, it's helpful to keep a list of the qualities and achievements that might make you eligible for certain scholarships.

Qualities that can make you eligible for scholarships include:

- **Interests**—Interests include subjects you've studied like history or geography; a passion for languages or writing; a hobby or enthusiasm that captures your imagination. Scholarships are also available for students intending to pursue a certain major (these may be college-based or private scholarships). Another interest-based qualification is the student's intention to enter a profession such as medicine, education or the law.
- **Values and beliefs**—Religious, political, moral or ethical beliefs are supported by many scholarship providers. The applications often require you to describe how you have put your beliefs into action.
- **Background**—There are scholarships for which family history and personal experiences make you eligible. Your parent's experiences or membership in a union, the armed forces, or clubs and associations may likewise qualify you to apply.
- **Associations**—Your own membership in a club, association or society, from the Future Farmers Organization to Mensa to the Girl Scouts.
- **Location**—States, municipalities and even countries offer money for college (the last being for students who are foreign-born).
- **Work**—As mentioned in chapter 11, employers and unions might offer

scholarships. McDonald's, for example, has a scholarship program for students who have worked at a McDonald's restaurant. UPS, the delivery service, has a similar program.

- **Minority or other group status**—Some scholarships use your status as a disabled person or a member of a particular ethnic group as the criterion of eligibility.

ELIGIBILITY LIST AND ACCOMPLISHMENTS RESUME

Here's a brainstorming exercise that will also result in an organizing tool: Using the criteria above, make a list of specific qualities and achievements that might make you eligible for a scholarship. See if you can list items in at least half the categories. Keep this list handy, because as you go through the process of searching for scholarships, it will help to broaden your thinking. New possibilities will emerge.

Many students find it helpful to put together an "accomplishments resume." Not only will this help you target your scholarship search, but it will also help when you apply for scholarships. It summarizes your past—talents, skills, awards and achievements—giving you a sense of where you've been and where you might be headed in the future. It is often helpful to provide a copy of your accomplishments resume to the teachers who will be writing letters of recommendation for you. They can use the resume as a source of additional material for their recommendation.

SEARCHING FOR SCHOLARSHIPS ONLINE

The easiest way to locate scholarships for which you qualify is to start online, with a free scholarship search service. To conduct an online scholarship search, you answer questions about your grades, test scores, intended major(s) and college(s), activities and interests. The service then creates your unique scholarship profile.

The service automatically matches your profile with scholarships in its database, presenting you with a list of scholarships for which you qualify. The search service will provide you with detailed information about each award, including the eligibility requirements, selection criteria, deadlines, dollar amounts, web site address and contact information for obtaining application materials. The better search services also provide tools to help you manage your scholarship results: marking favorites to apply for, tracking deadlines, comparing dollar amounts, making notes and sending automatic e-mail notifications whenever new awards for which you qualify are added to the scholarship database.

Keep your profile information up to date so that you don't miss out on any potential scholarship opportunities. When you update your profile—for example, if your GPA goes up—the service will rematch you with new scholarships for which you qualify. Update your online profile whenever new information arises. For example, if your mom or dad join a professional association, that might qualify you for additional scholarships.

Be sure to add every college or university that you are considering to your list of intended colleges. This way you will see all of the scholarships for which you are eligible at each of the schools. If you are still considering possible schools, the service might have a college search function which can help you search and compare colleges and universities on key criteria, including the number of scholarships you'd qualify to apply for at each school.

You will want to continue to update your profile throughout your college career so that you always know about any scholarship opportunities that are available to you. Remember that there are many scholarships available to fund your later years of college. Don't stop looking once you've enrolled for your freshman year.

Pay careful attention to the questions that the service uses to build your profile, and use them to add new information to the eligibility list you created in the exercise above. Your high school guidance counselor and college financial aid administrator should know as much as possible about you so that they, too, can steer you toward appropriate scholarships. The more complete your list, the better.

The profiles used by scholarship search services are often quite detailed. To maximize the number of matches, try to answer every question. Some questions include long lists of scores of hobbies, activities and employers. Read through them carefully, so that you don't miss any of your qualifications. By being thorough, you will increase the number of awards you match and your chances of winning a scholarship. It is worth taking the time. It takes most students only about thirty to sixty minutes to complete a scholarship search profile.

There's a side benefit to creating an online scholarship profile as well. As you learn more about certain scholarships, you start to decide which interest you, and why. You might realize that community service or athletics is really your most important interest after classroom study. In the next chapter, we'll discuss how the very process of applying for scholarships helps you make those big decisions about where to go to college and what to study.

Finding Scholarships

It's a good idea to complete a profile and start searching for scholarships by your junior year. Some scholarships are available to high school students (for example, summer internship programs) and the earlier you get into the game, the better you'll understand how it works. It's also never too early to know scholarship deadlines. But even if you are already in college, it is always worth looking and applying for scholarships.

We recommend searching at least two of the online scholarship search services. FastWeb is the largest and most popular, but it may be helpful to also search one of the other services. Most of the online scholarship databases overlap to a certain degree, so searching two databases will provide you with reassurance that you've found all the awards for which you qualify.

A note to parents: Searching for scholarships is one of the best ways to help your student. You can search the online databases yourself, or help your student fill out their online profile. You can certainly ask your employer, membership organizations, or for that matter, any of your friends, colleagues or acquaintances if they know about scholarships for which your student might be eligible.

Some people also like to perform online searches using their favorite web search engine to locate possibilities. Search engines are useful for locating the web sites for scholarships you might have heard about. LaNice Hagen, a junior at Florida State University, found several scholarships by searching the web sites of companies she knew about, using terms like "Burger King Scholarship" and "Rent-a-Center Scholarship." When you find a relevant scholarship opportunity, you might also check the "similar pages" link in the search engine. This is as much a memory-jogger as a way to locate specific scholarships, but be aware that this kind of open-ended search can lead you to some dead ends (such as scholarships scams, which we'll discuss in chapter 14). Also keep in mind that scholarship search web sites might have already done this type of research.

To summarize the steps of Internet scholarship search:

- Create a detailed profile at one or more scholarship search sites.
- Keep track of your favorite results and their deadlines.
- Evaluate and decide which scholarships to apply for.
- Update your online profile periodically.
- Use the information you find online to help your offline search.
- Use the repeating pattern we described earlier: locate/apply/repeat.

☑ **I Wish I Had Known . . .**

I wish that I had known about the availability of obscure scholarships. Everyone knows about the scholarships offered by Best Buy and Intel, but very few know about the $100, $200 or more smaller scholarships that are around.

—anonymous college student

SEARCH FOR SCHOLARSHIPS OFFLINE

An online search is the most important first step, but there are some steps you should take offline as well. You might not only find additional college money, but the search itself will turn up unexpected benefits—the chief one being that it puts you in closer touch with the people who can help you win the awards.

Anne Sandoval, guidance counselor of the Detroit Country Day School, describes how research reveals new possibilities you haven't considered:

> We tell students, please, contact your chamber of commerce. Contact your church, your synagogue, your temple, your ethnic organization. Have your parents contact the office of human resources at their company. There's a scholarship for students whose parents are East Asian physicians, from the Steel Workers Union and the Daughters of the American Revolution. Colleges have scholarships geared toward students in particular cities or counties or areas. If you're a golf caddy, there are the Chick Evans Scholarships. And on and on.

You should at least talk to the following:

Guidance counselors, teachers and **financial aid administrators** at local colleges are your first resource. They know about local scholarships—not just that they exist (you can find that online) but also community leaders who are involved with the scholarship. They know about state money. They have seen students apply and know a lot about how to win scholarships. They check essays and write recommendations, as you see in the next chapter.

Furthermore, the sponsors of scholarships themselves reach out to guidance counselors. Tom Holcombe of the Holland & Knight Charitable Foundation notes, "We circulate information about our essay contest each year to teachers and principals and guidance counselors at just about every public and private school in the country." The providers are interested in reaching the widest possible range of applicants.

Guidance counseling offices keep updated lists of these scholarships— sometimes on a school web site, sometimes on a bulletin board outside their office, and sometimes in handouts. Keep current with the information they provide!

Guidance counselors, teachers and the principal or other school leader can also help you decide which scholarships suit you best, and put you in touch with older students who won particular scholarships in the past. Show them your eligibility list and ask, am I missing any qualities or achievements? When they suggest a scholarship, ask, "What others are like this one?" and search for the same answer online.

Seek out these adults and these students, and ask them questions about how they located and won money for college. Parents can ask other parents how their children found and won money for college. Ask if they have any special tips for winning this particular scholarship. Try to take advantage of their hindsight.

Some scholarships require you to be nominated by your school. If you think you qualify for the award, ask your guidance counselor or principal about the nomination process. Ask them to consider nominating you, and provide them with a copy of your accomplishments resume. Sometimes they will nominate you by default because nobody else asked to be nominated.

College financial aid administrators at the colleges you are considering are prime sources of scholarship ideas, chiefly in the scholarships that are awarded by the college. Inquire about the opportunities at your first meeting. Do not be concerned that this will somehow harm your chances for admission to the school; they are dedicated specialists and their job is to help you find every opportunity. They already have a lot of information about you, and they might know of upcoming scholarships as well as current ones for which you qualify. They are also in touch with alumni, corporations and others who award scholarship money to students attending that college.

Bear in mind that the competition for scholarships that originate in a college is very intense. Because scholarships are awarded by a school only to students admitted to the school, you'll be competing with students just as talented and suited to the college as you.

Take athletic scholarships as an example: There are more than 500,000 high school seniors playing football, men's basketball and women's basketball.

Across these three sports there are about 25,000 positions available for college freshmen and only a fraction of those players are good enough to earn significant scholarship money for that talent. So even if you're a good athlete, look into all corners of your life to find ways in which you might be eligible.

School and public libraries have reference librarians skilled at helping you discover information in unexpected places. A good resource (suggested by Steve van Buskirk of the VFW National Office) are the reference books listing small family foundations. "You can find out who they gave [scholarship] money to for the last ten or fifteen or twenty years, and why. Then get in touch with those foundations." They may also have a bulletin board where they post information about new awards.

Another benefit of scholarship listing books is they help facilitate exploration. Many libraries include scholarship listing books as part of the jobs and careers section. Open a scholarship book to a random page, and look at the awards listed there. Maybe you aren't qualified for that particular award, but it may jog your memory, helping you expand your eligibility list. Or it may spark your interest in a field that is new to you, such as microbiology or genetic engineering. Most online scholarship databases tailor the results to just the awards that match your profile; scholarship books let you explore beyond the confines of your profile, giving you a sense of what might be available.

Before reading any book about scholarships, check the copyright date. If a scholarship listing book is more than one year old, it is too old to be useful. About 10% of scholarships change a critical piece of information each year, such as their address or selection criteria. If you're using old information, you may get a lot of "Return to Sender" mail when you send out letters seeking application materials. This is one of the reasons why we prefer online scholarship databases where information is updated on a daily basis.

Community leaders are naturally networked into your home town. They know about service organizations, churches, clubs and private foundations that provide scholarship money for local students.

Friends and neighbors might seem almost too obvious to list, but people often overlook them. Your school friends are in the hunt for scholarship money just like you. Double up on your research by sharing notes about scholarships you've discovered. Your neighbors might know of local awards you've overlooked, or be able to nominate you for an award from the local service fraternity.

Keep building that list of scholarships, online and in your files, throughout junior and senior years. After you graduate, update your profile online and keep your research going, because many scholarships are available for college under-graduates as well.

GOING FOR THE GOLD

There are scholarships distinguished not only by the amount of money you might receive, but also by the honor and distinction that comes with winning. They are national or international in scope, and they are also highly competitive. Pay close attention to the eligibility requirements and deadlines. Winning one of these awards marks you with a stamp of excellence that can open doors. (Some of these awards require nomination by the student's school and do not accept applications directly from students, so after you've checked out the web sites provided below, note the special conditions in your scholarship file.)

Robert C. Byrd Honors Scholarship Program

www.ed.gov/programs/iduesbyrd/index.html

This award is available to high school seniors who show exceptional ability and promise for postsecondary success. Winners receive a $1,500 renewable scholarship. Students may apply through their state education agency in their state of legal residence. Each state has its own deadline.

Coca-Cola Scholars Program Scholarship

www.coca-colascholars.org

This award is available to high school seniors in the U.S. who have a mini-mum GPA of 3.0 on a 4.0 scale. Award winners are selected based on academic excellence, leadership ability and a demonstrated commitment to their school and community. Character, civil responsibility and extracurricular activities are also considered. Fifty National Scholars receive $20,000 scholarships and 200 Regional Scholars receive $10,000 scholarships.

Collegiate Inventors Competition

www.invent.org/collegiate/overview.html#awards

To be eligible for this award students (individually or in teams) must create a new invention that can be reduced to practice or is a workable model. In addition, inventions must be reproducible and patentable. The grand prize winner or team will receive a $25,000 award, one undergraduate winner or team will receive a $10,000 award and one graduate winner or team will receive a $15,000 award.[65]

Gates Millennium Scholars

www.gmsp.org

The Gates Millenium Scholars program each year selects 1,000 African American, American Indian/Alaskan Native, Asian Pacific Islander American or Hispanic American students to receive awards for both undergraduate and graduate degree programs. The award makes it possible for recipients to study disciplines in which their ethnic and racial groups are currently underrepresented. The amount of the scholarship is determined by the student's unmet need after financial aid is awarded. While any major is eligible for an undergraduate award, graduate awards are focused on mathematics, science, engineering, education or library science.

Barry M. Goldwater Scholarship

www.act.org/goldwater/index.html

Influential senator and onetime candidate for president, Barry Goldwater was honored by the U.S. Congress in 1986, when it created this scholarship in his name. The students must intend to pursue careers in math, science or engineering, must be entering their junior or senior year and must be nominated by a member of a participating college's faculty. This scholarship covers tuition, fees, books and room and board up to a maximum of $7,500 per year. Second-year students who are currently enrolled in a two-year college but intend to transfer to a four-year college or university are also eligible. In keeping with the scholarship's focus, medical students are only eligible if they intend to pursue a research career.

Intel Scholarships

Intel Science Talent Search (STS)
www.intel.com/education/sts/

The Intel Science Talent Search is one of the most prestigious scientific research competitions for high school seniors in the United States. Winners are selected on the basis of their potential as future scientists and researchers. The first place finalist receives a $100,000 four-year scholarship, the second place finalist a $75,000 scholarship and the third-place finalist a $50,000 scholarship. Fourth-through sixth-place finalists receive $25,000 scholarships and seventh through tenth place finalists receive $20,000 scholarships. The remaining thirty finalists receive $5,000 scholarships. All finalists also receive a high-performance computer.

Intel International Science and Engineering Fair (ISEF)

www.intel.com/education/isef/

This is the world's largest science fair. Each year more than 1,200 students in grades 9 to 12 from more than forty countries are selected at regional science fairs to compete at the ISEF for more than $3 million in scholarships and prizes. The top three finalists receive the Intel Young Scientist Scholarship of $50,000, a trip to the Nobel Prize ceremonies in Sweden and a high-performance computer. A total of more than 900 individual and team awards are presented at the fair.

Jack Kent Cooke Foundation Undergraduate Transfer Scholarship Program

www.jackkentcookefoundation.org

Jack Kent Cooke left high school during the Great Depression, in order to help support his family. He went on to become a self-made millionaire (and the owner of the Los Angeles Lakers and Washington Redskins). Most of his fortune went to this foundation, which is focused on educating students with demonstrated financial need and academic excellence. This distinctive scholarship is specifically for students attending a community or two-year college, enabling them to transfer to a four-year college. The potential size of the scholarships is also distinctive—up to $300,000 over six years! Recently, the foundation added scholarships for graduate and professional study.

John F. Kennedy Profile in Courage Essay Contest

www.jfkcontest.org

The purpose of this scholarship is to promote understanding of political courage, the subject of Kennedy's 1956 Pulitzer Prize–winning book, *Profiles in*

Courage. Student essays must be focused on a factual example of political courage. The blue-ribbon judging panel includes U.S. senators and representatives, historians, journalists and civic leaders. The dollar amounts of the awards are relatively modest ($3,000, $1,000 and $500) but their prestige is enormous.

NIH Undergraduate Scholarship Program (UGSP)

ugsp.info.nih.gov

The National Institutes of Health (NIH) offers scholarships for students from disadvantaged backgrounds who are interested in pursuing biomedical, behavioral and social science careers at the NIH. The UGSP provides up to $20,000 a year for up to four years to pay for tuition, educational expenses and reasonable living expenses. Candidates must have a GPA of 3.5 or higher on a 4.0 scale or be within the top 5% of their class.

National Merit Scholarship Corporation

www.nationalmerit.org

The National Merit Scholarship Corporation (NMSC) sponsors the National Merit Scholarships and National Achievement Scholarships programs, as well as the Special Scholarships. These are among the largest scholarship competitions in the United States, with more than 10,000 students receiving college scholarships totaling $47 million. They are prestigious in part because they are so well known as signs of high academic achievement. High school students enter the competitions by taking the PSAT test, also referred to as the National Merit Scholarship Qualifying Test (NMSQT). There are a number of different scholarships within each program. Scholarship amounts range from $2,500 to renewable four-year full tuition scholarships.

Ronald Reagan Future Leaders Program

www.thephillipsfoundation.org/futureleaders.htm

The Ronald Reagan Future Leaders Scholarship Program provides scholarships of up to $10,000 to college undergraduate students who demonstrate "leadership on behalf of the cause of freedom, American values and constitutional principles." Winners of the scholarship are those who, in the words of the foundation, "are making significant, positive differences—often against great odds—to promote American values on college campuses where 'political correctness' usually reigns." Candidates must be U.S. citizens and currently college sophomores or juniors.

Siemens Competition in Math, Science and Technology

www.siemens-foundation.org

The Siemens Westinghouse Competition is one of the most prestigious scientific research competitions for high school students in the United States. Students submit research reports individually or in teams of two or three. The top individual and team winners at the National Competition receive $100,000 scholarships. The second- through sixth-place National Finalists receive scholarships ranging from $50,000 to $10,000.

Elie Wiesel Prize in Ethics Essay Contest

www.eliewieselfoundation.org/EthicsPrize

Nobel Peace Prize laureate Elie Wiesel writes, "What would education be without its ethical dimension? Many of us believe them to be inseparable. That is why this Prize in Ethics Essay Contest was established." The contest is open to full-time juniors and seniors at accredited four-year colleges and universities in the United States. There is a first prize of $5,000, a second prize of $2,500, a third prize of $1,500 and two honorable mentions of $500 each.

13

Winning Scholarships

The day after Thanksgiving, Matt drove Sarah and two of her friends to the mall. Dropping them off at the main entrance, Matt saw his friends Stephen and Jill drinking coffee outside a Starbucks. He honked, drove over to the curb and rolled down the window.

"What's going on?" he asked Stephen.

"We're waiting for Emily and Sam and Tina and some other guys," said Stephen.

"We're all going to hang out here for a while, and then go to a movie. Want to come?"

"Um, I have to get some stuff done for school," said Matt. Applications for two more scholarships were sitting on his desk at home.

Jill interjected, "I've got rehearsal from four to eight tonight, and then there's a party for everyone who's working on the play after that. It's at Devon's house. Maybe you can come to that?"

"I should be done by then," said Matt. He hoped he would be done. Matt actually found scholarship applications challenging and interesting. Each one asked something a little different, but there were similarities too, and he had adapted three different essays for ten scholarships so far.

"Laura's going to be there," said Stephen. He put his arm around Jill, who chuckled at Matt's suppressed smile.

"Yeah, okay. We're not . . . we're, um, never mind," said Matt, looking away to hide his expression.

Stephen reached into the car and batted him lightly on the arm. "Can't work all the time."

"Well, I'll try to make it," Matt said. Gotta get some money for school first, he thought. "See you." He drove away, thinking about his scholarship essays and thinking about Laura.

• • •

Winning scholarships is a matter of applying the right strategy and tactics to the right opportunities. In this chapter, we'll lay out a strategy for winning scholarship awards, and specific tactics for such steps as applications, interviews and letters of recommendation. We've drawn this advice from scholarship providers themselves, as well as students from the FastWeb "winner's circle," who have won substantial scholarship dollars. If you follow this advice, you will improve your chances of winning a merit scholarship.

First, a dose of perspective: You are not going to get a free ride to college through scholarships because you're a B student at a mediocre school and you have no hobbies or other talents. While there are many awards that don't depend on academic merit—there are even several that target average students—the awards that don't depend on grades require excellence in a different area of interest to the sponsor. Scholarship sponsors aren't going to give you money simply for breathing (only the federal government does that—and you still have to fill out the FAFSA!). They want to give money to the most talented qualified applicant, and you're only going to win if you match the scholarship's criteria, such as artistic, athletic or academic merit. In brief, you have to earn the award.

That said, if you excel in an area that resonates with a scholarship sponsor, you have a good chance of winning a large amount of money. As we saw in the last two chapters, there are thousands of different areas that interest sponsors. Let's learn from the winners and examine the qualities they have in common.

WHAT DO WINNERS HAVE IN COMMON?

Some scholarship winners are straight-A students; some are not. Some have enormous talent in music; many can't carry a tune. Some are natural writers and dash off their application essays in a couple of hours; some find writing an agonizing chore. Many are quite poor, but many winners come from middle-class or even wealthy families.

While scholarship winners are diverse in their circumstances, interests and backgrounds, they share certain attitudes and behaviors that enable them to win. Here are the qualities that paint the portrait of a winner:

Diligence. As in persevering. Conscientiously applying appropriate attention to a task. Paying attention to detail. Most scholarship applications take time to complete and hard work as well. Patti Ross, Vice President of the Coca-Cola Scholars Foundation, notes their online application requires diligent effort to complete: "It'll take you, probably, a good hour. Sometimes students think, There are only 250 scholarships, so why should I bother? Rather than that attitude, I would like students to recognize that every effort to secure a scholarship is worthwhile. Applications are designed to capture a snapshot of a student's record, so the goal is to provide as much accurate information as possible.

"The kids who complete it are the ones who historically are winners. They research, they find fellowship opportunities, they find travel stipends—other kids don't, because they don't put the hard work into it. It's not as if it just falls into their laps: They work hard to get this stuff."

Diligence means hard work, and it also means careful work. Pay attention to the details. Read the questions carefully, and make sure that you really answer them. Complete the applications fully, and apply for scholarships you think you can win. And when those hours seem long, remember the payoff mentioned by David Levy of Caltech in chapter 11: The time investment is worth the payoff.

Determination. If diligence means hard work, determination means talking back to all those doubts when the work seems endless. It means devoting full concentration and effort to succeeding. No winner we know said that winning a scholarship was easy, and the fact that much of the work has to be done while you are applying for admission to college AND doing school work AND maybe holding down a part-time job . . . it can seem overwhelming. But winners learn how to work in spite of the doubts and disappointments (and almost nobody wins every award to which they apply).

Winners are distinguished by their ability to overcome obstacles. They are highly motivated to succeed. When something stands in their way, they persevere and devote their full effort to solving the problem, instead of letting it block them. They may fail several times while striving for success, but they don't let that stop them from trying. Never give up.

Here are the phrases we hear from scholarship providers: "Winners are determined. They have a vision. They know what they want. They know what they want to study. They're motivated. They're passionate about learning. . . . They just make it happen."

Self-knowledge. Scholarship winners play to their strengths and you have to know yourself to do that. What do you excel in? What do you feel passionate about? And how well can you handle the particular scholarship application process? If it requires a public competition, for example, know that you do well in that kind of forum before you enter. If you feel confident taking a timed, Internet-based test, you've passed the first hurdle for a scholarship like the Common Knowledge Scholarship.

Recognizing your weaknesses is also important. If you get flustered when you are interviewed, practice. Ask your parents to run mock interviews, so that you become accustomed to the process. If your weakness is in a different area, conduct drills until you become proficient.

Begin with your most distinguishing characteristics, which are not always talents. Steve van Buskirk of the Veterans of Foreign Wars advises that the first question to ask is, "What is special about me?"

He says, "We all know students who make good grades, and have athletic or musical or some other talent, but there are all kinds of other factors that make someone unique. They include ethnicity, family history, special needs or circumstances. There're scholarships available for students who are overcoming disabilities or conditions like asthma, for just one example."

True Involvement. For most scholarships, the *quality* of your experience is just as important as its *quantity*. Scholarships identify excellence, and being truly accomplished in one activity trumps being mediocre at twenty activities. Excellence, as shown by your accomplishments, awards, grades and so forth also demonstrate diligence and determination. The depth and duration of your involvement are essential.

Debbie Kahler of the Elks National Foundation looks for leadership. She asks, "Is this student first chair in their orchestra? Are they student council president or newspaper editor for their local school? What kind of community service are they participating in? We don't just count up the twenty activities they did—we look at what positions they held, and the depth of their service."

What are you dedicated to? Liz Kerr, who runs the Patrick Kerr Skateboard Scholarship, describes its winners: "You could have a perfect score on your SAT and not give yourself to help other people, but [our winners, who are all skaters] have to have done something in their community. Ninety-nine percent have had public skate parks built. They're activists, some of them starting in sixth or seventh grade. They have lots of press clippings to validate their work. They have recommendations from teachers and other adults. They've put in sweat equity for years."

THE WINNING STRATEGY

There's one more shared quality that we've observed in scholarship winners. When it comes to scholarship applications, most use similar tactics, which together we call the winning strategy. Whether you land large scholarships or small, this is a way to give it your best shot.

Start early. Scholarship deadlines often fall earlier than college admissions deadlines. Take the actions described in Chapter 12 before the college admissions process dominates your time. Junior year is not too early.

Check the eligibility requirements. The first step for any specific scholarship is to make sure you qualify. If the application requirements specify that you must have a 3.7 or higher GPA and you have a 3.6 GPA, don't bother applying.[58] Most scholarship sponsors receive so many qualified applications that they do not have the time to consider applications that fail to satisfy the requirements. You may be a wonderful and talented person, but if your application is not qualified, the selection committee is not going to look at it.

In addition to the performance requirements, pay careful attention to eligibility rules. Some scholarships require you to complete standardized tests like the PSAT/NMSQT or SATs before you apply. Fill out an early FAFSA (as described in chapter 5) to establish financial information—some scholarships need to know those details. For example, the prestigious Gates Millennium Scholarships require recipients to be "Pell [Grant] Eligible," which you find out with the FAFSA.

BOOK TO WEB

Remember, you can estimate your Expected Family Contribution (EFC) at www.collegegold.com. This is another relevant standard used by scholarships that are focused on lower-income candidates.

CODE: 1024

Register online at FastWeb and study the relevant scholarship web sites (FastWeb has links to them), because they're unique. You can decide to save or discard different suggestions from the database.

Use up-to-date award information. Go to the scholarship sponsor's web site and check current dates and deadlines. If you are looking for information about scholarships in the library, use a book that is less than one year old. Check how frequently an online scholarship database is updated. The more frequently updated the information is, the less likely you'll miss something important or be relying on old information.

Customize. To maximize your chances of winning an award, you need to identify the criteria a selection committee will use to choose the winner. Sometimes the sponsor has published the criteria they use on their web site, but you should go further, learning about the organization's mission and purpose. What is the scholarship sponsor looking for in a winner of their award? A good example is the Intel Science Talent Search (STS). Many students think that the STS is looking for the best science fair projects. They aren't. The projects and the answers to the application questions are there to help them evaluate each candidate's potential as a future researcher. The project provides concrete evidence of your ability to conduct research.

Use your application to demonstrate how you match the objectives of the scholarship.

Remember that scholarship sponsors are evaluating applications, not applicants. Scholarship sponsors, like college admissions staff, are not inspired by generic applications. What guidance counselor Anne Sandoval of Detroit Country Day School calls "McApplications" are off-putting to the people who take great care judging entries to their opportunity.

You also need to ensure that your application and supporting materials contain all relevant information the committee needs to evaluate your candidacy.

It helps to critique your application from the sponsor's perspective, or ask a parent, guidance counselor or friend to critique it. Have you stuck to the subject? Have you answered all their questions? Have you related the topic of the scholarship essay to your personal experiences? (See essays, below.)

Do your research. Many scholarship sponsors post the stories and essays of prior year winners on their web site. Study these! You won't win by imitating or plagiarizing, but you can learn what is important to the sponsors. Do the winners tell personal stories? Are they talking about their hometown, their country or the world? Do the winners have anything in common with each other?

Learn more about the subject. Internet and library research are a great start, and don't forget the old-fashioned interview when you find an expert cited in your research. If you tell them you're applying for a scholarship and ask a few good questions, you will be amazed at their responsiveness.

Reuse, renew, recycle. You can adapt essays or research completed for school for scholarships based on similar subjects. Let's say you are interested in the Benjamin A. Gilman International Scholarship, which encourages students to study abroad. A social studies paper you wrote about mobile health care clinics in Southern Africa can be the basis of strong, relevant scholarship essay.

Research on topics that interest you can serve as the "core" for many scholarship applications. If you have carefully crafted an essay, you might reuse it for several scholarships as long as it is clearly relevant to each. That's not cutting corners; many scholarship organizations have similar criteria for awards. This step can also save time.

Apply for less competitive scholarships. Apply for the small local awards you identified with the tools in chapter 12. These awards are less competitive, and so your chances of winning them are greater. Examples include the local PTA scholarship, Dollars for Scholars scholarship, local cultural and religious organizations, local businesses and your parents' employers. You can also find information about local awards on bulletin boards at the local public library, local newspaper, town web site and from a guidance counselor or school financial aid office.[59]

Ask to be nominated. Some scholarships do not allow direct application by students, but instead require that the student be selected by their school. Don't ignore these awards. Identify the person in your school who handles nominations—it could be a teacher, a guidance counselor or the principal—and ask that person to consider nominating you. Give them a copy of your resume. If you're the only one who asked, and they are pressed for time, sometimes they'll nominate you by default.

Walk the talk. If you really are fascinated by the scientific debate about global warming, your application will show it. If you're *sort of, somewhat* or *slightly* interested, you won't win. You must demonstrate real devotion to the subject of the scholarship. Don't pad your application with exaggerated qualifications.

Follow up. Confirm that your application was received, especially if it was sent in the mail (you might want to send it "Certified—return receipt requested" or enclose a stamped, self-addressed postcard they can use to confirm receipt). Check in as winners (or semifinalists or regional winners) are announced.

If you win a renewable award, make sure you satisfy any requirements for retaining it in subsequent years. This may involve maintaining satisfactory academic progress, maintaining a minimum GPA, continuing to study in the same major, retaining full-time enrollment, submitting an annual progress report and providing a copy of your transcript each year. Some scholarships may require community service or other activities, so make sure you're absolutely clear about how to renew a scholarship you've earned through hard work.

Some scholarship programs will allow students to apply twice (e.g., once as a high school senior and once as a college freshman, or once as a college senior and once as a first-year graduate student). If you didn't win the award the first time, write a letter asking for a copy of the reviewer's comments on your application. Some scholarship sponsors are willing to provide you with a copy of the comments. These comments are often quite specific. If you address the problems in your next application, it can help you win. Seeing the comments can also help you improve your future applications to other award programs.

A good example of this is the National Science Foundation Graduate Fellowship. Students who were honorable mentions as college seniors have won the NSF fellowship after fixing the problems noted in their previous application.

HOW MANY SCHOLARSHIPS?

Students often ask if they should apply for many scholarships or just a few, and the answer depends on their particular mix of strengths.

Scholarship money is partly a game of numbers, and all things being equal, the more you apply, the better your chances of winning. Obviously you can't win if you don't apply, and even if you are extremely talented, your chances of winning any particular scholarship are low, since you are competing with many other equally talented applicants.

Student Maxim Pinkovskiy, winner of several prestigious scholarships, offers this advice to students who feel they should concentrate on fewer awards: "I would probably not recommend taking sixteen scholarships, filling out rudimentary applications and sending them in, unless that's really the only thing that is possible. The applications should be a labor of love. Once you have found scholarships, either from a large search directory like FastWeb or maybe through your own research, you should put your all into it."

The winning strategy combines these two approaches: Apply to every award for which you are qualified, but do not sacrifice the quality of your applications by becoming an application factory. For some, this will mean many, many hours of devoted work in order to prepare good applications for many scholarships. For others, it will mean intense work on just a few (perhaps very lucrative or distinguishing) scholarships. Your effort will depend on your need, dedication, time and eligibility. It's common sense to spend more time applying for scholarships that are a good fit with your background, strengths and interests. Sometimes you'll find many of those, but more likely you'll choose some favorites out of the universe of scholarships you find. If your time is limited, focus your effort on the scholarships you are most likely to win.

Don't let the size of the award put you off. Every penny helps, and winning an award adds a line to your resume that can help you win other awards or get a better job after you graduate. The less lucrative scholarships are often less competitive, so you have a better chance of winning them.

Steve van Buskirk of the Veterans of Foreign Wars National Headquarters scholarships recalls "a young fellow—bright, a good athlete, but with nothing that really set him apart from others. He was very diligent, however, and with a little bit of guidance from me and some other people, he won many scholarships of $500 and $1,000. He wrote a ton of essays, but he managed to pull together enough to pay for four years of college."

FROM APPLICATION TO AWARD

What happens to your application once it's completed? The details of judging scholarships vary, but there are some typical steps.

First, incomplete or inappropriate applications (i.e., the student doesn't match criteria) are winnowed out from the larger group and discarded.

The remaining applications go through a general review. Many national organizations have local and regional competitions in which the

continued

winners advance to the next level. For others (federal government scholarships, for example), a general review of all submissions identifies finalists.

As applications advance, they are closely scrutinized by judges—usually volunteers with an interest in the institution (for example, alumni/ae of a school might volunteer to judge entries in a school-based scholarship). Often essays are scored on several criteria, and the aggregate score from several judges determines whether the applicant will go on to further consideration. Different dimensions of the scholarship criteria are judged and scored separately, then combined in a uniform mathematical score. Sometimes different criteria are weighted—for example, long experience in an activity might mean more than the language used in an essay. Letters of recommendation are read and reread. At this point in the process, applications are being compared to one another.

Perri Green, Contest Coordinator of the American Foreign Service Association scholarship program, describes the final round:

> The final twenty-five go to the judging panel who read all the essays and pick the winners. If there's a tie, we'll look at the score in the previous round. If that doesn't work, we look at having an original topic. Essays are scored 33% on research excellence, 33% on original thought and 33% on style and quality.

Perri continues:

> Winners are able to take a personal incident and apply it to an international incident and then show how the foreign service played their role. For example, a student wrote about human trafficking because in her community, someone was discovered keeping a human slave [literally]. The student researched where slaves come from in the third world, and then cited a specific instance in which a foreign service officer was able to do something about it.

Finalists are often interviewed (see section on interviews, below), or they must demonstrate the particular talent on which the scholarship is based—musical performance, for example. Some national scholarships turn this final pass into a great group experience, in which finalists from all around the country gather to meet, to learn from each other and the sponsors and ultimately to compete for the final honors.

This can be an amazing experience. Most winners describe it as one of the best experiences of their lives. It builds instantaneous lifelong friendships. It can also be a humbling experience, when you meet someone who is smarter or more talented than you. That can spur you into a more energetic pursuit of your interests. There's a powerful synergy that arises when you put a few dozen bright kids together.

Competitions and contests, particularly in academic subjects, put the applicant through a rigorous process similar to the playoffs in sports. The pressure of competition can refine a student who shows a lot of potential into a polished gem. Every student deserves to be pushed to the limits of their abilities, and then a little bit farther. The benefits of the process itself can have an impact long after the last prize is awarded.

Finally, the sponsor's judges apply their best efforts to make clear decisions in all the hard-to-quantify qualities like leadership, character and potential. Even though organizations attempt to standardize decision-making in the interest of fairness, the awarding of a scholarship often depends on the excellence of the judging.

APPLICATIONS

Scholarship providers find you through the application process: Online or on paper, you send them an application form and, usually, additional material such as an essay, letters of recommendation and other material supporting your claim to the scholarship. It's often followed by an interview or a competition. The rest of this chapter will walk through these basic steps.

The first section of a scholarship application should be easy. All you need to do is read and follow the instructions. If you don't do the following, your application won't even be considered:

- Include all requested materials.
- Prove you meet eligibility requirements.
- Get every required signature.
- Submit as many copies as required, formatted exactly as requested.
- Keep the essay relevant.
- Check your spelling and proofread your application (and have a friend proofread it too!).

Look at it this way: You're already going to a lot of effort to apply for the scholarship, so don't put your application in the incinerator with a pointless oversight. Just following the rules eliminates much of the competition: A prestigious scholarship provider told us that as much as 75% of their applications are rejected because they don't have a teacher's signature, bibliography or the correct number of unidentified copies (this helps judges remain impartial), or they include an essay that isn't relevant to the topic!

Online applications are convenient and growing in popularity. At some sponsor web sites, you can complete a full application online. Others simply use the online application to prequalify you for the scholarship and then require you to submit additional materials (either online or offline). Some sites allow you to work online for a time, save your work and come back later to complete the application. There is no standardized online application, so give yourself some time to complete one, because you're bound to be asked some questions you haven't seen. If you apply online, use the same professional presentation points mentioned above.

Two more notes on this first step:

- **Be accurate.** Answer questions as completely and correctly as you can. If you list community service organizations to which you belong, for example, list their full, correct names.
- **Don't exaggerate.** Stretching the truth can hurt your application. For example, if you list photography as a hobby on an application for a science scholarship, don't be surprised if you're asked to explain the chemical reactions that make photography possible during your interview. Selection committees are good at detecting when a student exaggerates, and the dishonesty will cause you to lose a scholarship you might otherwise have won.

Incidentally, if a scholarship application, online or otherwise, asks for money or a social security number or other private information, beware. These are tip-offs that you may have encountered a scholarship scam (see chapter 14).

ESSAYS

Few steps in the college financing process inspire as much stress as the scholar-ship essay. True, the essay is the heart of many a scholarship, and unless re-search and writing come naturally, you might feel some serious performance anxiety.

You don't have to be a natural writer to write a winning essay. Remember that most scholarship judges are as interested in the content of the essay as the style. The stories you tell, the research you show, the personal connection you make to the subject of the scholarship can mean as much or more than a gracious prose style.

There are some straightforward rules for writing good essays (you've heard them in English class).

Choose a theme carefully. The rambling stream-of-consciousness essays most students write are not distinctive enough to win awards. Choose a theme you can really develop, one that can be uniquely yours. Write about something you find fascinating.

Scholarship winner Rachael Massell says she started with a simple purpose, and arrived at a simple theme: "How do you capture yourself in 500 words? How are you different from everyone else? One essay I used for all of my college appli-cations and a lot of my scholarship applications was about interviews I'd done with community members that had grown up in my town. With classmates, I compiled a rich oral history into a play. I wanted to talk about how coming from a small town like that and living there my whole life really has contributed a lot to who I was."

Rachael's tactic of using the same essay for college admissions and scholar-ships is efficient, and we like it. Remember the caution about "McApplications," though, and customize your essay to suit the recipient. An essay about your cousin who served in the Persian Gulf could be the core of a number of topical essays. Here are five examples:

- Your personal reaction to your cousin's letters home.
- The choice to serve in a time of obvious danger.
- How U.S. foreign policy affects ordinary American families.
- The politics of oil.
- Democracy and dictatorship.

Write an outline. Then rewrite it. Even accomplished fiction writers outline their work. Using an outline will allow you to present your arguments and ideas in a structured and cohesive manner that supports your conclusions, yielding a more powerful essay. Express one main idea per paragraph and one point per sentence.

👍 **TRY TALKING FIRST**

If you find it difficult to write essays, try talking about the essay topic while recording the conversation. After you're done, transcribe the recording and edit it into essay form. This will give you a good start on your essay. Since the act of writing often interferes with the flow of ideas (most people can think and speak much faster than they can write or type), speaking into a tape recorder can help you capture your ideas and emotions better than starting at a blank piece of paper.

Make it personal. Self-evaluation is appropriate when you are writing about how an experience affected you. But do not limit the essay to how you felt about the experience. Instead, also talk about how it affected your future actions. By linking your feelings to concrete examples and actions, you allow the committee to judge how the experience affected you through a tangible result.

Maxim Pinkovskiy, now a junior at Columbia, emphasizes the personal connection that students should make: "They should think back to things that they've learned in school, things that they have directly experienced and see what unique lessons they can draw from them. So that the essay is not just *a* response to the topic, but it's *their* response to the topic, what *they* as individuals with such and such a background with such and such experience can bring to the table."

What do you find interesting? Chances are, if you are passionate about a topic, you'll be able to write a more interesting essay about the topic.

Be specific. Another key to a memorable essay is to be very specific. Narrowing your essay's theme forces you to do good research. Perhaps you'll teach the judges something they didn't know.

For example:

- Not "War is bad," but "How do we quantify in dollars the civilian cost of war?"
- Not "We should save the earth," but "Can the die-off of frog species in Costa Rica since 1990 be attributed to global warming?"
- Not "Homelessness is dreadful," but "How a homeless family I know (from my church-based work) copes with the contradictions of the Virginia welfare system."

Give concrete examples. If you say that one of your best qualities is leadership, tell a specific story where you demonstrated leadership. Similarly, a question about community service should not be answered with a vague "I like helping others and feel that it is important," but should include specific examples where you have helped others.

This can have a big impact on whether you win the award. If your application is filled with vague and abstract answers, the selection committee doesn't have any way of evaluating your qualifications. Selection committees never accept an applicant's self-evaluation at face value. If you give them concrete examples, they can form their own opinion and cite those experiences and accomplishments as evidence in support of their opinion. Concrete examples also make an application more memorable.

Keep it fresh and interesting. Try to avoid editing the life out of your essay. Safe essay topics are often boring. You should write an essay that is memorable and captivating without being offensive. Engage the reader, and tell them something interesting that will make them want to know more about you. For example, two decades ago a student wrote an essay for his college admissions applications about depositing checks from Playboy at the bank. When he was a child, he regularly wrote puzzles for *Games Magazine*. At the time, *Games Magazine* was owned by Playboy Enterprises, so his checks would arrive from Playboy Enterprises, Magazine Division, with no further identification of the publication. Imagine a twelve-year-old boy depositing a check like that at a small-town bank. When the tellers would look at him strangely, he would wink and say, "Oh, didn't you see it? It was in the March issue." He closed the essay with a custom puzzle he wrote for each college. The topic of his essay was a bit risqué, but it made his application stand out.

Proofread your essays. When the selection committee is evaluating your application, all they can see is what you submitted. If your application is filled with typographic, spelling and grammar errors, it will form a bad impression. Most word processing programs have built-in spelling and grammar correction tools. Use them. Then print out the essay and copyedit it manually. Spelling correction algorithms are not currently capable of correcting valid word spelling errors, in which one word is substituted for another, such as "principle" for "principal." For example, about 10% of the time the word "it's" or "its" is used, the other word should have been used.

ESSAY QUESTIONS

Often a scholarship application will ask you to write an essay based on a specific question, and it's helpful to think about *why* the scholarship sponsor asked that particular question. FastWeb has identified the following seven categories of essay questions.

Your academic plans. Some scholarship applications will ask you to write about your major or field of study. These questions are used to determine how well you know your area of specialization and why you're interested in it.

Past-present-future is often a good structure to use for describing your academic and career goals. Talking about the past tells the reader how you became interested in the field and the depth and breadth of your experience. Talking about the present tells them how you are executing your plan. Talking about the future lets them evaluate your potential contributions to the field.

It is important to demonstrate your commitment to the field of study. If your essay is wishy-washy and unmotivated, the selection committee will wonder whether you are a good investment. They do not want to award you the scholarship only to see you switch majors midway through your academic career.

Samples:
- How will your study of _____ contribute to your immediate or long-range career plans?
- Why do you want to be a _____?
- Explain the importance of (your major) in today's society.
- What do you think the industry of _____ will be like in the next five or ten years?
- What are the most important opportunities and challenges your field is facing today?

Current events and social issues. To test your skills at problem-solving and check how up to date you are on current issues, many scholarship applications include questions about problems and issues facing society.

Samples:

- What do you consider to be the single most important societal problem? Why? How would you solve it?
- If you had the authority to change your school in a positive way, what specific changes would you make?
- Pick a controversial problem on college campuses and suggest a solution.
- What do you see as the greatest threat to the environment today?
- Discuss the strengths and weaknesses of the democratic system of government.

Personal achievements. Scholarships exist to reward and encourage achievement, so you shouldn't be surprised to find essay topics that ask you to brag a little.

Samples:

- Describe how you have demonstrated leadership ability both in and out of school.
- Discuss a special attribute or accomplishment that sets you apart.
- Describe your most meaningful achievements and how they relate to your field of study and your future goals.
- Why are you a good candidate to receive this award?

Background and influences. Who you are is closely tied to where you've been and who you've known. To learn more about you, some scholarship committees will ask you to write about your background and major influences.

Samples:

- Pick an experience from your own life and explain how it has influenced your development.
- Who in your life has been your biggest influence and why?
- How has your family background affected the way you see the world?
- How has your education contributed to who you are today?

Future plans and goals. Scholarship sponsors look for applicants with vision and motivation, so they might ask about your goals and aspirations.

Samples:

- Briefly describe your long- and short-term goals.
- Where do you see yourself five or ten years from now?
- Why do you want to get a college education?

Financial need. Many scholarship providers have a charitable goal: They want to provide money for students who are going to have trouble paying for college. In addition to asking for information about your financial situation, these committees may want a more detailed and personal account of your financial need.

Samples:

- From a financial standpoint, what impact would this scholarship have on your education?
- State any special personal or family circumstances affecting your need for financial assistance.
- How have you been financing your college education?

Random topics. Some essay questions don't seem directly related to your education, but committees use them to test your creativity and get a more well-rounded sense of your personality.

Samples:

- Choose a person or persons (living, dead or fictional) you admire and explain why.
- Choose a book that affected you deeply and explain why.
- Pick one of your greatest weaknesses and explain how you are compensating for that weakness.
- If you could be any inanimate object, what would you be? Why?

LETTERS OF RECOMMENDATION

Scholarship sponsors want to know more than your opinion about yourself, and so they ask you to provide one or more letters of recommendation. They want to read the opinion of someone who is familiar with your background and knows you well. This is a great time to learn how to get effective recommendations, because you will need them at school and later in your career.

Your critical choice is *who* will make the recommendations. You have to ask the right persons to do this. Of course they should be able to write well, and there are several other important factors affecting your choices.

Depending on the nature of the scholarship program, you should consider asking your teachers or professors, your employer, your coach, the director of a community service organization at which you volunteered your time and anybody who knows you well. (Never, however, ask a family member to write a letter on your behalf.)

Choose people who are relevant to the sponsor's goals. For example, ask a science teacher to write a letter of recommendation for a science scholarship, not your English teacher. If writing about community service, ask someone who directs the service program, not a friend who served with you. All else being equal, it is better to ask someone who has known you longer and who is more impressed by your qualifications. (It is even better if they can compare you with other students, especially students who have won the award previously.)

Ask each person whether they can write you a *good* letter of recommendation. You should pick people who can not only write well, but write well about you. If they seem reluctant to recommend you, ask them to suggest someone else who might be a better choice.

Meet with each person you've chosen, and tell them about the scholarship and its sponsor. Let them know why you think you deserve the scholarship. If you've written an essay, give them a copy. Provide them with a copy of your accomplishments resume, so that they have a summary of your background. Request that they relate the recommendation specifically to the scholarship, and the sponsor's mission and goals. A generic "to whom it may concern" letter is a weak recommendation.

Provide the recommender with a stamped and addressed envelope and any required forms. Give them two or three weeks to write the letter. Follow up after ten days, and gently remind them of the deadline (ask whether they have sent in the recommendation or need more information from you).

Do not ask to see a copy of the letter, even if they offer to give you a copy. If the recommender provides you with a copy of the letter, the selection committee may suspect that the letter isn't as candid as it might have been otherwise.

However, when the scholarship selection process is over, you might want to request a copy of the recommendation for your files. One well-written recommendation might be shared with future recommenders as a model.

Send the writer a thank-you note after the letter has been mailed. In all likelihood you will ask them to write additional letters for you. Once they've written one letter on your behalf, the second letter is much easier. If you send them a thank-you, it will give them a good impression and make them more willing to spend time writing you additional letters in the future.

SCHOLARSHIP INTERVIEWS

Your application was perfect, your essay was brilliant, and now you are in the home stretch . . . and then they ask you to interview live and in person with a scholarship judge.

It's natural to feel a little nervous. The scholarship is on the line. You might not be comfortable or confident talking about yourself. Fortunately, you can turn what feels like an impending interrogation into a revealing conversation.

Remember that they expect you to be nervous. Of course a scholarship judge is comparing you to other candidates, but remember that he or she is hoping you'll do well. Most of the time, the interviewer is a volunteer whose job is to identify the most appropriate candidates, not destroy your ego.

The biggest difference between a stellar interview and a mediocre one is your level of preparation. With that in mind, use the following techniques to do your best.

Stay relevant. Your interviewer wants to know more about you, in addition to what you wrote in the essay. When an interviewer asks you to "tell me about yourself," they don't want to hear your life history and how you like vanilla ice cream. Instead, tell him or her about your relevant background and qualifications for the award.

Prepare stories. People are hard-wired to tell and hear stories. They make you memorable. Be prepared with very specific stories about your schoolwork, activities, athletic or artistic accomplishments that are relevant to the scholarship. Saying "I raised some money" is boring. Specific details about how you got sponsors for a three-day walk to find a breast cancer cure, and how you kept going through the last two hot, rainy October days, the people you met and the way the event changed you are gripping.

Prepare questions. Specific and intelligent questions about the scholarship, the sponsor and its mission, and the interviewer's connection to the scholarship help turn the interview into a conversation. Have at least five real questions (and check to see that the answers are not on the application or the web site). Stay away from questions about money or requirements. Try to turn the interview into a conversation instead of an interrogation.

Practice answers. Athletes and artists know there is simply no substitute for practice . . . and scholarship interviews are no different. Try this: Have an adult friend (or parent) sit with you in an office or coffee shop, and ask you some of the questions below. Dress exactly as you would for the interview. Answer the questions, then both of you critique your performance after the practice interview. If you really want to rehearse, try videotaping your performance . . . [60] then go back and do it better the second time!

Practice is one way to prepare for the ultimate interviewing skill, which professional interview coaches call "presence." You have to connect to the interviewer in a meaningful and authentic way. You have to make a good impression from the first minute of the interview. Here are common-sense keys to presence:

Review current events. Before any interview, it is a good idea to read a national newspaper like the *New York Times* or *Wall Street Journal* and a news magazine like *U.S. News & World Report* or *Newsweek*. Better yet, make it a habit to read a newspaper or news magazine on a regular basis. Some interviewers like to ask your opinion about current events, and a blank stare doesn't help.

If you are asked a question about a controversial topic like politics, discuss the key issues. Base the discussion on reason, not emotion.

Arrive a few minutes early. If you are unfamiliar with the location, scope it out before the day of the interview. You don't want to arrive late because you got lost. Give yourself plenty of time to get there, not just because it's polite, but because you'll want to be thinking about the interview, not how late you are.

It is generally a good idea to use the bathroom at home before you leave for the interview.

Dress for success. Wear professional attire (men — a suit and tie; women — a suit or professional outfit). If you wear a T-shirt and jeans, you won't win the scholarship. If you don't have a suit, wear conservative clothing, such as a sweater or dress shirt. You and your clothes should be clean and neat. Get a haircut if necessary. Trim your nails. Brush your teeth. This is not selling out — it's showing respect.

Show your manners. Smile. Shake hands firmly. Make eye contact. Say,

"Thank you for seeing me." Don't smoke or chew gum. It helps to be positive and upbeat. Don't trash your school or the college financing system—instead, show in your demeanor that you're excited and grateful to talk about the scholarship.

Be decisive. When answering questions about why you chose a particular activity or college major, do not show uncertainty about your choice. The scholarship sponsor wants to support students who will graduate with a degree in a particular major, or continue the activity that concerns the sponsor.

Listen and clarify. If you're unsure about a question, ask the interviewer to say more. If you truly don't know an answer, don't try to fake it or dwell on your response. Say, "I'm afraid I don't know the answer to that. Can you tell me more?"

Avoid extreme answers. Never use "never" or "always," since it always sets you up for a challenge to your answer.

Be concise. Avoid long-winded answers when a shorter answer will work just as well. Get to the point. Don't spend too much time answering the question. Don't chatter for the sake of saying something. Know when you've sufficiently answered the question. But don't answer in monosyllables either.

Expect the unexpected. Some interviewers ask unusual questions or do strange things simply to see how you will react. It is okay to pause to think before answering any question, so long as the pause is short. (It is better to think before answering than to answer before thinking.)

During the Westinghouse Science Talent Search competition (now the Intel Science Talent Search), the candidates were interviewed by Glenn Seaborg, Nobel laureate. One of the students told the following anecdote about his interview: "During my interview with Glenn Seaborg, he asked me, 'What is the fifty-fourth element of the periodic table?' I didn't have the faintest idea what the answer was, as I had never memorized the periodic table of the elements. I started using what I remembered about the layout of the periodic table to mention some of the properties of the fifty-fourth element (i.e., that it must be inert), when I started laughing uncontrollably. I had just noticed that Dr. Seaborg's tie was a periodic table of the elements, and element 54 (xenon) was clearly visible on the tie."

Expect interviews to differ. Rachael Massell observes, "Interviews are all different. For local scholarships, the interviewer would want to talk about people that we knew in common, or what I thought about local events. They knew a lot about my high school, so I didn't have to explain a lot about my background. In national scholarship interviews I would spend a lot of time talking about where I was from and how that came into play with who I was, and what I wanted to do."

Finally, expect these common interview questions in addition to specific discussion about the scholarship:

- Tell me about your interest in [academic subject]. Why do you like studying that? Will that be your major in college?
- How have your personal experiences prepared you for college?
- Why did you do [name of activity]?
- Why do you want to study [name of major/field]?
- What's most important to you about a college education?
- What are your strengths and weaknesses?
- What's your biggest accomplishment? Your biggest regret?
- What was the last book you read?
- What frustrates you?
- What are your hobbies?
- Discuss an obstacle you encountered and how you overcame it.
- Discuss a mistake you made and what you learned from it.
- How involved are teachers, friends and family in your work on [subject]?
- What are your favorite classes and activities at school?
- What do you know about [the scholarship sponsor]?
- Have you ever had to work with someone you didn't like? How did you deal with the situation?
- Why do you want to win this scholarship?
- What qualifies you for this scholarship?
- Why shouldn't you get this scholarship?
- What will you do if you don't get this scholarship?
- How do you handle pressure and stress?
- What field do you think will be important twenty-five years from now?
- That was an unoriginal/stupid answer. Don't you have any better ideas? (Yes, sometimes you will be asked aggressive questions intended to throw you off!)
- What do you think is the benefit, beyond money, of winning this scholarship?
- Is there anything you'd like to add?
- Do you have any questions?

If the interviewer gives you a puzzle or problem and asks you to solve it, solve it aloud. Each step of the way, say what approaches you are considering.

The purpose of this type of question is not to see if you can solve the problem, but to see how you approach solving problems and how you react when you can't figure out how to solve a problem. It is not unusual for interviewers for a highly selective scholarship to give you a problem for which there is no known solution or for which the solution is very difficult because they don't want you to be able to solve the problem.

After the interview, send a thank-you note to the interviewer. (And when you receive that scholarship, send a thank-you note to the scholarship provider!)

WINNING A COMPETITION

The ultimate "interview" for a scholarship is a competition, in which you go head-to-head against fellow students. Competitions exist in all academic subjects and most activities—mathematics, science, speaking, debate, spelling, musical performance, athletics and on and on.

Competitions don't create champions, they identify them, and you have to be skilled in the subject just to get past the starting line. Enter if you (and an impartial observer, like a teacher) are reasonably confident of your ability. It's a badge of honor even to reach the regional playoffs for one of these; some national competitions award smaller scholarships to those who make the semifinals. Don't worry about being disappointed if you lose. Most students lose several competitions before they win one, and they quickly forget about their failures. Just don't let one loss stop you from entering more competitions.

Your fellow competitors will probably try to seem more confident than they really are. Don't let this psych you out. Focus on the task at hand, not the competition. You need to speak up when you have an answer, and correct or amplify the points raised by others. Sometimes teamwork matters.

☑ **I Wish I Had Known . . .**

I wish I had been better prepared to present myself more effectively in order to gain merit-based scholarships.

—*Britney Frankston, freshman*
Cal Poly San Luis Obispo

In many competitions, time limits are an additional source of pressure. First, take a deep breath and relax. Then, scan the questions, and answer all the easy questions before moving onward to the more difficult questions. Don't rush—careless errors can be the difference between winning and losing the competition. It you finish early, spend the time checking your work. Check it several times, if you can. Try solving the same problems several different ways.

Don't worry if some of the questions seem too easy. Most competitions include a few easy questions to build confidence and to help contestants relax.

In multiple choice tests, it can help to eliminate the clearly incorrect answers. It is difficult to write four good wrong answers. Sometimes the nature of the wrong answers can give you a hint as to how to solve the problem or the kinds of errors they are expecting contestants to make.

A key to winning competitions is to practice and drill. Take a previous year's exam under realistic conditions to let you get used to the setting. Score your answers, and review your wrong answers. Don't just look at the correct solution, but identify where you went astray. This will help you avoid pitfalls in a real competition. The more time you spend practicing, the better you will perform.

If you're really talented, you will occasionally find an error in one of the

A WINNER'S ADVICE

Lubna Malik, who won several national scholarships, offers this calming advice: "Don't worry about money first. In America, there are so many loans and grants and scholarships for people who don't have enough money to get an education. Even if you take out some loans, it'll be worth it if you're getting the best education.

"I think you should apply to colleges that have great overall programs. After coming to Princeton, I definitely realized that the type of student you're with at a school makes a huge difference because they are the people you're competing with. And competing with people who are as like-minded as you and who are trying their hardest and have very, very high aims in life—that is just something amazing that you can't get anywhere else."

questions on an exam, such as a question with two correct answers. Don't over-think the question, or you'll end up providing the wrong right answer. It is best to supply the answer they expect. Then, to provide backup, use some of your scrap paper to explain the error and the solutions, and turn it in with your answer sheet.

Award ceremonies can be nerve-wracking. Often they start by announcing the honorable mentions, and eventually work their way up to the first place winners. Toward the end, you get increasingly nervous, because either you won a top prize, or you won nothing at all.

Paying for college is hard. Scholarships offer a world of help. In the next chapter, we'll caution you about some potential danger zones—in scholarships, money management and other parts of the process—that could thwart all the good work you've done. We'll teach you how to protect your investment of time and money, so that you'll get the best possible outcome.

ADVICE FOR PARENTS

You can't win the scholarship for your child, but you can help in all the steps that go into winning.

- Proofread and critique your child's essays, but don't rewrite them. Are they interesting? Could anyone else have written them? They should reflect your child's unique experience.
- Help your child prioritize scholarship opportunities, and remember that many small scholarships add up!
- Make a list of friends or coworkers your child might interview for an essay, and introduce them.
- Have your child practice his or her interview style in front of you (or better, in front of a trusted adult friend).

14

Danger Zones

Matt followed his parents into the meeting room at a local hotel. The room was starting to get crowded, with thirty to forty families already in attendance. A few minutes after everyone settled into their seats, a good-looking man jumped up in front of the screen at the front of the room and announced in a booming voice: "Good morning! My name is Robert, and I'd like to welcome you to our free financial aid seminar, sponsored by American Student Aid Foundation.

"I've got a lot of material to cover, so take careful notes. After the seminar, we'll break out into your personal interviews. I apologize for our holding the seminar in this hotel room, but space was not available at the local college campus."

Matt slouched in his chair. To him, the guy sounded more like a salesman than a guidance counselor. Lynn nudged him at the word "interviews."

Robert dimmed the room lights and clicked on a projector. The screen flashed,

$6 BILLION

UNCLAIMED!

"You probably don't know, but more than $6 billion in scholarship money goes unclaimed each year," Robert called. His voiced lowered. "That's billion with a capital B. And a lot of these scholarships just don't get enough qualified applicants because nobody knows about them."

Robert continued, "There are also billions of dollars in aid awarded each year by the federal government. We can help you complete the Free Application for Federal Student Aid, to make sure you get as much money as possible."

Robert put up slides and graphs at a dizzying pace. Matt's parents were scribbling notes furiously, but were having trouble keeping up. Finally, after about an hour, the seminar was over, and the families were assigned to one of six "counselors" for the personal interview. Matt was assigned to Robert.

Robert shook hands with Matt and his parents, and said, "You're probably worried about how you're going to be able to afford to send Matt to an expensive college like Caledonia or the University of Ohio, right?"

Matt wondered how Robert knew where he had applied. He hadn't told him. Maybe his parents had mentioned it when they talked to his assistant on the phone?

"The good news is there is a lot of money available, and we can help you get it," Robert said. "It's amazing what doesn't get advertised. Did you know that there are even scholarships for left-handed redheaded tennis players?"

"My little sister Sarah plays tennis," Matt replied.

"We can help her too, when she's ready for college."

"She's fifteen, so she's not there yet," said Matt. "Anyway, why do you think I'm qualified?"

"With your good grades you qualify for many awards. There are millions of scholarships. We can match you up with all kinds of scholarships you didn't even know existed . . . the ones I told you go unclaimed."

"Well, I've used several free online scholarship sites and found almost a hundred scholarships. Aren't the scholarships you're talking about on those sites?" Matt asked.

Robert grinned at Lynn and Jim, as if to say they had a very clever boy. "Excellent question!" he replied. "We certainly recommend using the online scholarship databases. But we have a special relationship with many scholarships that you can't find in any national database or book. There are scholarships that do not depend on grades or athletic ability or financial need. We can help make sure you get your fair share."

"What scholarships are available for me besides the ones I already found?" Matt asked.

"It might interest you to know that we work with a number of foundations that are right here in Ohio, Matt. They're for Ohio students, and you are a legal resident of Ohio, right?"

"Sure."

"Now, the seminar you just attended was absolutely free, no charge, nada. But if you want us to help you apply for scholarships and complete the FAFSA, there's a small annual fee of $475. If you pay for all four years at once, there's a 15% discount, for a total of $1,615."

Lynn interjected, "That's a lot of money. Can't we get help completing the FAFSA from Ms. Breen at Manchester State, and from Matt's guidance counselor?"

Jim added, "There's also a toll-free hotline run by the U.S. Department of Education. It's on their web site."

Robert bristled a little, then resumed his easy smile. "Well, let's think about this. Whose interests do college financial aid administrators represent? Who pays their salary? The college, right?"

"They work there, sure, but . . ." Jim began.

Robert cut him off. "Matt's guidance counselor probably has a caseload of 400 students. How much time has she been able to give you, Matt?"

"But that's still a lot of money. Why can't we complete the forms on our own?" Jim responded.

"You could, but you might not get as much money. Let me ask you a question. Do you do your own taxes?"

"We use H&R Block."

Robert smiled. "So you pay a tax preparer to help you get all the deductions you deserve. We are the same. We are experts. We present your finances in the best light, ensuring that you get as much federal aid as possible." He drew a form out of his shiny leather portfolio. "Here's our contract. As I noted, we have a 15% discount if you pay for all four years today."

"We're not sure," Lynn said.

"It's a small amount of money compared to the cost of a college education. Wouldn't you do anything to help prepare Matt for the future?"

"Yes, but . . ."

"There's also no risk. We guarantee that Matt will get at least $2,000 in financial aid. It's free money."

When Jim and Lynn still hesitated, Robert added, "We can only help so many students. If you wait too long to sign up, you won't get as much aid. Many of these scholarships are awarded on a first-come, first-served basis."

Jim said, "We need some time to think about it. It's a lot of money, and I left my checkbook at home."

Robert rose and shook his hand. "Thank you for coming to our seminar. I'll hold Matt's space for the next three days. If you mail us the contract with a check when you get home, we can get started right away."

Back in the car, Matt said to his parents, "Ms. Breen told us that if you have to pay money to get money, something's wrong. It's probably a scam. She also said to be suspicious if anyone guarantees you'll get scholarships."

"You're probably right, dear," Matt's mother said. "But we need to check out anything that might help."

Matt sighed. The hard part about this spring was the fact that it wasn't quite all nailed down . . . yet. He was going to college, he knew that, but he had not heard from a dozen scholarships for which he'd applied. He would not hear for weeks. He thought he had uncovered every possibility, but now this seminar guy tells him that he's missed all kinds of money . . .

• • •

Because paying for college is complicated, you might encounter difficulties working through the process. Because paying for college is costly, those difficulties can lead to expensive mistakes. Because paying for college is complicated *and* expensive, the territory unfortunately includes danger zones—times and places that can get you into trouble. Fortunately, these danger zones are avoidable if you recognize them. In this chapter, we'll discuss the most costly danger zones, which include:

- Financial aid and scholarship scams.
- Paying to locate scholarships.
- Deciding whether to use paid consultants or services.
- Problems with money management.

Jim Sumner, Dean of Admission and Financial Aid at Grinnell College, is concerned about vulnerable families seeking money for college. "Many people think that there are enormous untapped buckets of money spread around the country, and it's just waiting to pay for your college," says Jim. "More often than not, people get sucked into these expensive entrepreneurial entities that say, 'You give us a few hundred bucks we'll find you plenty of money.' I worry that people believe that and they're forced to waste a lot of money and time."

This chapter will warn you about common pitfalls, mistakes and outright dangers you might find during the process, and help you avoid both unnecessary "help" and outright scams.

SCAMS

Students and their families looking for college financing are frequent targets of scam artists. Some of these are deceptive, and some are simply illegal. They tend to find victims among people who can least afford college, but anyone can be a target.

In the 2006 *College Gold* survey, 5% of students responded that they had encountered scholarship or financial aid scams. Students specified that they had lost from $25 to as much as $6,000!

Guidance counselor Lori Johnston describes how a scam almost ruined a typically hopeful family:

> *I knew the son of a single mom who worked in a sandwich shop. He didn't have money to go to the dance or the field trip. He was on a free lunch program. He and his mom got a letter that said, "We've reserved this time for you and your student," so they attended one of those seminars where they guarantee financial aid and scholarship money. When they got there, of course, there were sixty other people whose time had been "reserved." And then they got a general sales pitch, and then they met individually with someone who said, "Oh, for $2,500 we can get this for you . . ."*
>
> *They put that $2,500 charge on their only credit card, and ended up getting information that I could give them free. Fortunately, they came in to my office all thrilled, saying, "Gosh, look what we're able to get, look what they said they're going to help us with. . . ." We went to the Better Business Bureau and Federal Trade Commission and ended up taking the charge off the credit card.*

Some of the most common scams are these:

Free seminar. You may receive a letter advertising a free financial aid seminar or "interviews" for financial assistance. Sometimes the seminars do provide some useful information, as described above.[61] Often, however, the seminar is a cleverly disguised sales pitch for consulting services you don't need. If you're interested in a seminar, ask your guidance counselor or financial aid administrator about it; he or she might be able to tell you whether it's worth your time and money. Also please note that even if the seminar is held on a college campus, it may still be a scam. Many colleges sometimes rent space to the public, especially during the summer. Often scams will rent space without the aid office knowing about it, in an effort to suggest that the college is endorsing their service.

Scholarships for profit. This scam looks just like a real scholarship program, but requires an application fee. The typical scam receives 5,000 to 10,000 applications and charges fees of $5 to $35. These scams can afford to pay out a $1,000 scholarship or two and still pocket a hefty profit, if they happen to award any scholarships at all. This amounts to an illegal lottery.

The scholarship prize. This scam tells you that you've won a college scholarship worth thousands of dollars, but requires that you pay a "disbursement" or "redemption" fee or the taxes before they can release your prize. If someone says you've won a prize and you don't remember entering the contest or submitting an application, be suspicious.

Scholarships that never materialize. Many scams encourage you to send them money up front, but provide little or nothing in exchange. Usually victims think that they simply didn't win the scholarship.

The advance-fee loan. This scam offers you an unusually low-interest educational loan, with the requirement that you pay a fee before you receive the loan. When you pay the money, the promised loan never materializes. Real educational loans deduct the fees from the disbursement check and never require an up-front fee.

Investment required for federal loans. Insurance companies and brokerage firms sometimes offer free financial aid seminars that are actually sales pitches for insurance, annuity and investment products. When a sales pitch implies that purchasing such a product is a prerequisite to receiving federal student aid, it violates federal regulations and state insurance laws.

There are several recent trends in scholarship scams:

- Seminar scams are becoming more prevalent.
- Scholarships for profit are becoming more brazen in admitting that they are operating a for-profit business that redistributes the students' applica-

tion fees as scholarships (after skimming a percentage off the top). They are relying on student gullibility.

- The fine print on the scholarship checks offered by some scams authorize the scam, if the check is deposited, to debit your account for a monthly fee.
- A web site might promise you a scholarship if you complete a survey and take the offers of a certain number of advertisers. But the survey is never-ending, the offers involve your spending more money than you are promised and the promised scholarship never materializes.
- Scholarships designed to gather personal information for marketing or identity fraud purposes.

👍 CONSUMER RULES OF THUMB

1. If you must pay money to get money, it might be a scam.
2. If it sounds too good to be true, it probably is.
3. Spend the time, not the money.
4. Never invest more than a postage stamp to get information about scholarships.
5. Nobody can guarantee that you'll win a scholarship.
6. Legitimate scholarship foundations do not charge application fees.
7. If you're suspicious of an offer, it's usually with good reason.

It's easy for unscrupulous businesses to locate college-age students, their parents or families, and you might be approached out of the blue by persons who seem to have a valuable service to offer and may know a lot of details about your background. Here are some additional red flags that will alert you to possible deceptive "opportunities":

Unusual requests for personal information. If the application asks you to disclose bank account numbers, credit card numbers, calling card numbers, or Social Security numbers, **don't.** If they call and ask you for personal information to "confirm your eligibility," "verify your identity" or as a "sign of good will," **hang up immediately.** Identity thieves are slathering to grab a piece of the dollars spent on college aid—or misuse your information a hundred other ways. In 2003, an identity thief in Arizona received education money from the federal government for forty-three separate identities—most stolen from prison inmates!

The more recent online schemes called phishing and pharming are also a threat. Basically, these are friendly-looking e-mails or web sites that solicit information such as credit card numbers, passwords and Social Security numbers. The e-mails or web sites might appear to be from familiar institutions such as large banks. The best defense: Don't give the information! You can learn more about these practices at www.antiphishing.org.

No telephone number. Most legitimate scholarship programs include a telephone number for inquiries with their application materials. The scholarship sponsor will have a telephone number listed with Directory Assistance. Foundations do not have unlisted numbers.

Masquerading as a federal agency. If you receive an offer from an organization with an official-sounding name, check whether there really is a federal agency with that name. Don't believe someone offering a scholarship opportunity from the U.S. Department of Education or similar-sounding name, as the U.S. Department of Education does not charge fees for education grants and loans. Don't trust an organization just because it has an official-looking "governmental" seal as its logo or has a prestigious-seeming Washington, DC, return address.

Claims of university, government, Chamber of Commerce or Better Business Bureau approval. The federal government, U.S. Department of Education and the U.S. Chamber of Commerce do not endorse or recommend private businesses. If a financial aid seminar is held in a local high school or college facility, call the guidance counselor or financial aid office to find out whether it is an approved event.

Suggesting that they are a nonprofit, charitable organization when they are not. For example, an organization with "Fund" or "Foundation" in its name is not necessarily a charitable foundation and may even be a for-profit business. IRS Publication 78 (apps.irs.gov/app/pub78) lists all tax-exempt charitable organizations.

Unsolicited scholarship opportunities. Most scholarship sponsors will only contact you in response to your inquiry.

Failure to substantiate awards. If the organization can't prove that its scholarships are actually awarded and disbursed, be cautious.

Notification by phone. If you have won a scholarship, you will receive written notification by mail, not by phone.

Disguised advertising. Don't believe everything you read or hear, especially if you see it online or in an e-mail message. Unless you personally know the person praising a product or service, don't believe the recommendation.

A newly formed company. Most philanthropic foundations have been established for many years. If a company was formed recently, ask for references.

Runaround or unspecific information. Demand concrete answers that directly respond to your questions. If they repeat the same lines again and again, the caller is probably reading a standard pitch from a boilerplate script.

Abusive treatment. If the caller swears at you or becomes abusive when you ask questions, or gives you a pressured sales pitch, it's probably a scam. Hang up.

Sometimes a scam persists for years before people catch on to it. If you believe the offer is a scam, report it to the Better Business Bureau and to the Federal Trade Commission at www.ftc.gov or call toll-free, 1-877-FTC-HELP (1-877-382-4357); TTY: 1-866-653-4261.

It's not much fun to contemplate all the wrong turns you can make in a complex process like paying for college. It's even less fun to think about the people who are willing to take your time and money without giving much of value, or even trying to scam you. Hang up on the quick-money schemes, and toss those deceptive brochures in the trash. Ask the questions in this chapter of anyone who offers help for pay. Instead of paying for services you don't need, or scholarships that don't exist, turn to proven, trustworthy people and resources. That's where you'll find help and advice that will get you on your way to a great college career.

PAYING TO LOCATE SCHOLARSHIPS

Do not waste your money on fee-based scholarship-matching services. The largest and highest quality scholarship databases are all available for free on the World Wide Web—these include FastWeb, The College Board and Peterson's services. It takes only about half an hour to search any of these databases.

Paid scholarship-matching services do not award scholarships and do not apply for scholarships on your behalf, and they don't select the winning students. All they do is provide a list of the names and addresses of scholarships that superficially match your profile. It is then up to the student to contact the scholarship sponsor for current information and application materials—exactly what the student would do if they found a scholarship using a free service.

Some fee-based scholarship services have engaged in false and misleading marketing tactics designed to give you an unreasonable expectation of success. Some of the more common statements include:

"Millions of scholarship dollars go unclaimed!" We mentioned this in chapter 2, but it bears repeating: You might be told that millions or billions of dollars of scholarships go unused each year because students don't know where to apply, but this simply isn't true. There is no huge pool of unclaimed money just waiting for you to "claim your fair share."

"Guaranteed winnings!" There's no way they can guarantee you'll receive funding, because they have no control over the decisions made by scholarship sponsors. Also, such "guarantees" often come with complicated, hidden conditions that make them extremely hard to redeem.

"Everybody is eligible!" All scholarship sponsors are looking for candidates who best match certain criteria. Scholarships are awarded according to a variety of merits and needs, but some set of restrictions always applies.

"A 96% success rate!" When they refer to a 96% success rate, they are describing their success in matching students against the database, not the number of students who receive money.

"You must use our service to qualify for aid!" Scholarship-matching services match you to a list of awards, but it is not necessary to use their service to prequalify for an award. Scholarship-matching services do not control who wins an award.

"Awards are given on a first-come, first-served basis. Time is limited. Apply now!" Although most programs have deadlines, very few give out scholarships on a rolling basis. Scholarship-matching services that use this claim are trying to rush you into using their service without thinking.

"We represent big-name companies who need a tax write-off." If a company claims to represent big companies "who give away scholarships for tax purposes," be suspicious. The firms that do manage scholarship programs for big-name companies—including Scholarship America, ACT Recognition Program Services and the Oregon Student Assistance Commission—never charge an application fee.

FINANCIAL AID CONSULTANTS

Sometimes the financial aid process can seem overwhelming, and that's easy to understand. In the 2006 *College Gold* survey, 38% of respondents said that completing forms and/or paperwork was the most stressful part of getting financial aid. Although this book includes every tool and tip you need to navigate the waters of financial aid, some people wish to consider additional help. Furthermore, many families are approached by people or businesses calling themselves financial aid consultants. It's tempting to give the process over to someone calling themselves an "expert."

There are several dangers in this situation, however. Anyone can call himself/herself a financial aid consultant, however unqualified they might be.

If you believe you need help beyond what *College Gold* offers, please, consider these questions:

Do you really need a consultant? You aren't going to save any time, since you need to fill out a consultant's forms with the same information as is presented with the FAFSA. You'll still have to gather your records and get the answers to detailed questions about your finances. You're not paying for something you couldn't do in this case—just "outsourcing" the work to see it gets done.

Will a consultant take responsibility for the work he or she does? For example, would they expose themselves to penalties if they prepare a FAFSA with false information? If not, avoid them. Ask the consultant for examples of information or advice they can provide that is not generally available in books such as this one or web sites like FinAid.org. Ask them what they can provide that is not offered free by college financial aid administrators, or 1-800-4-FED-AID.

What are their credentials? A consultant who has worked in the financial aid office at a university, or who is a CPA (Certified Public Accountant) or CFP (Certified Financial Planner), will be more likely to be able to help you than one who has no experience as a practicing financial aid professional. CPAs and CFPs have earned their certifications by passing rigorous tests from national organizations. They are qualified to help with financial planning, although some of them might not make recommendations that are optimal from a college financial planning perspective (e.g., saving in the child's name for the tax advantages).

What specific help do you need? You might not need a full range of services. Most families or individuals are perfectly capable of filling out the FAFSA. Also, college financial aid offices process most of the federal grant and loan programs for you; you don't need a consultant to tell you whether you are eligible for the Federal Pell Grant. If you need just a little help filling out your financial aid forms, ask your guidance counselor or college financial aid administrator. Many schools and public libraries run free workshops and offer free help in filling out the financial aid forms accurately. The National Association of Student Financial Aid Administrators (NASFAA) and the Lumina Foundation for Education sponsor College Goal Sunday (www.collegegoalsundayusa.org) where you can get free help completing the FAFSA. Do not pay for things you can do yourself; do not pay for multiyear "packages" of services.

BOOK TO WEB

You can find help with the FAFSA from the Department of Education at www.studentaid.ed.gov/completefafsa or by calling 1-800-4-FED-AID. Help with completing the CSS/Financial Aid PROFILE is available online at profileonline.collegeboard.com.

Financial aid consultants often argue that the schools will not tell you how to take advantage of the loopholes in the need analysis process to maximize your eligibility for financial aid. However, there's no need to pay a financial aid consultant for this advice. Every legal tip they give can be found in chapter 5 in the section titled "Maximizing eligibility for student aid," with additional and updated information on www.collegegold.com. You should know that using a financial aid consultant will cause your FAFSA and school aid applications to be more heavily scrutinized.

Try calling your campus financial aid office before using a consultant. Although a financial aid administrator will rarely recommend a consultant, he or she will certainly tell you about past problems they've had with particular consultants. Financial aid administrators get particularly upset about consultants who hurt the family by giving financially unsound or unethical advice, or introduce errors or delays into the FAFSA process.

As a general rule, unless the family is truly poor, a decrease in the EFC will yield an increase in eligibility for student loans and work-study, not grants. Carefully consider whether it is worthwhile paying a fee for what in most cases amounts to increased eligibility for student loans.

As with any business, there are good consultants and there are bad consultants. Some consultants are reasonably priced, charging $50 to $100 for a comprehensive set of services, and others line their own pockets by charging hefty fees of $250 to $5,000 for the same services. Most consultants act in an ethical and professional manner, while others will encourage you to commit fraud. If you choose to work with a financial aid consultant, be alert to these red flags:

- Beware of any consultant who guarantees that you will receive a certain amount of financial aid. Such guarantees are on their face fraudulent, since the consultant cannot guarantee something the depends on your performance.

- Beware of any consultant who refuses to sign the FAFSA, because that's a good sign that he or she is encouraging you to commit fraud. Paid consultants are required to sign the FAFSA, even if they don't fill out the FAFSA on your behalf. Remember, you can be fined and imprisoned for providing false or misleading information on the FAFSA. Financial aid administrators are very good at identifying fraud and the U.S. Department of Education is instituting new procedures to catch fraud, including sharing information with the IRS.

- Beware of any consultant who encourages you to overestimate your income when completing the FAFSA. This will make you eligible for less aid. Unethical consultants do this so that they can provide the correct income figures later, making it appear as though they've saved the family money. They might even claim that they "negotiated" with the financial aid office to get you more aid, when all they did was supply the financial aid administrator with the correct financial information.

- Some consultants drum up business by sending letters to local parents advertising a free financial aid "seminar" (the opening scene in this chapter is an example). The seminar is little more than a sales pitch for their services, with a few well-known facts about financial aid thrown in. More useful seminars, without the sales pitch, are given by guidance counselors and college financial aid administrators. (Holding the seminar at a college does not guarantee that it is approved by the college.)

- Be wary of any consultant who encourages you to use strategies that seem unethical. For example, while it is legitimate to reduce your assets by paying off your credit cards, it is completely illegal to lie about your assets.

- Never agree to pay a fee based on the amount of aid received. Pay a flat fee, and know from the beginning exactly what services you'll receive.

MONEY MANAGEMENT PROBLEMS

When you're dealing with a lot of money, the risks of managing it incorrectly go up proportionately. When you're dealing with loans, as most students going to college are, the risks are that much greater. There are three questions in particular that cause a lot of confusion and/or grief in this process—whether to put money in children's names, defaulting on loans and dropping out of school.

In whose name to save? A common money management problem concerns the question of whether to place savings or other assets in the name of the child or the parents. With little or no income, children are taxed at a lower rate than their parents, so interest, dividends and other increases in assets (like capital gains on stock or bonds) are taxed at a lower rate. However, under current financial aid formulas, there are significant benefits to saving the money in the parents' name, despite the relatively meager tax savings of the child's lower tax bracket. Some of the more important reasons include the following:

- In calculating financial aid, child assets are assessed at a rate of 35%[62]— that is, 35% of the asset is included when calculating the expected family contribution. Parent assets are assessed on a bracketed system, with a top rate of 5.64%. Simply put, the college includes only up to $5.64 of every $100 parent assets, but $35 of every $100 in children's assets.

- Many parent assets are sheltered from the need analysis process. For example, an asset protection allowance based on the age of the older parent shelters a portion of the family's investments. For the typical parents of college-age children (median age 48), this asset protection allowance amounts to approximately $45,000 to $50,000. In addition, money in qualified retirement plans, such as an IRA or 401(k), is sheltered as an asset.[63] Also, the federal formula (but not the formulas used by many schools) ignores the value of the family's primary residence. There are no asset protection allowances for money in the child's name, so money in the child's name is not sheltered.

- Money in the child's name is legally the property of the child, so the child could spend it on whatever they want when they reach the age of trust termination for the custodial account.[64] If the parents set up a more complicated trust fund to restrict the use of the money (e.g., a Spendthrift Trust, a Section 2503(c) Minor's Trust, or Crummey Trust), it can negatively impact need assessments, since the full remaining value of the trust gets counted as a child asset each year. Voluntary restrictions on access to principal have no impact on need analysis; the full value of the trust fund must still be reported as an asset of the beneficiary to the extent that the beneficiary will eventually receive income and/or principal from the trust.[65] The only trust funds that are ignored by need analysis are involuntary trust funds established by court order (e.g., to pay for future medical expenses) and trust funds where ownership of the trust is indeterminate or in dispute (e.g., a will is currently being contested in court). Even blind trusts must be counted as assets.

Thus, placing money for college in the child's name is generally a mistake for most families. Families should save in the parent's name.

If you saved money in the child's name (e.g., in an UGMA or UTMA account), there are two methods of undoing the damage. Since the money is legally the child's, you cannot simply transfer the money into the parent's name. The child does not have the legal capacity to gift the money to the parents, and it would be a breach of the parent's fiduciary duty to appropriate the funds. An improper transfer could also result in gift taxes or other taxes being owed to the IRS. Acceptable methods of addressing this situation include:

- **Spending the money for the child's benefit on non-parental obligations.** Nothing prevents the parents from spending the money for the child's benefit, so long as the money is not spent on expenses that are normally considered *parental obligations* (e.g., food, clothing, shelter, medical care). A review of the parent's expenses might identify some that can be paid for using the child's funds, such as summer camp, a computer or a car. Of course, the money can also be spent for the child's education, and the parents should spend down any remaining funds for the child's college education before using their own funds. Clearly, we are not advocating that you spend the money on products and services you weren't already considering, but rather that you allocate the expenses to the child's account where possible. You can then set aside a similar amount in the parent's name with the intention of using it for the child's education.

- **Rolling over the assets into the custodial version of a qualified tuition plan.** Starting on July 1, 2006, assets of a dependent student held in a section 529 college savings plan (see appendix) or prepaid tuition plan are treated as an asset of the parent for federal student aid purposes. So the parents could liquidate the child's UGMA or UTMA account and roll the funds over into a custodial 529 college savings plan or a custodial prepaid tuition plan. The account will be titled the same as with the original custodial account, and the beneficiary will be restricted to the child, but the account will be treated as a parent asset during need analysis.

If there is still money left over in the child's name, the good news is that starting on July 1, 2007, the assessment rate for child assets will be dropping from 35% to 20%.

☑ **I Wish I Had Known . . .**

I wish I had known to have my parents only save money in their names.

—anonymous freshman
Augustana College

Defaulting on loans. A loan is in default when the borrower fails to pay several regular installments on time—usually ranging from six to twelve months[66]—or otherwise fails to meet the terms and conditions of the loan. If you default on a loan, the university, the holder of the loan, the state government and the federal government can take legal action to recover the money. The scary ones include:

- Turning your loans over to a collection agency.
- The government suing you to recover the full amount owed.
- Collection costs of as much as 18.5% of the amount owed.
- Garnishment of your wages (up to 15%!).
- Withholding of federal/state income tax refunds.
- Withholding of Social Security benefit payments.
- . . . even withholding of lottery winnings!

. . . and you won't be eligible for any further federal student aid. Furthermore, Congress has made it extremely difficult to escape student education debt through bankruptcy.

There is no statute of limitations on this debt! Defaulting on student loans can really ruin your credit rating—if you can't handle repaying low-cost loans like federal education loans, other lenders will be unwilling to lend you money.

Dropping out of school. Unfortunately, financial problems are the leading cause of students dropping out of college. Life doesn't stop because a student is enrolled, and typical reasons for a student hitting the wall financially include sudden changes in family income, a sudden loss of a business, medical problems or one of the other reasons listed on pages 236–237.

It's difficult to consider the possibility of things going wrong while a student is in school, but it makes sense to be aware of such possibilities. Parents might die or get divorced, or financial resources might run dry before college is completed. Non-traditional students (see chapter 16) with families might find their financial resources stretched beyond what they initially anticipated.

Dropping out of school does not absolve you from the obligation to repay your education debts. Furthermore, if you drop out of school you may be obliged to pay back part of the unused portion of your federal *grant* money, not just loans. If you drop out and don't pay back loans, getting back into school to complete a degree is that much harder. If you owe money to the college, the college may refuse to release your transcripts until you repay your debt.

If there's any change in your situation, let the financial aid administrator know, even midyear, because a midyear professional judgment adjustment is possible. Most schools have some contingency funds such as emergency loans to help with such situations. You might, for example, become eligible for the Federal Pell Grant if your EFC changes in the middle of the year.

By this time, a student should know basic money management. Melissa Ibanez of the University of Pittsburgh at Bradford says at the very least, a student needs to understand how credit cards and debit cards work, how to balance a checkbook and how to budget. If you didn't cover that territory early in the process, as described in chapter 4, make sure you do now. Many colleges run workshops to help their students learn basic financial literacy.

The habits of good money management apply to paying for your education. Don't borrow over your head. Use scholarship money for education, not something else.[67] Live within your means or even a little bit under them. Don't lie on your financial aid forms. If you think you need help, ask for it. The financial aid office, private scholarship organizations and private lenders want to see you graduate and succeed, not fail.

15

Decision Time

Matt's letters from colleges arrived in March—first the expected acceptance at Ohio State Mansfield, and then a series of letters in fast succession—a thick envelope from the University of Ohio, followed by another acceptance from Caledonia. When a single, thin envelope arrived from Oberlin, Matt was not surprised. He had doubted he would be accepted. The next day, letters arrived from the financial aid offices of Caledonia and Ohio, and Matt scanned them briefly for deadlines, then carefully copied and filed them. He did the same with a letter from Ohio State Mansfield. On March 14, Matt learned that he had won a scholarship for $1,000 from the Richland County Foundation, a local community foundation in Mansfield.

On the last Saturday in March, Matt and his parents sat down once again at the kitchen table, calculators at hand, and spread out the letters from the financial aid offices.

"First, let's see if there are any places we simply cannot afford," suggested Jim. Matt suspected he meant Caledonia.

Lynn spoke to Jim. "Honey, instead of looking at it that way, let's start by comparing them all to one another. They might not be as different as you think."

"Okay," said Jim, and then to Matt: "If you really think Caledonia is the only place for you, we'll see if we can make it happen. I just don't want to jeopardize Sarah's chances of going to a good school as well."

"I like Caledonia, I like Ohio as well," said Matt. Then he fell silent, studying the different-looking award letters, looking for comparisons.

• • •

You have been accepted to several colleges. You have received each college's financial aid package. Based on everything you've done and everything you know, which college will you attend?

You have some time to decide. Usually college acceptances and financial aid offers are made from mid-March to mid-April, and your commitment date—when you have to declare which college you'll attend and send a deposit payment—is usually the common reply date of May 1. That means you have roughly a month to make a commitment, and to make the right choice, you must take a few more steps.

First, you have to understand each college's financial aid offer, and compare them to each other.

You have to weigh the financial facts against each college's particular strengths and weaknesses.

You should look at the family budget one more time. If your financial circumstances have changed recently, you might return to the financial aid administrator to request a "professional judgment" adjustment to your financial aid package.

And if, despite the best financial aid offers, your favorite college still seems financially out of reach, you must explore alternatives.

In the end, your decision is as much about the unknown future—what your experience will be at one college versus another—as it is about the hard dollar figures. It is an emotional, personal decision.

A note before we walk through the decision-making process: You can and should continue your quest for scholarship money through this period and even beyond. If you earn more awards, you must notify the financial aid office of the college you finally decide to attend. The most likely outcome will involve replacing some of your loans and/or work-study employment with the scholarship award . . . a good outcome.

Let's deal first with the factual component of an emotional decision, and compare the actual costs of different colleges that want you on their campus next year.

SAMPLE AWARD LETTER

This is a sample letter from the financial aid office of a typical state university (see over). It contains the components described in chapters 1–9. For this student, total aid is the same as total need. Loans make up $4,700 of the aid package, and the EFC is $1,800, so the out-of-pocket cost (the amount you would be paying if you accepted no loans) is $6,500. The self-help level (sum of packaged work and loans and unmet need) is $6,100.

This and another award letter will be compared in the next section of this chapter.

COMPARING AID PACKAGES

Your financial aid award is the complete package of the grants, scholarships, loans and work-study employment that a college financial aid office has at its disposal. Its components are decided on an individual basis by the office, and it is presented to you in a detailed award letter. We've placed the figures from two sample award letters side-by-side on pages 220–221.

When evaluating award letters, first one needs to put them on an apples-to-apples basis. Compare loans to loans, grants to grants. Award letters from two schools might well be formatted differently. To understand the relevant differences between two award letters (or among several) you should compare the components that make up the packages directly, as well as the net costs. If one school is packaging the Federal PLUS loan, which is intended to cover the EFC, but others aren't packaging Federal PLUS, you need to separate it out.

Your EFC should be the same at each school, because it comes from the FAFSA (and the resulting Student Aid Report).[68] If you're eligible for a Federal Pell Grant, it should show up in all the packages.[69] Resources you've earned, like scholarship money, should be uniform in all packages to make comparison possible. If not, call the financial aid office and make sure they're included.

Check whether the colleges include the same expenses in the COA figures. Besides obvious direct costs like tuition, fees and room and board, do they include reasonable estimates of transportation, health fees and personal expenses? If not, estimate these and add them to the cost of attendance. You might have to use different figures; for example, if one school is close and another across the

State University
Office of Student Financial Aid

Financial Aid Award Notification

Mary Q. Student   <DATE>
100 Main Street   Award Year: 2006–07
Anytown, ZZ 00000   SSN: 000-00-0000

Dear Ms. Student:

The Office of Financial Aid of State University is pleased to make the following
award for your attendance at State University in the 2006–2007 academic year.

Fall Enrollment: Full-Time   Housing Status: On-Campus
Spring Enrollment: Full-Time   Dependency Status: Dependent

Sample Public College

EXPENSES (COA)

Tuition and Fees	$6,000
Room and Board	$7,250
Books and Supplies	$600
Student Health Insurance	$1,000
Miscellaneous/Personal	$1,800
Transportation	$550
TOTAL EXPENSES	**$17,200**

> Most of these figures are school charges; expenses like transportation might vary.

EXPECTED FAMILY CONTRIBUTION (EFC)

Parent Contribution	$1,256
Student Contribution	$544
TOTAL EFC	**$1,800**

> This should be close to the figure on your Student Aid Report. If not, the Financial Aid Office has applied its "institutional methodology." You might want to clarify with the Financial Aid Office.

RESOURCES

ABC Employee Scholarship	$500
PTA Scholarship	$250
TOTAL RESOURCES	**$750**

> Here, "resources" means additional money you have available beyond the EFC. In this case, two local scholarships have added $750 to the total dollar amount you pay.

Decision Time

FINANCIAL NEED			
COA	$17,200		
—EFC	–$1,800		
—Resources	–$750		
TOTAL FINANCIAL NEED	**$14,650**		

"Need" has a specific meaning here: It's what remains after your minimum expected EFC and resources are deducted from the total one-year cost of attendance.

AWARD INFORMATION			
GRANTS	Fall	Spring	Total
Federal Pell Grant	$1,125	$1,125	$2,250
Federal SEOG	$375	$375	$750
College Grant	$2,000	$2,000	$4,000
State Grant	$775	$775	$1,550
WORK			
Federal Work-Study	$700	$700	$1,400

The "college grant" might be described as a scholarship, for example, "The Governor Smith University Scholarship." It does not need to be repaid.

LOANS (NEED-BASED)			
Federal Perkins Loan	$850	$850	$1,700
Federal Stafford (Sub)	$1,500	$1,500	$3,000
TOTAL AWARDS	**$7,325**	**$7,325**	**$14,650**

Remember that "awards" include college-based loans, which you have to pay back, as well as grants from government and college. In this case, awards cover 100% of the need.

Awards Available for EFC:			
LOANS			
Federal Stafford (Unsubsidized)	$250	$250	$500
Federal PLUS Loan	$650	$650	$1,300
TOTAL AWARDS			
AVAILABLE FOR EFC	**$900**	**$900**	**$1,800**

These awards, like other components in the package, are optional. In this case, the college has made federal loans available to cover the EFC which was calculated above. The unsubsidized Stafford loan will be offered to the student, and the PLUS loan is offered to the parents.

country, your annual transportation costs will be different. You might need new clothing if you're moving to a different climate. If your actual costs are substantially different than the costs listed in the school's student budget, you can ask the school to adjust the cost of attendance. Common adjustments include a one-time expense to buy a personal computer and an adjustment for child care expenses. As much as possible, you are trying to compare your total cost of going to each college.

You are entitled to accept or reject each individual piece of aid. So you can turn down the loans or work-study, if you wish. Applying for financial aid does not obligate you in any way to take on additional debt, or commit you to work-study. Refusing to accept part of your aid package, however, will not increase the rest of the aid package to compensate.

Unsubsidized Federal Stafford loans and Federal PLUS loans are often not considered part of the financial aid package from a college, since these financing options are intended to help families reach their Expected Family Contribution (EFC). However, we'll include payments for them in the examples below because they are ultimately loans you have to pay off.

We recommend looking at financial aid packages together with the cost of education because a more expensive school will necessarily offer a larger aid package. What really matters is net cost and out-of-pocket cost, since they tend to reflect the true cost to the family. **Net cost** is the difference between the cost of education you determined and the financial aid offered by the college. It reflects the amount of additional money you will need now to be able to attend the college. **Out-of-pocket cost** is the difference between the cost of attendance and all forms of gift aid, with loans excluded. Although education loans are a form of financial aid, they do need to be repaid. The out-of-pocket cost corresponds to the amount you would be paying if you accepted no loans.

We don't recommend basing your decision by the grant/loan ratio or the total grants because they really aren't meaningful. A college with a high percentage of grants could nevertheless be more expensive for the family because of a higher Cost of Attendance.

The net cost will be the same at most schools (a significant difference in net cost might indicate that you provided some information to one school but not the others, and if this is the case, you should provide missing information to schools.)[70] The out-of-pocket costs, however, can vary significantly from school to school, depending on such factors as endowment size, differences in state aid that depend on the location of the college, size of the student aid budget, outside scholarship policy and availability of merit aid. Your family then will need to decide which is more important: the financial factors or the non-financial factors.

Compare the total packages. Don't assume the school that has the lowest Cost of Attendance (COA) or which gives the most grants will be the most affordable.

Compare loan types. Remember that the federal government pays interest on subsidized loans while you are in college (see chapter 7). Unsubsidized loans require you to pay interest from the moment you receive the loan. Different

COMMON TERMS

For reference, here's a review of common terms and calculations from earlier chapters. Not every term will be used in every financial aid package; we're supplying them here because terms adopt different relevance depending on how you look at the financial aid package.

Terms:
COA (Cost of Attendance)—the full cost of attending the college for a year.
EFC (Expected Family Contribution)—your family's (or, for independent students, your own) contribution to the total COA, as determined by the federal needs methodology (the result of your filling out the FAFSA).
RESOURCES—Money that is restricted for educational expenses such as a scholarship or veterans education benefits.
PACKAGED LOANS—Our term for the total loans offered through the college.

Calculations:
FINANCIAL NEED = COA – EFC – RESOURCES
FINANCIAL AID = WORK + LOANS + GRANTS
NET COST = COA – FINANCIAL AID – RESOURCES
             = UNMET NEED + EFC
OUT-OF-POCKET COST = UNMET NEED + EFC + LOANS
                        = COA – GRANTS – WORK – RESOURCES
SELF-HELP LEVEL = WORK + LOANS + UNMET NEED
UNMET NEED = FINANCIAL NEED – FINANCIAL AID

loans can have different interest rates and fees. Calculate the total cost of each loan, including interest and fees, so that you can compare them side-by-side.

Compare the requirements. Are all the awards in your first year renewable for subsequent years? Will terms change? Grants might be replaced by loans, making your education more expensive as you go. A grant or scholarship offer that requires the 3.0 cumulative average to continue, and isn't guaranteed, might not be as good for you as an offer that's two or three thousand dollars less, but only requires satisfactory academic progress.

Cost of Attendance (COA)

EFC	+	Unmet Need	+	Resources
		+		
Loans	+	Work	+	Grants

Financial Need

EFC	Unmet Need	Resources
	+	
Loans	+ Work +	Grants

Self Help Level

EFC	Unmet Need	Resources
	+	
Loans	+ Work	Grants

Financial Aid

EFC	Unmet Need	Resources
Loans	+ Work +	Grants

Net Cost

EFC	+	Unmet Need	Resources
Loans		Work	Grants

Out of Pocket Cost

EFC	+	Unmet Need	Resources
	+		
Loans		Work	Grants

Decision Time

The differences in aid packages can be significant in terms of lifestyle as well as long-range financial planning. For example, one school might offer a larger "college grant" or "academic scholarship"—a grant you don't have to pay back, whereas another might have larger loans, which you must pay back. Or, one school might put together a package with more work-study money, which means the student will spend more hours working in a part-time job.

Identify whether there is any "gapping"—i.e., whether any portion of demonstrated financial need is not being met. If so, find out why. Some colleges make a practice of meeting full demonstrated need with the financial aid package, while others have insufficient funding to cover the financial need of all students, leaving a gap for the family to fill.[71] If there's a gap, check with the school to see whether there was an error. If the gap was caused by school policies (e.g., all students from families earning more than $50,000 a year are left with a $1,000 gap), ask what you can do to eliminate the gap. You might be able to fill the gap with outside scholarships. If the gap remains, you and your family will have to decide whether it is worth stretching your finances even more to allow you to attend this school as opposed to a different college that provided a more generous—and gap-free—financial aid package.

Two model financial aid packages appear on pp. 220–221, one from a sample public school and one from a sample private school. We've set them side-by-side for comparison. The analysis at the end shows that, in this example, the more expensive private school has a lower net cost but a higher out-of-pocket cost.

Comparing expenses and resources:

- Total expenses at the private college are higher.
- Total EFC is identical.
- Total Resources money is identical.

. . . So the family's financial need is greater at the private college.

Comparing grants:

- Federal Pell Grants are identical.
- Federal SEOG is different (private college offers $1,750 more).
- College grant money is very different (private college offers $8,750 more).
- State grant money is slightly different (private college offers $150 more).

Sample Public College

EXPENSES (COA)

Tuition and Fees	$6,000
Room and Board	$7,250
Books and Supplies	$600
Student Health Insurance	$1,000
Miscellaneous/Personal	$1,800
Transportation	$550
TOTAL EXPENSES	**$17,200**

EXPECTED FAMILY CONTRIBUTION (EFC)

Parent Contribution	$1,256
Student Contribution	$544
TOTAL EFC	**$1,800**

RESOURCES

ABC Employee Scholarship	$500
PTA Scholarship	$250
TOTAL RESOURCES	**$750**

FINANCIAL NEED

COA	$17,200
–EFC	–$1,800
–RESOURCES	–$750
TOTAL FINANCIAL NEED	**$14,650**

AWARD INFORMATION

	Fall	Spring	Total
GRANTS			
Federal Pell Grant	$1,125	$1,125	$2,250
Federal SEOG	$375	$375	$750
College Grant	$2,000	$2,000	$4,000
State Grant	$775	$775	$1,550
WORK			
Federal Work-Study	$700	$700	$1,400
LOANS (NEED-BASED)			
Perkins Loan	$350	$350	$700
Federal Stafford (Sub)	$1,500	$1,500	$3,000
TOTAL AWARDS	**$6,825**	**$6,825**	**$13,650**
UNMET NEED	$500	$500	**$1,000**

Awards Available for EFC:

	Fall	Spring	Total
LOANS			
Federal Stafford (Unsubsidized)	$250	$250	$500
Federal PLUS Loan	$650	$650	$1,300
TOTAL AWARDS FOR EFC	**$900**	**$900**	**$1,800**

Analysis: Total aid is $1,000 less than total need, so there is unmet need of $1,000.

- $3,700 of the aid package is in the form of loans, and the EFC is $1,800, and the unmet need is $1,000, so the out-of-pocket cost is $6,500.
- Self-help level (sum of packaged work and loans and unmet need) is $6,100.

Sample Private College

EXPENSES (COA)

Tuition and Fees	$22,500
Room and Board	$8,100
Books and Supplies	$900
Student Health Insurance	$1,000
Miscellaneous/Personal	$1,800
Transportation	$850
TOTAL EXPENSES	**$35,150**

EXPECTED FAMILY CONTRIBUTION (EFC)

Parent Contribution	$1,256
Student Contribution	$544
TOTAL EFC	**$1,800**

RESOURCES

ABC Employee Scholarship	$500
PTA Scholarship	$250
TOTAL RESOURCES	**$750**

FINANCIAL NEED

COA	$35,150
–EFC	–$1,800
–RESOURCES	–$750
TOTAL FINANCIAL NEED	**$32,600**

AWARD INFORMATION

	Fall	Spring	Total
GRANTS			
Federal Pell Grant	$1,125	$1,125	$2,250
Federal SEOG	$1,200	$1,200	$2,400
College Grant	$6,375	$6,375	$12,750
State Grant	$850	$850	$1,700
WORK			
Federal Work-Study	$1,000	$1,000	$2,000
LOANS (NEED-BASED)			
Perkins Loan	$1,000	$1,000	$2,000
Federal Stafford (Sub)	$1,750	$1,750	$3,500
College Loan	$3,000	$3,000	$6,000
TOTAL AWARDS	**$16,300**	**$16,300**	**$32,600**
UNMET NEED	**$0**	**$0**	**$0**
Awards Available for EFC:			
LOANS			
Federal Stafford (Unsub)	$0	$0	$0
Federal PLUS Loan	$900	$900	$1,800
TOTAL AWARDS FOR EFC	**$900**	**$900**	**$1,800**

Analysis: Total aid is the same as total need, so there is no unmet need.
- $11,500 of the aid package is in the form of loans, and the EFC is $1,800, and the unmet need is $0, so the out-of-pocket cost is $13,300.
- Self-help level (sum of packaged work and loans and unmet need) is $13,500.

Comparing self-help level:

- Federal work-study is different (private college offers $600 more).
- Federal Perkins loan is different (private college offers $1,300 more).
- Subsidized Federal Stafford loan is different (private college offers $500 more).
- Unsubsidized loans are not identical, but net amount is the same.
- Total financial aid is $1,000 less than total need at the public college, so the public college has unmet need. The private college has no unmet need.

In this example, the gift aid in the private school package does not entirely compensate for its higher COA. But it has no unmet need, while the public school does, so it has a lower net cost. Assuming living expenses are identical, the private school has a higher out-of-pocket cost, however, due to more loans in the financial aid package.

Which one costs less depends upon which way you compare the packages, and we recommend comparing them in two ways:

COMPARISON 1—NET COST

You find the net cost of a year at college by subtracting the total aid package and resources from the cost of attendance. This identifies how much money the family is going to have to come up with on their own—from savings, current income, unsubsidized Federal Stafford loan, Federal PLUS loan, private education loans, home equity loans/lines of credit, scholarships, education tax benefits, etc.

Subtract the aid package (not including Federal PLUS loans and unsubsidized Federal Stafford loans) and resources from COA to arrive at a net cost. This is a raw analysis that indicates whether you can afford to pay for the school.

In the examples above,

Public: COA of $17,200 – Aid package $13,650 – Resources $750 = Net cost of $2,800

Private: COA of $35,150 – Aid package of $32,600 – Resources $750 = Net cost of $1,800

. . . with this method, the private school net cost is $1,000 less.

COMPARISON 2—OUT-OF-POCKET COST

We also recommend looking at the cost when one subtracts just gift aid (grants, scholarships, federal work-study) from the COA. This is a useful way of looking at the differences between college aid packages, because it combines loans, EFC and any unmet need. Assuming you can afford all financial aid packages, this calculation tells you which ones are more expensive. (Subsidized loans are nice, but you still have to pay them back, and bear in mind that the more you pay in loans, the greater your cost, because of interest charges.)

In the examples above,

Public: COA of $17,200 – Total Gift Aid $10,700 = $6,500
Private: COA of $35,150 – Total Gift Aid $21,850 = $13,300

. . . with this method, the private school out-of-pocket cost is $6,800 more, even though it offers a little more than twice the gift aid of the public college.

BOOK TO WEB

Our award letter comparison tool makes it easier to compare financial aid packages and college costs online, on an apples-to-apples basis. It automatically calculates the net cost and out-of-pocket cost, highlights any unmet need and helps you identify significant differences in costs (both overall and for specific line items) between two or more colleges. You'll find it at www.collegegold.com.

CODE: 1060

Additional differences in the examples above might require verification. Note how some of the elements of the student budget, such as books and supplies and transportation, are estimated by the public college to be $600 less than at the private college. If the public college is low-balling the figures by $600, this would mean that even though the net cost of the public college is $1,000 more than at the private college, the true net cost might be as much as $1,600 more. This is not to say that the public college offer is deceptive, but to trigger an inquiry—why are their estimated expenses $600 less? (Conversely, why do books and supplies, and transportation at the private college cost $600 more?) Call the college and get details; the differences might be relevant to you.

Some differences might be beyond the college's control. For example, if you're choosing between an out-of-state college and an in-state college that would allow you to live at home, your transportation costs will be different. You will have to decide whether the benefits of an out-of-state college outweigh the added costs.

COMPARE COLLEGES

When you've established the most relevant differences between financial aid packages from different schools, it's time to consider whether one college is more important to you than another.

If the best college is also the one at which you'll spend the least money, you're done. The choice is rarely that clear-cut, however, and it gets really difficult when the college of your dreams costs much more than your least expensive alternative. Can you actually put a dollar value on the education you'll get? What about the experience, the lifelong relationships, the connections with alumni? If you want to go on to graduate school, will one college put you in a better position than another?

Whether you think one college will give you a better start in a career, the value of colleges ultimately depends on what you make of it. Excelling at your second-choice school—financially, socially or academically—might be better for your career or mission or personal happiness than struggling at an institution that seems more prestigious.[72]

Cathy Simoneaux, Director of the Office of Scholarships and Financial Aid of Loyola University, New Orleans, makes this point: "Parents will say, 'My kid can go to the state university for free. If he goes to Loyola [a private school], we're going to get in debt.' And that's true. The education that a student gets at a large state school, however, is vastly different from one at a private school." You have to compare the intangibles as well as you can.

Financial aid administrators we interviewed offered these questions to help you compare colleges:

Does location make a difference? Some students don't mind whether their college is in the middle of a city or the middle of cornfields. To others, location is a critical factor for all sorts of reasons. Students who were raised in sunny locales might not be happy in the snow belt, with cloudy days most of the year.

One issue that families should definitely discuss: How far away from home the college is located, which can be both a financial and emotional decision.

What's the best class size for me? Some students do just fine in classes with 200 students. Others respond to the greater attention and accountability of a smaller class size.

What size college do you prefer? Do you want to attend a small college (under 3,000 students), a medium-sized school (3,000 to 10,000 students) or a huge public institution (more than 10,000 students)?

What relationship is important with my professors? This question is related to class size—how important is it that the professors know you well? In larger classes, the tutorial sections might be taught by graduate students and junior faculty, while the main lecture is presented by a more established professor. Will you have the opportunity to work one-on-one with the faculty?

What type of college—two-year or four-year, public or private—is best for me? Are you seeking a bachelor's degree or an associate's degree? Are you unsure whether college is right for you, or are you planning on getting a PhD? Do you want to start off at a lower-cost two-year institution, and later transfer to a four-year college?

Do I have a single focus? Smaller or more specialized colleges might not offer the same range of experiences, people and opportunities as larger schools. But they may offer more personalized attention.

Is this my last school or the next step? Students who believe they will attend graduate school must consider the longer-range costs[73] and whether a less expensive undergraduate program will equip them just as well for graduate studies.

How about facilities? Buildings, playing fields, studios and performance spaces can make a real difference to an athlete or an artist. The intramural and extramural sports offered by the college may matter to the serious athlete.

Does the religious affiliation of the college matter? Are you interested in a religiously affiliated college? Are there churches, synagogues and mosques or religious campus groups if you require them?

What will happen through four years? Is the financial aid package renewable? What rules do you have to follow to renew? If the student intends to take his/her junior year abroad, for example, what programs are available at each college? What if a parent loses his or her job? These are questions you may ask the financial aid office, and you should.

Will it be just four years? Joseph Russo, Director of Student Financial Strategies at Notre Dame, poses this hidden possibility: "A really astute consumer will ask the college how long a typical kid takes to graduate. The national statistic is 30% of the students who start in four-year schools finish on time in four years." Six years at a "less expensive" college might cost more than four years at another.[74]

If you discuss the pros and cons of each college separately from the financial issues, you'll develop a sense of whether the school that will cost the least is the right school . . . or whether the college that will require you to borrow more money is worth the debt.

Vince Pecora, Director of Financial Aid at Towson University, compares the choice between colleges to any purchase. "You have to distance yourself a little and decide how each school will meet your needs," says Vince. "For example, someone who wants to be a teacher might gravitate toward an out-of-state college which costs two or three times more than a school in his or her state. That difference will take a long time to pay off on a teacher's salary. You need to think about return on investment while embracing knowledge for its own sake."

The process of comparing schools poses the question: How much do you really know what life at each school will be like?

"I encourage students to go back and visit their top choice institution — maybe do an overnight to make sure that it's the right fit," says Ellen Frishberg, Director of Student Financial Services, Johns Hopkins University. It's a great suggestion. You know a lot more about schools because you've gone through the admissions, financial aid and scholarship processes. You might even know more about yourself. Now is a good time to return to schools you're considering to get a personal feel for them.

Ultimately, your focus should be on the student. Bob Shorb, Director of Student Aid and Family Finance at Skidmore College, observes, "Some families only gravitate toward the college with the highest merit award for their child, but I find that half the time it's the wrong school and the student ends up transferring out. It's a matching process, and students have to find a place that's going to take them to the next level academically. Typically, that could be more than just one institution."

ALL THOSE OTHER EXPENSES

After determining the differences among offers, a family's next step is to consider the full financial impact of each choice in the context of its full financial life. You did background work on this in chapter 4 when you thought about the family budget, spending habits and debt. This step is a reality check, and should be taken for several reasons:

- To decide if the best offer is, in fact, affordable.
- To determine whether a "lesser" offer coming from a favorite college might be affordable.
- To decide whether other financial factors—savings, spending, taxes[75]—make a difference.
- To demonstrate your best efforts before requesting more aid from a favorite college (which we'll explain in the next section).

First, take a hard look at the actual costs you calculated in the beginning of this chapter. Simply put, can you afford the total monthly payments of the proposed loans—both those administered by the college and direct loans? Can you afford them for the life of the loan? How will it affect your ability to pay for other expenses you anticipate for the near future, such as the cost of college for a younger sibling, saving for retirement or a predictable expense in a small family business?

Really important reminder: Assuming the financial aid package is described for one year, remember that you will probably have to borrow more in subsequent years. A payment of $200 per month might seem affordable now, but a

---

👍 **RULE OF THUMB**

"We encourage families to sit down and honestly look at their finances. And it's very hard for parents to have that discussion with their children, and it's very hard for eighteen-year-olds to really understand the financial challenges parents face sometimes."

—*Cathy Simoneaux, Director of the Office of Scholarships and Financial Aid at Loyola University New Orleans*

total payment of $800 + per month after four years of college might be out of sight. Base your calculations on four years of college (including the inflation calculation we mentioned in chapter 3).

If the student intends to pay back loans after school, how much will that cost each month? What is the total debt load, and what percentage of your expected income after graduation will that require to pay off? If you intend to enter a certain job field after school, what's the average entry-level salary of that position?

BOOK TO WEB

There are several salary search engines on the Internet. Go to content.salary.monster.com to begin basic research.

When David Levy, Assistant Dean and Director of Financial Aid at Caltech, presents options to parents in group meetings, he always talks about some ways to save money: "We talk about ways to save money on buying college textbooks, on room and board costs . . . you know, you don't necessarily have to buy the most expensive meal plan that the college offers."

The college that offers the best package might actually cost more in total yearly expenses, so once again it's time to study where the expenses mount up.

Look again at transportation and lifestyle expenses. If the college is a long way away, how much airfare will you pay, and is the bus, train or standby travel an alternative? Do you need to return home twice a year, or can you stay and work on-campus during the summer? Does the student really need a car at college? If you plan to have a car on campus, find out the costs of car insurance, gas and maintenance and college parking permits.[76] In addition to saving money on meal plans, are there expenses like clothing, entertainment, laundry and other incidentals that you can cut a little? If you will be attending an out-of-state public college, can you find a way to qualify for lower in-state tuition? Can you accumulate credits before college by taking AP tests, CLEP, or advanced standing exams which give you college credit?

Although living at home can help save on room and board, it increases transportation costs. Financial aid will not cover the cost of purchasing and maintaining a vehicle, parking and insurance. It generally does provide a small allowance based on distance to the school. Commuter students often find themselves disconnected from campus life and lose some of their time to the daily commute. Part of the benefit of a college education is the opportunity to learn from your fellow students.

Some other places to look for savings:

- Compare dorm/meal plan living with living off-campus and buying your own food (some colleges require freshmen to live on campus).
- Replace a cell phone with pre-paid phone cards or e-mail, or find the cheapest cell plan available.
- Replace monthly fee services, such as DVD rentals through the mail, with à la carte buying (but don't stack up late fees!). Do you really need DVD rentals?
- Replace memberships or season tickets (to sports events, ski clubs and the like) with à la carte buying.
- Cancel paid subscriptions to magazines and online services; replace them with free services or use the school library.
- For entertainment, attend campus-sponsored events, performances, lectures, movies. Many are offered free or at a reduced cost.
- If you'll need a computer, find out whether the college has a discount computer purchase program. The college may also publish minimal specifications for computers that are connected to the campus network.
- If you think you'll live off-campus, be realistic about the cost of utilities in addition to rent, including Internet access and air-conditioning.
- If you will be attending college far away from home, visit home only once a year. Try getting a summer job near school and staying in the dorms for the summer. Often summer jobs pay better wages near a college campus.

Saving money is a choice that financial aid administrator Melissa Ibanez puts clearly: "Live like a student today, or live like a student after college, as you pay off your loans. One key to good budgeting is to see today's expenses as tomorrow's debt. If taking the bus instead of owning a car means you'll pay $100 a month less after college, the bus starts to look better."

If you'll be traveling late at night, however, or will be traveling to an internship as part of your education program, owning a car might be necessary. If so, do you need a new car, or will a roadworthy hand-me-down suffice?

The tradeoffs are not always easy, and here's a common one: Parents might be reluctant to cut back on retirement savings to free up money for a college loan payment. They'd be postponing their retirement and giving up a substantial tax break. We've heard experts come down on all sides of this example — some saying that retirement savings are critical long-term investments, others pointing out that younger parents might be twenty-five years away from retirement, with plenty of time to save.

In general, we don't advocate cutting back on retirement, savings, insurance or other actions that tend to improve or protect a family's financial future. However, even those items are a matter of the individual situation, and once again, you've got to make the best possible decision based on the largest possible amount of options you can perceive.

EDUCATION TAX BENEFITS

Education expenses can have tax benefits, and while these benefits will not change the amount of financial aid a college offers, they can reduce your total cost of education, and thus should be part of your planning.

There are numerous eligibility requirements for these benefits in the tax code, and they can change year by year. A full-length version of this information, including eligibility requirements, is online at www.collegegold.com.[77]

You may not use multiple tax benefits for a single expense (that's double-dipping), so pay careful attention to restrictions. For example, you cannot use the Hope Scholarship and the Tuition and Fees Deduction for the same student in the same year.

Hope Scholarship. The Hope Scholarship provides a $1,500 tax credit per student per year for higher education expenses during the first two calendar (tax) years of postsecondary education. The amount of the credit is 100% of the first $1,000 of qualified tuition and related expenses per student and 50% of the second $1,000 of qualified tuition and related expenses. Scholarships and financial aid do not count as qualified tuition. Only out-of-pocket expenses count.

There is an income phase-out for incomes from $43,000 to $53,000 (single filers) and $87,000 to $107,000 (married filing jointly). These phase-outs are indexed for inflation. You cannot use the credit if you are married filing separate returns.

Lifetime Learning Tax Credit. The Lifetime Learning Tax Credit provides a tax credit of up to $2,000 per taxpayer for education expenses. The amount of the credit is equal to 20% of the first $10,000 of qualified tuition and related expenses paid by the taxpayer.

Unlike the Hope Scholarship, the Lifetime Learning Tax Credit does not vary according to the number of students. This means that if you have multiple children in school at the same time and your tuition bills total more than $10,000, you only get the credit for the first $10,000 paid. The credit is relative to the total amount of tuition paid, irrespective of the number of children in school.

Qualified tuition and related expenses include expenses for any course of instruction at an eligible educational institution to acquire or improve job skills. This means that the credit may be used by students enrolled at least half-time in a degree program.

Unlike the Hope Scholarship, the Lifetime Learning Tax Credit may be claimed for an unlimited number of years.

The Lifetime Learning Tax Credit has the same income phase-outs as the Hope Scholarship. You cannot use the Hope Scholarship with the Lifetime Learning Tax Credit for the same student in the same year, but you can use them for different students' educational expenses in the same year.

Deduction for student loan interest. You can deduct up to $2,500 in student loan interest, even if you don't itemize deductions. The deduction is phased out for taxpayers with adjusted gross incomes of $50,000 to $65,000 (single filers) and $105,000 to $135,000 (married filing jointly). Taxpayers who are married but file separate returns are not eligible.

The interest must be paid on a qualified education loan for you, your spouse or a dependent. Eligible education expenses include tuition, fees, room and board, books, supplies and equipment, transportation expenses and other necessary expenses (as included in the school's student budget). A qualified education loan is defined as a debt borrowed *solely* to pay higher education expenses.

Parents who do not qualify because of the income phase-outs should consider having their child borrow the funds. Not only does the Federal Stafford loan have a lower interest rate than the Federal PLUS loan, but the student is less likely to exceed the income phase-outs.

According to regulations published by the IRS on May 7, 2004, education loan origination fees and capitalized interest qualify as deductible education loan interest. Students and parents can claim the deductions for past years by filing amended income tax returns.

The regulations also clarify that only the person legally obligated to repay the education loan may take the interest deduction. If someone else makes payments on a student's education loans, the student gets to take the deduction, not the other individual. For example, if a grandparent helps the student out with a few loan payments, the student takes the deduction, not the grandparent.

Interest on private education loans qualifies, with some restrictions. See www.collegegold.com for details.

Employer education assistance. Your employer may provide you with up to $5,250 in employer education assistance benefits for undergraduate or graduate courses tax-free each year. The benefits must have been paid for tuition, fees, books, supplies and equipment. Travel, lodging and meals are not included. Courses involving sports, games or hobbies are not included, unless they are required as part of a degree program or are related to the business of your employer.

Payments above $5,250 may also be tax-free if they represent a working condition fringe benefit. This means that if you had paid for the expenses, you would have been able to deduct them as an employee business expense. Talk to your employer if you think this is the case.

TUITION AND FEES DEDUCTION

Taxpayers can deduct up to $4,000 in tuition expenses as an exclusion from income, even if they don't itemize deductions. The deduction is phased out for taxpayers with adjusted gross incomes of $65,000 to $80,000 (single filers) and $130,000 to $160,000 (married filing jointly). You can use it in conjunction with tax-free distributions from Coverdell Education Savings Accounts, qualified tuition programs and education savings bonds, provided that different education expenses form the basis for each benefit.

Although the original deduction ended for the tax year 2005, as of this writing it appears likely to be extended by Congress.

You cannot take the deduction and use the Hope Scholarship or Lifetime Learning Tax Credit for the same student in the same year. However, since this deduction is taken as exclusion from income, it reduces adjusted gross income, and can make the family eligible for additional need-based aid during the next year. That can potentially make this deduction more attractive than the Hope Scholarship or Lifetime Learning Tax Credit, if the additional aid is in the form of grants instead of loans.

In addition to tax benefits for expenses, there are significant benefits for college savings plans, which are described briefly in the appendix, "Saving for College."

PROFESSIONAL JUDGMENT

Because the FAFSA and federal aid formulas do not account for all circumstances affecting a family's ability to pay for college, Congress has authorized college financial aid administrators to compensate for special circumstances on a case-by-case basis. This authority is broadly referred to as professional judgment.

Professional judgment is applied on a case-by-case basis after individual review of the student's situation. It is optional and not mandatory. Nationwide, approximately 5% of Federal Pell Grant recipients and about 1% of undergraduate students receive professional judgment adjustments.

It is a subjective process. There is no requirement that financial aid administrators reach the same decision in similar cases, so long as there is no discrimination. Professional judgment cannot alter eligibility restrictions set by law, for example, by changing a student's marital status to what it was after the time the FAFSA was filed.

In general, the financial aid administrator can use professional judgment to adjust input data elements on the FAFSA and/or to override a student's dependency status. The decision of the financial aid administrator is final. There is no appeal. By law, neither the school's president nor the U.S. Department of Education can override the financial aid administrator's decision.

"Professional judgment is both an art and a science," explains Joseph Russo of Notre Dame. "The science side of it is formulas, consistency, regulations and rules to be organized and fair. The art side is also important: Compassion, common sense, asking, does this really make sense for this family?"

There are three types of changes a financial aid administrator may make to a student's application:

Corrections. Information on the original application was not accurate as of the application date. Corrections are permitted at any time.

Updates. Information on the original application was accurate as of the application date, but has since changed and the application no longer accurately reflects the student's situation. A handful of data elements may be updated in accordance with regulations, such as changes in dependency status or household size. Updates to dependency status may be made at any time, so long as they are not due to a change in the applicant's marital status. Updates to household size can only occur if the FAFSA is selected for verification.

Adjustments and overrides. Information on the application is accurate, but special circumstances justify a change. Adjustments may only occur through an exercise of professional judgment.

Special circumstances are not required to be circumstances beyond the family's control. Even a voluntary income reduction, such as a wage-earner quitting his or her job to take care of the family full-time or a wage-earner voluntarily forgoing a bonus, can be considered. Private elementary and secondary school tuition for the student's siblings also represent a special circumstance, even if the decision to send the children to private school is entirely voluntary.

Special circumstances can also include an anticipated drop in the student's income (i.e., the student quits his job to attend school full-time), not just a change in the parent's income.

☑ I Wish I Had Known . . .

That my family income was going to change drastically, because I then would have qualified for grants.

—Alexandra Murphy, freshman
Salem State College

Financial aid administrators are not limited to the following circumstances, nor are they required to use professional judgment in these circumstances. They review each family's situation on a case-by-case basis.

Items that might lead to an adjustment include:

- Medical or dental expenses not covered by insurance.
- Recent unemployment of a family member.
- Death, disability, incapacitation or serious illness of a wage-earner.
- Temporary layoff or furlough of a wage-earner.
- Drop in income due to fewer hours (i.e., no overtime) or reduced salary or elimination of bonuses.
- Wages included moving expenses.
- Bankruptcy or foreclosure.

Decision Time

- Custodial parent remarries after application date.
- Recent divorce of the student's parents (i.e., to separate the income of the custodial parent from the non-custodial parent).
- Termination of a child-support agreement (i.e., the custodial parent will no longer receive child-support payments during the award year).
- Alimony payments that are not deductible on the family's income tax return.
- A parent being called to active duty in the armed forces.
- Children with special needs.
- Unusually high child care costs.
- Tuition expenses at an elementary or secondary school.
- Elder care expenses (e.g., nursing home fees).
- Change in income due to recent retirement.
- Additional costs incurred as a result of a student's disability.
- Other changes in a family's income, a family's assets or a student's status.
- The number of parents enrolled at least half-time in a degree, certificate or other recognized educational program.
- Proceeds of a sale of farm or business assets if the sale resulted from a voluntary or involuntary foreclosure, forfeiture, bankruptcy or an involuntary liquidation.
- Unusual capital gains.
- Roth IRA rollovers.
- Casualty losses due to weather (hurricane, tornado, flooding and other natural disasters), fire, theft, acts of God or terrorism.

There are plenty of circumstances that do not qualify for professional judgment, even though they certainly affect a family's ability to pay tuition. Having high levels of credit card or other consumer debt is a consequence of a voluntary consumer choice to live beyond their means, and not a special circumstance. Other discretionary expenses, like vacations, tithing or car payments will not qualify for professional judgment. High mortgage payments and standard living expenses like utilities or property taxes do not qualify as special circumstances.

> ## SENIOR YEAR SHOCK
>
> "Changes in circumstances can come at any time in a college career. I knew a student at Macalester who wasn't particularly noteworthy; just an average family situation and an average financial aid need. About a month before he started his senior year, one of his parents passed away very unexpectedly, and the family was thrown into complete financial disarray. We reevaluated the family's financial situation from top to bottom and we were able to take action that made it possible for him to stay, study and graduate on time."
>
> —Brian Lindeman, Macalester College

DEPENDENCY OVERRIDE

Students may get more financial aid if they are declared independent of their parents (the unquestioned reasons for this were discussed in chapter 5). Financial aid administrators have the authority to change a student's status from dependent to independent in cases involving unusual circumstances. Items that might lead to a dependency override include:

- an abusive family environment (e.g., sexual, physical, or mental abuse or other forms of domestic violence).
- abandonment by parents (e.g., no contact or financial support for more than a year).[78]
- incarceration or institutionalization or extended hospitalization of both parents.
- parents lacking the physical or mental capacity to raise the child.
- parents' whereabouts unknown or parents cannot be located.
- an unsuitable household (e.g., child removed from the household and placed in foster care).
- married student's spouse dies or student gets divorced.

Decision Time

Nationwide, approximately 2% of undergraduate students annually become independent through such dependency overrides.

The U.S. Department of Education has published guidance (page AVG-24 of the 2006–2007 Application and Verification Guide) indicating that the following circumstances do *not* merit a dependency override, either alone or in combination:

- Parents refuse to contribute to the student's education.
- Parents are unwilling to provide information on the application or for verification.
- Parents do not claim the student as a dependent for income tax purposes.
- Student demonstrates total self-sufficiency.

In short, a student cannot become independent just because the parents are unwilling to help pay for the student's college education (as opposed to an inability to pay).

SIMPLE ERROR

"Sometimes in the process of reviewing the aid package you just find a mistake. Last year a low-income student came in to tell me that he wasn't going to be attending college. He showed me his student aid report, and right away I saw a very simple error—a number was placed incorrectly on the form. We were able to correct the error online in five minutes, and his new student aid report proved he was eligible for 100% aid."

—*Lori Johnston, Hastings High School*

HOW TO REQUEST A PROFESSIONAL JUDGMENT REVIEW

If you believe that special circumstances qualify you for a professional judgment, make an appointment with the college's financial aid office to appeal the decision. Tell the office the reason for your appeal when you make the appointment, and ask what documentation you need to state your case. A professional judgment appeal can be done via letter as well. Just explain the unusual circumstances and provide photocopies (not originals) of relevant documentation. Also include your telephone number in the letter so they can call to ask questions.

You must arrive at this meeting with complete documentation supporting your appeal, and that documentation will vary depending on the special circumstance. In addition, it is very helpful if you can say exactly how much more aid you might need.

Professional judgment is not the same as bargaining. It is more about making a complete case than it is about persuading the financial aid office to bend its rules (which it can't, according to law, and shouldn't, according to fairness). Accordingly, you should arrive at the meeting with an understanding of what you can do to help remedy the situation.

Ellen Frishberg of Johns Hopkins describes the most helpful posture for a family this way: "They describe their circumstances and add, 'We know we can pay this much, and we can cut back a little here, and we're willing to borrow, but we can only borrow so much for the following reasons. . . .'

" 'We're willing to borrow' are the magic words," says Ellen, "because that opens up more possibilities for the aid office to help."

If you can be precise about how much more you need, so much the better. Stating, "We have to find a way to get another $3,500 per year" starts a more fruitful conversation than, "Give me more."

Here is an example of a successful professional judgment case (stick with us because even this simple case requires a lot of documents):

A family which has recently been hit with severe medical expenses requests a change to the Adjusted Gross Income (AGI) figure from their previous years' tax forms, which was used to calculate their aid package. Their medical expenses are much higher this year than last year, so they can't afford the family contribution set by the college.

The college can subtract the family's additional unreimbursed medical expenses from the AGI, giving a new (lower) figure.[79] Plug this into the formula, and the result is a lower EFC figure, yielding an increase in financial need and consequently a higher aid package in the form of greater grants, loans or other considerations.

The family in this example would provide proof of all out-of-pocket medical expenses (after insurance payments). The family should also project further out-of-pocket medical costs it anticipates throughout the year.

For a complete picture, the family should also document any impact the medical condition would have on family income. That means deducting lost income and adding such income as disability insurance payments or workman's compensation.

That's a lot of paper, but the more you can document your case, the more likely you'll achieve a professional judgment in your favor. The law requires the financial aid administrator to make their decision in such a case on the basis of adequate documentation, so the process is driven by documentation.

Notice how the adjustment is driven by the nature of the unusual circum-

NEGOTIATION

Although very few schools actually negotiate a financial aid package in the usual sense of bargaining back and forth, there are nevertheless a handful that will match other schools' financial aid offers. Usually these schools use a rigid policy, matching only offers from a limited number of schools that the college considers to be its peers (i.e., similar quality schools for which the college competes for students). Usually the peer schools are in the same geographic area and cost about the same. The schools never get into bidding wars for students.

One area where a few schools will sometimes negotiate is their outside scholarship policy (i.e., how the school reduces the financial aid package when the student wins a private scholarship). Federal regulations require the school to reduce the financial aid package to compensate for outside scholarships when total aid exceeds demonstrated financial need, so the school cannot increase the amount of financial aid you receive.

continued

However, there is a little wiggle room in deciding how to configure the aid package. For example, the school could reduce loans before reducing grants. Since grants are better than loans, replacing a loan with all or part of an outside scholarship will benefit the student more than replacing a grant. (This is only done for students who are bringing in a large amount of outside scholarships.)

If you want to try negotiating with a school, present a better offer from a competing college and indicate that you will matriculate at the school if they will match the other school's offer. If the school is one of the few that matches other institutions' offers, they will ask for a copy of the other school's award letter. They will compare it with their own financial aid package, and also the costs and student budget at each school. If there is a genuine difference in out-of-pocket costs, they might match it (or at least come a little closer) or they might not.

Do not ever try the practice of sandbagging, in which you get a larger offer from one school, bring it to another, and when the second school matches it, return to the first school asking for more. This creates mistrust and will almost certainly backfire.

The schools that will match offers from competing schools are open about the practice and encourage the students to submit competing offers. This doesn't mean you'll necessarily get a better offer after the second review, just that they are willing to take a second look in response to new information, including better offers from their competition.

stance. The application of professional judgment is not only justified by the unusual circumstance, but also the amount of the adjustment is directly connected to the financial impact of the unusual circumstance on the family. The financial aid administrator uses this to adjust the inputs to the formula, but cannot otherwise modify the federal need analysis methodology.

DOS AND DON'TS

A cooperative, professional attitude really does help your case, so remember the following:

- The decision of the financial aid administrator is final. You may appeal a final decision only if critical circumstances have changed.

- Many decisions cannot be changed, because they are based on federal or state regulations or laws.
- A change in eligibility for an award does not guarantee a larger award. Some changes, in fact (such as increased capital gains), could mean a lesser award.
- A dependency override can sometimes lead to an increase in the EFC, when cash support from the parents was previously sheltered by the parents' higher income protection allowance.
- It is legitimate to reveal the details of aid packages offered by other schools as long as you keep the focus on the specific reasons for the aid.
- You might be asked to start an appeal online or in writing, and let it work through the system, especially at a large school.
- The process takes time. Depending on the timing, you might have to secure your registration before the appeals process is concluded, to avoid late registration fees. Ask the financial aid administrator how the appeals process deals with this. *File an appeal as early as possible.*

Much of the typical financial aid package has been determined by law and regulations, but at colleges that give merit aid, you might feel justified in appealing its amount. The decision is subjective, and up to the college (often the admissions office or the office of the President), but if you can keep the tone of the conversation balanced, you will often find a receptive audience.

There are a few stratagems that drive financial aid administrators crazy, and all reflect a misunderstanding—or disrespect—toward the financial aid function.

Don't compare the quality of schools offering you aid. Financial aid administrators too often hear, "Well, my kid got more aid from . . ." followed by a long list of schools that they regard as less prestigious or less appropriate for the student. Those are very difficult conversations, because you're asking them to compare not only the money but the quality of the schools.

Do not haggle over tuition with the financial aid office. Tuition is set by the college administration, and aid administrators are not auto salesmen. Although you might have heard the term "tuition discounting," you are not talking about discounting a product but constructing a financing package. Financial aid is a policy-driven process. You will not be able to get more aid by bluff, bluster or bargaining skill. Rather, the key to getting more aid is to ensure that the school has complete information about the family's financial circumstances.

Don't walk into the office on May 1 having paid your admission deposit and then try to convince the financial aid office that you can't afford the college after all. They have been working hard with families who provided that information weeks or even months before.

Don't start the conversation with "My neighbor Patti got more." ("Sometimes I think we're like airlines," says Ellen Frishberg. "It feels like every seat has a different price.") You are not Patti, and the reasons she got more are confidential. The school cannot discuss Patti's financial aid package with you because of federal privacy laws.

The conclusion of your conversation(s) brings you back to the fundamental decision of this chapter: Which colleges can you afford, given the final financial aid packages you are offered?

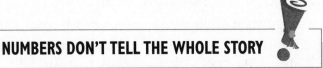

NUMBERS DON'T TELL THE WHOLE STORY

"The numbers on the application forms don't necessarily tell the whole story. Right after September 11, 2001, a student called me from New York. He said, 'I've got a really tough situation, Mr. Levy. I don't know what to do. Both of my parents perished in the World Trade Center and now I'm living with my high school counselor. . . . I don't know what to do about filling out my financial aid application.'

"There is no way to know something like that by looking at the numbers in an application for financial aid. But I was able to get a statement from the student, his high school counselor and a member of the clergy from the congregation to which the student belonged, and we were able to help the student."

—*David Levy, Caltech*

WHAT IF IT'S STILL NOT ENOUGH?

You have received your final financial aid packages from all schools that accepted you. The time to commit to a school with a tuition deposit is approaching . . . and you are still not certain you can afford your first (or second) choice of schools. Before you make that commitment, consider the other possibilities in this section. We are not offering a prescription for making money appear out of thin air, but a set of options that help you get the best possible outcome—a good education at the right school at a price the student or family can handle.

Know your payment options. You will find greater flexibility in the way you are being asked to pay, although not in the amount. Financial aid offices are becoming more astute about helping families structure payments. Daniel Barkowitz of MIT suggests this example: "Let's say that the family has a balance of $20,000. For most families who are asked to pay $20,000, a ten-month payment plan of $2,000 a month is not affordable. And for most families $200 to $400 a month on a long-term loan is eminently affordable. So now we say, "Okay, let's end the *financial aid* conversation and start the *financing* conversation, which is to say: How do we find the combination of programs that best works for your individual family circumstances? If the family says they can afford $400 a month, that's great—we find a combination of loans and payment plans to make a $400 monthly payment. More and more colleges are moving in this direction."

Look for additional scholarships. Steve Borkowski of FastWeb notes that you can continue to search for scholarships beyond the commitment date. Keep your profile updated to be sure you're getting the most relevant results. Don't forget to stay in touch with community organizations who grant scholarships. Additional scholarship money might offer some relief even after you've made the decision to accept a high family contribution.

Stay close to home. A student might consider attending a nearby college to save living expenses, and continue to live with his or her parents. Clearly, there are personal issues to consider, like a student's developing sense of independence. For some families, it's the right choice.

Community college. There is the option of attending a low-cost community college nearby, planning to transfer to another institution after one or two years. This tactic is sometimes suggested by financial aid administrators to families who cannot afford the college they want, even with the best possible aid package. If you want to consider this route, discuss it with the financial aid offices of colleges that have accepted the student. Some colleges have "articulation agreements" that make it easier for students to transfer from a community college to a four-year institution. Some states, like California, Florida and Pennsylvania, guarantee admission into one of the state's public four-year colleges for students who receive an associate's degree from one of the state's two-year colleges.

Consider a part-time job. If work-study isn't part of your aid package, ask if it's a possibility. Many colleges have more jobs available than they have students to fill them. Research the campus and surrounding community to find other viable employment options.

Check your government money. Review chapters 5 to 7 to be sure you're borrowing the maximum you can in subsidized loans and the unsubsidized Federal Stafford loan. If you still don't have enough money to cover the gap after maximizing your subsidized loans and other low-cost education loans, you can approach a private lender for a Federal PLUS loan or an alternative (private) education loan (chapter 8).

Consider accelerated programs. It might be possible for you to obtain your degree in less than four years. For long-term planners, especially those considering graduate school after undergraduate, this can represent a significant savings. You will have to take on a higher course load, but it can cut your costs significantly.

Consider delaying a year. Some students take a year between high school and college to earn money by working full-time. If you wish to explore this, check with the colleges as soon as possible to find out their policy regarding delays by admitted students. Most colleges will allow students to defer their admission for up to a year (in some cases, two) for various reasons. It is common among very religious Jews, for example, to take off a year between high school and college to study at a religious school in Israel. Students from other religions may go on a church mission to another country. Deferments are also often granted for military service and humanitarian service (e.g., Peace Corps), medical conditions, foreign academic scholarships (e.g., Marshall or Rhodes scholarships—obviously for graduate study), family responsibilities and financial reasons. One has to apply for a deferment after one is admitted. If you were admitted off of the waiting list,[80] you will probably not be eligible for a deferral.

Consider cooperative education. Cooperative education enables students to alternate work and study in a more career-oriented program than traditional work-study jobs. The programs are voluntary and vary from one college to another. You can learn more about cooperative education at www.co-op.edu.

Review ways to save money. We've listed ways to save money elsewhere in this book; we mention it again here because often the clearest perspective on where you can and can't save money comes when you are forced to choose between your dream school and another option. Taking a hard look at your finances might identify other ways to save.

Ask for help. Sometimes there are resources you've been reluctant to tap. Perhaps you didn't want to go to grandparents or other relatives requesting a gift or loan, but when that could make the difference between one school and another . . . it might be worth the discussion.

Even if you don't end up at your first choice institution, these strategies are ways to get the best possible college situation you can.

Once your decision is made, you can roll up all you've learned, and get ready to move on to school, which is the subject of this book's final chapter.

16

Moving On

It was after school in April, and Matt was starting a three-day trip to the University of Ohio and to Caledonia College, to make a final decision on which school he'd attend in the autumn. All that work, all those forms, all those scholarship applications had resulted in this: a real choice between two very different, and very good, colleges. As for the money—Matt and his family had worked their way to the point that the money wouldn't force his decision one way or another. His next step in life was up to him, not his parents' checkbook.

Even though he probably wouldn't have time to practice, Matt decided to bring the guitar along, and he strapped it securely behind the driver's seat of his truck. Sarah dribbled a basketball nearby. Matt thought, she's doing that kid-sister thing—ignoring me but staying close. He realized, perhaps for the first time, that Sarah would be the big kid next year—the only kid in the house. I wonder if she's looking forward to that, he thought.

Lynn emerged from the side door of the house, holding something small. Jim followed. As Matt hoisted his backpack behind the passenger seat, she pressed it into his hand—five $20 bills.

"You let us know what they say at both schools, honey," she said.

"Hey, Mom, I don't need this," Matt said, holding out the money.

"Yes, you do," said Lynn. She closed his outstretched hand on the bills. "Use it for something fun. Take your host student out for a burger. Come back with a sweatshirt from the college you decide on. And bring a second one for Sarah."

Jim said, "That means you'll have to decide which sweatshirt to get. If you go to Ohio, she won't wear anything with Caledonia's name on it."

Matt sat in the driver's seat. "Well, there are choices. Big school vs. little school. Great sports vs. great arts. Public vs. private. Affordable vs. expensive . . ."

"Not so bad when you add up all the pieces," said Jim.

Lynn closed the door of the truck. "In the end, there's not so much difference that you should make the decision based on money." And Jim added, "Stick to the things we discussed last night, buddy. Whichever college you choose is fine with us."

"Thanks, Dad. Thanks, Mom," said Matt. He started the engine and called to Sarah, "See you Tuesday, Sis!" Sarah caught the basketball rebounding off the garage, then turned and waved.

To his parents, Matt said, "I bet I'll know right away after seeing them both. . . ." Catching his mother's look, he added quickly, "And I promise I'll call you."

"Tonight, when you get in," said Lynn.

"You got it," said Matt. He backed the car onto the street, waved and drove west.

•   •   •

Matt's road trip to make his final decision marks the beginning of one of life's great journeys—moving from home to college. For students and their families, this time marks the end of one way of life and the beginning of another. This time also begins a transition to a new level of financial and personal responsibility. A host of new opportunities and potential pitfalls arise about this time.

This final chapter of *College Gold* will help ensure that your venture into the brave new world of college life goes well. We're going to talk about money (of course!), and also about certain specific situations for nontraditional and graduate students that require somewhat different consideration.

Transitions don't always mean a complete break with the past, so let's talk first about carrying forward the good habits you've practiced into your college years, beginning with the management of your hard-won financial aid.

KEEP THE PROCESS GOING

Michael J. Bennett, Director of Financial Aid at Brookdale Community College, summarizes the challenge a freshman faces: "Despite everyone's best efforts, we find a student's first year receiving financial aid is filled with learning a complex process and navigating offices. This includes filing a FAFSA, responding to follow-up letters/e-mail messages, navigating web sites/online Self-Serve Financial Aid/phone systems, obtaining books and receiving loan balances/stipend checks. We hope that at the end of that year, a student has obtained some new technology skills, met some new people, talked with other students and realized 'I can do this.' We want our students to know how to seek out and access important information at the time it's needed the most."

It's up to you to keep the process going, and you don't have to do it alone. Even before you arrive at school, we suggest you keep in touch with the financial aid office. Don't be shy about asking questions concerning any topic, such as: "When is this payment due? When and how do I renew? What are the restrictions?" There are no stupid questions. One of the unspoken benefits of college work is a growing ability to look down the road . . . not just to the next exam but to next year, and five or ten years down the road.

On the next page you'll find a punch list for students to use in their first year of college concerning financial aid, and financial opportunity such as summer jobs:

Following the freshman year, it's mostly a matter of repeating steps you've taken previously. Open and *read* the letters and e-mails from your financial aid office, the U.S. Department of Education and/or private lenders; complete paperwork before deadlines; study your financial aid statements and, if you have questions, bring them quickly to the attention of your financial aid administrator.

☑ I Wish I Had Known . . .

I wish I had known the total package price and not just tuition. I did not think about books or laundry. I did not think about health insurance, which is a big deal to independent students such as me.

—*Diesha Frye, 2nd semester freshman*
Virginia State University

FINANCIAL AID TO-DO LIST FOR COLLEGE STUDENTS

Fall:

- Reconnect with your financial aid office. Complete any remaining financial aid paperwork.
- Set up a budget and time management calendar for the year, including financial aid and scholarship deadlines.
- Visit your academic advisor/career center to discuss courses, career building and other activities.
- Gather the financial records and materials you need for next year's FAFSA. The form is available January 1, and you **must file a renewal FAFSA to be eligible for aid next year.** Same with the CSS/Financial Aid PROFILE.
- Join clubs and community service groups in areas of interest.
- Do a scholarship search at FastWeb.com and apply for scholarships.
- Participate in any college-level competitions that are relevant to your interests, such as the Putnam competition for math majors.
- Confirm rules for renewing any multiyear scholarships you have won.
- Build relationships with professors, counselors and activity supervisors. This will help you obtain recommendations for jobs and graduate school.

January–February:

- Complete the FAFSA as soon as possible after January 1 to continue receiving financial aid next year. You must renew every year for most forms of aid.
- Maintain a resume or portfolio[81] that includes academic records, extracurricular activities, honors and volunteer work. Post your resume online (www.Monstertrak .com is a site dedicated to matching students with internships as well as jobs).

Spring:

- Meet with your faculty advisor to discuss plans for summer and next fall.
- Register for fall classes.
- Renew your financial aid package for next year.
- Explore options such as: study abroad, double major, co-op programs, international internships, mentoring programs and independent study.
- Continue to search and apply for scholarships as part of your routine.
- Apply for summer jobs, internships and volunteer opportunities.

KEEP ON TOP OF THE MONEY

Your college's financial aid office can help you keep track of scholarships, grants and loans that they administer. Beyond that money, you are directly responsible for the other sources of income. All loans, whether from your college or private sources, have payment terms and requirements (During entrance and exit counseling, which is required by the federal government for all students with federal education loans, the school will review the terms and repayment options with you.) Scholarships might have requirements such as maintaining a certain GPA or major. Keep your files updated and mark renewal deadlines on your calendar. Maintain a list of all of your loans and scholarships and their requirements.

Keeping on top of money means creating a budget and sticking to it. We've given tips for creating a budget and places to save money in chapters 4 and 14. There are a few additional habits that help while students are in college:

Spend within your limits. Don't run out of money at the end of a semester because you've spent poorly. Get into the habit of asking for receipts and recording your expenses against a budget; it's a good lifelong habit. Just knowing where the money has gone is enough to help many students control their spending. When you feel the urge to splurge, consider whether you're over budget.

Spend education money on education. Some scholarships come with no strings attached. Before you upgrade to a spiffy new laptop computer, use the money to cover books, fees and other necessary educational expenses. Prioritize your expenses into mandatory and discretionary categories, taking care of the mandatory expenses first. If you've budgeted the money for living expenses, don't upgrade them (i.e., buy a more expensive cell phone plan) in the middle of the year, only to run out of money early.

Pay bills on time. If your bills are sent to a collection agency, it can harm your credit, which hurts your chances of being approved for future student loans, or the purchase of a house or car. Set up a bank account with automatic online bill-paying and keep your account funded to avoid late fees.

Watch out for peer pressure, marketing and other temptations. Don't let friends, cool advertisements or "free" premiums pressure you into spending money you shouldn't. Avoid lending money.

Be careful with credit cards. A credit card can be incredibly convenient for managing your money. It can save money, for example, by enabling you to purchase discount travel tickets online or by giving you a small rebate on your purchases. A credit card can be a great help in an emergency, and wise use can help establish a good personal credit record. Credit card misuse, however, causes a world of trouble for students (or anyone else, for that matter). It's tempting to go over budget. When you use plastic, it doesn't feel like you're spending real money—it feels the same whether you're spending $10 or $500, and a lot of small charges can add up fast. It's easy to rack up monthly interest payments until you're actually paying far more for the original purchase than you intended. You can get in over your head without much thought.

If you as a student decide to get a credit card, observe some good habits:

- Select a card that does not charge an annual fee.
- Look for low annual percentage rates (APR). The higher the interest, the more you will have to pay later.
- Ask about additional fees like late payment, charging over your limit and maintaining a balance.
- Remember that the rates for cash advances are usually higher than your interest rate on regular purchases.
- Read the fine print on introductory offers. Interest rates usually go up considerably after only three or six months.
- Have only one card with a low credit limit. A card with a limit of only $500 to $1,000 will help you control your spending.
- Only get credit cards that provide a grace period of at least twenty days. If you pay the balance in full during the grace period, no interest charges will accrue.
- Pay off your credit card balances in full with each statement. If you are carrying a balance, it means you are spending beyond your means. Stop using the credit card for new purchases if you're forced to carry a balance, and pay the monthly bill!

You might feel more comfortable with a debit card, which deducts purchases directly from a bank or other account like a checkbook. No more money—no more purchases. It's a disciplined approach that works for many.

Consumer Reports magazine (consumerreports.org) and Bankrate.com publish periodic ratings of credit card deals, and offer excellent advice on managing credit.

Good money management also looks ahead to the years when a student and/or parents must pay back loans. "I'll worry about that tomorrow" is not a plan; you must now consider the impact educational debt will have on your budget when you leave school. Debt has an impact on which jobs you pursue. If you go on to graduate school (see below), you might be able to postpone (defer) payments for undergraduate loans, but they won't go away.

Financial aid offices and lenders can supply information on how much you'll have to pay, and for how long. If you have not yet taken out any loans, the following examples illustrate typical payments.

The rule of thumb we mentioned earlier, "Don't borrow more than your first year's pay," is a rough way to estimate what you can afford. Another way to judge: Monthly payments for all your loans should be no more than 10% of your gross income (depending on other debts, interest rates and the like).

As you'll see from the two examples that follow, college loan payments match other typical payments. For example, a ten-year loan of $25,000 at 6.8% (the current Federal Stafford loan interest rate) will cost $288 per month, or about as much as the monthly payment on a mid-sized car loan.

BOOK TO WEB

You can find monthly payments, using any combination of loan amounts and interest rates, with the online calculators at www.collegegold.com. The online calculators automatically create a monthly payment schedule for the life of the loan.

CODE: 1022

GOVERNMENT LOAN CONSOLIDATION

Another type of government education loan that should generally be considered later in college or after graduation is the consolidation loan. We're including it here because the programs for government and private education loan consolidation are different (see chapter 8 for information on private loan consolidation).

Loan consolidation combines several student or parent loans into one bigger loan from a single lender. The consolidation is like a refinance, with the proceeds from the consolidation loan being used to pay off the balances on the original loans. Consolidation loans are available for most federal education loans. They often reduce the size of the monthly payment by extending the term of the loan beyond the standard ten-year repayment plan. (For anything other

PAYBACK TIME

Graduate with subsidized Federal Stafford loan totaling $19,000:

Loan Balance:	$19,000
Loan Interest Rate:	6.8%
Loan Term:	10 years
Minimum Payment:	$50
Monthly Loan Payment:	**$218.65**
Number of Payments:	120
Cumulative Payments:	$26,238.45
Total Interest Paid:	$7,238.45

Note: The monthly loan payment was calculated at 119 payments of $218.65 plus a final payment of $219.10.

It is estimated that you will need an annual salary of at least $26,238.00 to be able to afford to repay this loan. This estimate assumes that 10% of your gross monthly income will be devoted to repaying your student loans. If you use 15% of your gross monthly income to repay the loan, you will need an annual salary of only $17,492.00, but you may experience some financial difficulty.

These results assume that the student is paying the interest charges on any unsubsidized loans and is not capitalizing the interest while in school. If the student is capitalizing the interest, the cumulative payments and total interest charges will be higher than shown here.

Parents paying off Federal PLUS loan of $10,000:*

Loan Balance:	$10,000
Loan Interest Rate:	8.5%
Loan Term:	10 years
Minimum Payment:	$50
Monthly Loan Payment:	**$123.99**
Number of Payments:	120
Cumulative Payments:	$14,877.99
Total Interest Paid:	$4,877.99

* Reminders: Federal PLUS loan payments begin sixty days after the first funds are disbursed, so this cumulative figure actually has been arrived at over four years, but payment began in the freshman year. Also, as of this writing, borrowers can get a slightly lower rate by consolidating loans.

Assuming that 10% of gross monthly income goes to repay this loan, parents will need to earn at least $14,878 per year to be able to afford to repay this loan. Most U.S. households make much more than this, but parents also tend to have much larger financial responsibilities than childless graduates just starting out. Another way to look at this: Parents need to dedicate $1,488 of yearly net household income to paying off the loan.

than standard ten-year repayment, one must consolidate the loans.) The reduced monthly payment may make the loan easier to repay for some borrowers. However, extending the term of a loan increases the total amount of interest paid over the lifetime of the loan.

Here's the basic formula: The interest rate on consolidation loans is the weighted average of the interest rates on the loans being consolidated, rounded up to the nearest ⅛ of a percent and capped at 8.25%.

It is a common misconception that a student can consolidate only once in a lifetime. Borrowers can consolidate multiple times, so long as each consolidation adds a previously unconsolidated education loan. For example, if you have three separate loans, you can initially consolidate two loans together. Then to consolidate again you can consolidate the two already consolidated loans with the third loan. The key benefits of a consolidation loan include replacing multiple payments with a single payment[82] access to alternate repayment plans (see below); and access to various forbearances and deferments.[83] An additional benefit of consolidation includes resetting the clock on the deferments and forbearances that are limited to three years, such as the economic hardship deferment.

Also, since PLUS loans have a fixed interest rate of 8.5% and consolidation loans cap the interest rate at 8.25%, if you consolidate PLUS loans by themselves you effectively reduce the interest rate by 0.25%. This will save you hundreds of dollars in interest over the lifetime of the loan.

There are, however, a few drawbacks to consolidation, including the following:

- When a borrower consolidates during the grace period, the borrower has to begin repayment immediately and loses the remainder of the grace period, including possibly eliminating interest benefits on subsidized loans.
- The borrower may lose some of the favorable loan forgiveness provisions on the Federal Perkins loan when it is included in a consolidation

loan. The federal government also will no longer pay the interest on Federal Perkins loans while the student is in school or during periods of deferment.

- Extending the repayment term may increase the total interest paid over the lifetime of the loan.

Consolidation simplifies the repayment process but can result in a slight increase in the interest rate. Students who are having trouble making their payments should consider some of the alternate repayment terms provided for by consolidation loans. Income contingent repayment, for example, adjusts the monthly payments to compensate for a lower monthly income. Graduated repayment provides lower payments during the first two years after graduation. Extended repayment allows you to extend the term of the loan.

LOAN DEFERMENT

We touched on earning loan forgiveness through service, in chapter 9. You can also receive a temporary suspension—called a deferment—of certain federal loan payments for specific situations such as maintaining at least half-time enrollment in school (including graduate school), up to three years of unemployment, up to three years of economic hardship, and up to three years of active duty military service during a war or national emergency. During this period you don't have to make any payments of principal. You also don't have to pay interest on subsidized loans (e.g., Federal Perkins and subsidized Federal Stafford loans or subsidized Federal Direct Stafford loans) or any consolidation loan that includes only Federal Direct Stafford loans and subsidized Federal Stafford loans.[92] On any other federal education loans the interest continues to accrue and must either be paid by the borrower or capitalized (added to the loan principal). To obtain a deferment, you must submit a deferment application to your lender; deferments are not automatic. Continue making payments on your loan until you are notified that your deferment request has been granted. Otherwise, your loans might go into default for nonpayment.

Remember that going into default on your federal loans triggers the unpleasant consequences we described in chapter 14. Furthermore, you cannot get deferment on loans that have gone into default—so try to anticipate payment trouble. If you think you won't be able to keep up your payments, you must contact the financial aid office or loan servicer immediately—and don't assume that just notifying them means you can stop paying the loans. Deferment requires paperwork and approval is not automatic. **Direct Loan** borrowers should contact the Direct Loan Servicing Center at the following numbers:

> Phone: 1-800-4-FED-AID (1-800-433-3243)
>
> Fax: 1-800-848-0984
>
> TTY: 1-800-848-0983
>
> www.dlservicer.ed.gov

Federal Family Education Loan (FFEL) borrowers should contact the lenders or agencies holding the loans. Federal Perkins borrowers should contact their loan servicer or the school that issued the loan.

If you are temporarily unable to meet your repayment schedule but are not eligible for a deferment, you may receive **forbearance** for a limited and specified period. During forbearance, your payments are postponed or reduced. Whether your loans are subsidized or unsubsidized, you will be charged interest. If you don't pay the interest as it accrues, it will be capitalized.

For example, you may be granted forbearance if you are:

- Unable to pay due to poor health or other unforeseen personal problems.
- Serving in a medical or dental internship or residency.
- Serving in a position under the National Community Service Trust Act of 1993 (forbearance may be granted for this reason for a Direct or FFEL Stafford loan, but not for a Direct or FFEL Federal PLUS loan).
- Obligated to make payments on certain federal student loans that are equal to or greater than 20% of your monthly gross income.

NONTRADITIONAL STUDENTS

Are you married, returning to college after a long absence or going to college for the first time in midlife? Are you over twenty-four, a veteran or have you decided to attend college in pursuit of a passionate interest after years in a career? Do you have children? Then you're a nontraditional student, a member of a fast-growing cohort. Nontraditional students tend to have different financial and lifestyle issues than the "traditional" two- or four-year student attending college right after high school. Financial pressures are part of this picture, and a significant second source of stress is time pressure.

Here are typical danger zones for nontraditional students, most of which have a financial component.

- Housing—especially for married students.
- Family pressures—spending less time with your family and increasing the pressures on your family budget.
- Child care/day care—both availability and affordability.
- Managing a schedule that includes work and study.
- Fitting in, or feeling different from other students, because you are older, or farther away from your days in school, or more experienced.
- Doubts about the investment of time and money (is this for me; is this a good career move?).
- Lifestyle changes, such as giving up recreation, hobbies and social activities.
- Sticking with it as the money runs low and/or the debts pile up.
- Loss of income from returning to college.
- Adding to debt from previous education.

Federal and college-based money for school is generally available to non-traditional students under the same rules and restrictions that traditional students must follow. While this means that nontraditional students are eligible for the same student aid programs, no special accommodations are made for non-traditional students. For example, the cost of attendance figure—the student budget—is based on the incremental increase in costs associated with the student pursuing a college degree. The EFC figure does depend on family size (and some child care costs can be accounted for), but current law does not allow the EFC to go below zero. Most schools will adjust the cost of attendance to include the rent of a larger apartment, but they'll be reluctant to make adjustments for more tangential expenses such as health insurance for family members. There's a limit to what they can do within the constraints of the law. The law does, however, include dependent care and child care within the definition of cost of attendance, so you can ask for an adjustment to cover those expenses. In most cases these adjustments will increase eligibility for student loans, not grants.

Although many schools restrict eligibility for the school's own financial aid programs to the first bachelor's degree, some schools will waive the restrictions when the student is an adult returning to school to earn a second degree in preparation for a career change. Generally you must be enrolled at least half-time (and in some cases full-time) to qualify for financial aid.

Nontraditional students are more likely (though not certain) to be independent of their parents—see the rules for independence in chapter 5.

Many scholarship and fellowship programs do not have age restrictions, and there are no age restrictions on eligibility for federal student financial aid. Older students should conduct a search for aid and scholarships just like younger students.

Some scholarships are specifically intended for nontraditional students. Here are four brief examples:

Talbots Women's Scholarship Fund. This award is available to women who are determined go back and get their undergraduate degree. Selection is based on financial and need and past achievements. Five women returning to a four-year institution will receive $10,000 scholarships and 50 women will receive $1,000 awards. (Go to www1.talbots.com and write "scholarship" in the search box.)

Datatel Returning Student Scholarship. Undergraduate and graduate students currently attending a college or university who uses the products of software developer Datatel are eligible. Students must be returning to school after a minimum five year absence. An essay discussing the issues surrounding a returning student is also required. Fifty award recipients will receive $1,500 scholarships. (Find it at www.datatel.com/global/scholarships/)

Possible Woman Foundation Scholarship. The Possible Woman Foundation Scholarship is available to "women who are returning to school after a hiatus, changing careers, seeking advancement in their career or work life, and stay-at-home moms entering the work place and in need of additional education/training." Recipients must be U.S. citizens who are at least 25. Selection is based on need, leadership, community involvement and an essay. Awards range from $3,000 to $5,000. (Find it at www.possiblewomanfoundation.org)

Wal-Mart Higher REACH Scholarship. This award is offered to students who have been out of high school for at least one year, or have received their EED. Recipients must deomonstrate financial need and be Wal-Mart employees who have been with the company for at least one continuous year. Awards of up to $2,000 are available (Go to www.walmartfoundation.org and click on "what we fund" and then "scholarships.")

Nontraditional students—and some traditional undergraduate students as well—can benefit from the College-Level Examination Program (CLEP), a test that grants college credit to students based on knowledge learned through professional experience, independent study, adult courses or advanced high school courses. The CLEP is recognized by about 2,900 colleges and universities, and is administered by the College Board. The CLEP is comprised of thirty-four different tests in a variety of subjects, much like the SAT Subject Tests. Most students who take the CLEP are older, returning students.

Usually students take CLEP tests to pass out of first- or second-year courses at the college freshman and sophomore level. Instead of paying full tuition for classes about a subject you already know, you can take a CLEP test and move into more advanced classes, or even reduce the time you spend in college, thus saving money as well.

Ask your college whether they recognize CLEP test results, and if so, which tests they recognize. Most colleges that accept CLEP results will give credit for only certain tests. In addition, almost all colleges limit the number of CLEP credits they will grant.

There are three less well-known tests that are recognized by many colleges and universities: the DSST (DANTES Subject Standardized Tests—found at www.getcollegecredit.com), the TECEP (Thomas Edison State College Examination Program—found at www.tesc.edu/students/tecep/tecep.php) and the ECE (Excelsior College Examination, formerly called the Regents Exam and ACT PEP—www.excelsior.edu).

One option for nontraditional students, especially working students, is distance education, which has evolved from old-fashioned correspondence courses to sophisticated online universities. Online distance education is now a multibillion-dollar industry and growing fast. In 2005 Congress changed the rules governing eligibility for federal student aid, making students at purely online universities eligible for federal student aid. Although at this writing the Department of Education has not yet issued formal regulations, this means that students taking courses at some online universities may be eligible for Federal Pell Grants and Federal Stafford loans.

GRADUATE SCHOOL

Federal student aid accounts for the largest percentage of aid received by graduate and professional students. The process for acquiring financial aid for graduate school is like the process for undergraduate aid (you fill out a new FAFSA, work

ALTERNATE ROUTES

You might also consider "alternate routes" to your dream school—different paths to the same ultimate goal—such as the following:

You can save a lot by completing your general education requirements at a community college, state university or less expensive school and then transferring to complete the degree. A less competitive school might offer merit aid to attract talented students. There are even scholarships to help you do this, such as those awarded by the Jack Kent Cooke Foundation (see chapter 12).

Michael J. Bennett of Brookdale Community College comments, "Almost half of the students in this country attend community colleges. They provide an accessible and affordable education for families. Two years at a community college saves you almost $24,000 that would have been spent at a public university and $72,000 (or more) at a private university. Many students also attend local community colleges during the summer terms, and transfer credits back to their institution to ensure they graduate in four years."

If you graduate from a prestigious university, few people will care that you spent your first two years at a community college. Likewise, if you intend to go on to graduate school, few people will ask about where you got your undergraduate degree. Often, it is easier to get into graduate school at an institution if you attended a different undergraduate institution, since many colleges limit the number of their own undergraduates that they'll admit to the graduate school to prevent "inbreeding."

A good rule of thumb is that private four-year colleges cost twice as much as public four-year colleges, and public four-year colleges 1.5 times as much as public two-year colleges. (These figures are total cost, not just tuition.)

Transferring can complicate the financial aid picture, however. You have to reapply for financial aid at the new school, and your previous financial aid package does not transfer with you. The courses you took at the community college do not necessarily earn you credit to a four-year degree. Some schools restrict financial aid for transfer students, or may only have financial aid for students who transfer at the beginning of the ac-

continued

ademic year. You have to investigate this option carefully with the college you are targeting as your ultimate destination, so talk to an admissions counselor to be sure your credits will transfer, and learn as much as you can about the financial aid policy.

Most public colleges and universities charge considerably less tuition to in-state students in comparison to students from out of state. The out-of-state public four-year total is about 1.5 times the in-state public four-year total. Pick a college in your state to keep costs down. Investigate regional student exchange programs, in which some states offer reduced tuition rates for students from nearby states.

If your heart is set on going out of state, consider moving a year before starting college. After you've established residency (usually one or two years), you should be eligible for in-state tuition. Policies vary from school to school and state to state, so be sure to check with your school of choice.

If you're planning to earn multiple degrees, you can save a year's tuition by enrolling in a combined degree program. Some schools will allow you to combine a bachelor's degree with a master's degree or a master's degree with a doctoral degree. Some colleges may offer a program that combines a bachelor's degree with an M.D. Other colleges offer an accelerated three-year program, or will allow you to graduate early if you complete all the requirements ahead of schedule. You can do this by taking a somewhat heavier load, such as an extra course every semester, or by taking classes during the summer. Some schools do not charge extra tuition for taking additional classes.

with the financial aid office and so on). Some programs, such as the Federal Perkins Loan, have higher dollar limits, acknowledging the higher cost of most graduate study; graduate students may annually borrow $6,000 vs. $4,000 per year for undergraduate students in the Federal Perkins Loan program. The total limit of $40,000 that you can borrow as a graduate or professional student must include any Federal Perkins Loans you took out as an undergraduate. Likewise, the Federal Stafford Loan allows graduate students to borrow up to $20,500 per year (at most $8,500 subsidized) with a cumulative limit of $138,500 ($65,500 subsidized) including any undergraduate loans. Even higher limits are available for medical school students.

Other federal programs, such as the Federal Pell Grants, are available only to undergraduate students.

As noted in chapter 7, Congress created a new loan program for graduate and professional students, effective July 1, 2006, called the **Graduate and Professional Student Federal PLUS Loan.** It is an unsubsidized loan, similar in many ways to the parent Federal PLUS loan, and here in brief is how the program will work. (It is just getting under way, so some details might be changed by the Department of Education).

Annual Loan Limit: Limited to Cost of Attendance (COA), minus aid received, as certified by the school.

Cumulative Loan Limit: None.

Impact on Other Loan Limits: Does not affect eligibility for Federal Perkins, Stafford or Parent Federal PLUS loans.

Interest Rate: Fixed 8.5%.

Loan Fees: Total 4% (3% origination and 1% guarantee).

Repayment: Repayment begins sixty days after the loan is fully disbursed.

Deferrals: Repayment of principal is subject to deferrals, including the in-school deferment for pursuing a course of study at least half-time, a three-year forbearance during which the borrower is seeking and unable to find full-time employment and a three-year economic hardship forbearance. In-school deferments do not apply to periods when the borrower is serving in a medical internship or residency, but medical students remain eligible for the economic hardship deferment during that time.

Capitalization of Interest: During any deferral of principal payments, interest may either be paid monthly or quarterly, or it may be capitalized no more frequently than quarterly. Capitalized interest is not counted as exceeding the annual loan limit.

Grace Period: There is no grace period on these loans.

Eligibility: Borrower does not have an adverse credit history. (Note that Graduate and Professional Student Federal PLUS loans do not use any kind of a debt-to-income ratio or FICO score, unlike private education loans.)

Consolidation: Borrowers will be able to consolidate the Graduate and Professional Student Federal PLUS Loan with other loans they take, including Federal Stafford and Perkins Loans, and also Parent Federal PLUS Loans borrowed to pay for their children's education.

School as Lender: Although schools administer the program, they may not originate Federal PLUS and Consolidation Loans. Such schools will have to refer the graduate and professional students to other lenders for this loan, just as they have to refer undergraduate students to other lenders for the Federal Stafford loans.

Fellowships and assistantships are forms of financial aid for graduate students that do not need to be repaid. Typically, these include a full or partial tuition waiver and a small stipend for living expenses. Assistantships require that the graduate student perform teaching or research duties. The living expense stipend is typically taxable. The tuition waiver may or may not be taxable, depending on whether the graduate student is a degree candidate and whether the tuition waiver portion of the award represents a fee for services. (See IRS Publication 970 at www.irs.gov/pub/irs-pdf/p970.pdf for details.) Assistantships are largely offered by academic departments within colleges and universities, so in addition to working with your graduate school's office of financial aid, talk to the department where your study will take place. Fellowships may be offered by academic institutions, corporations, government agencies (e.g., National Science Foundation, NIH, U.S. Department of Energy, U.S. Department of Education) and foundations (e.g., Hertz Foundation, Ford Foundation, Guggenheim Foundation, Spencer Foundation, Sloan Foundation).

Graduate student awards are generally called fellowships, not scholarships. You can think of a fellowship as a scholarship for graduate students.

International fellowships include some of the best known and most prestigious awards in education. They are highly competitive and often the course of study less structured than typical graduate school curricula. Here are some of the top awards:

Gates Cambridge Scholarship (www.gates.scholarships.cam.ac.uk) Funded by The Bill and Melinda Gates Foundation, recipients of this award must be graduate students from outside the United Kingdom who are accepted to study at the University of Cambridge. Winners are worldwide; in 2005 they represented thirty-five countries. The award covers full tuition for 230 students at any one time, with 100 new students selected annually.

Fulbright Program (www.fulbrightonline.org) The famous Fulbright is an exchange program designed, in the words of its sponsor the U.S. Department of State, to "increase mutual understanding between the people of the United States and the people of other countries. . . ." Fulbright Scholars receive funding for independently designed, yearlong projects. It awards approximately 6,000 new grants every year.

German Academic Exchange Service (DAAD) Scholarship (www.daad.org) Institutions of higher education in Germany support this award for undergraduate students, graduate students and faculty members to study at universities in Germany. DAAD programs range from summer studies to research internships. It's a large and diverse program, with over 50,000 students and researchers receiving funding each year. The DAAD works with partner universities in the U.S. (a list of partner universities is available on the web site).

Marshall Scholarship (www.marshallscholarship.org) A British-sponsored program named for Secretary of State William Marshall, this scholarship funds students to study for graduate degrees at United Kingdom colleges in any field of study for two years. Applications are made at British Consulates in eight U.S. regions.

Rhodes Scholarship (www.rhodesscholar.org) The U.S. sends two candidates from each of sixteen regional districts to study at the University of Oxford in England. Scholars receive two years of funding and may be eligible for a third. Students are not restricted to a single course of study; the scholarships "seek excellence in qualities of mind and in qualities of person which, in combination, offer the promise of effective service to the world in the decades ahead."

Watson Fellowship (www.watsonfellowship.org) This is definitely a "moving on" award—you must leave the U.S. for one year. Founded by the family of the founder of IBM, the grant is for independent study (that is, you must design your own project) and travel outside the U.S. You must be a senior graduating from one of forty-eight participating colleges (listed on the web site).

Research grants can be a substantial source of money for graduate study, especially advanced work. Most are more like some of the fellowships just mentioned because they are won by spelling out a specific course of study and research. There are some research grants awarded by specific institutions that are searchable online, just like scholarships.

In the short term, research grants (even small ones) help you build a reputation as a committed scholar and forge the connections you'll need to generate more opportunities once you complete your degree. Working in the field at research sites or institutions provides a great opportunity to meet other experts in your field.

Graduate research grants are awarded by governments, universities and private organizations. One of the largest sources of grants, for example, is the

National Science Foundation (www.nsf.gov), which awards graduate-level grants every year in subjects ranging from astronomy to writing (on scientific subjects).

Research grants can be awarded with specific restrictions on how the money is to be spent, so be sure to clarify any questions about expenditures upfront with the granting institution.

Afterword

Our fictional narrative ends with the best outcome: Matt Gordon has a choice of schools to attend, and financial considerations won't force the decision upon him. We hope *College Gold* helps you to have the same kind of freedom.

Learning to pay for college can either be a frustrating puzzle or an exciting project. If you can make it the latter, the payoff will go far beyond just money. You'll practice work habits that will help carry you through college and beyond. If at all possible, parents and students should mark this transition to adulthood by working together.

Don't leave paying for college to chance, or put it off until the last possible moment. If after reading this book you are still unclear about anything concerning your college financing plan, we hope you'll remember to enlist the help of your guidance counselor or financial aid administrator. They are the heroes and heroines of this large and complicated undertaking. Also remember that updates and much more advice are available at three web sites: www.collegegold.com, www.fastweb.com and www.finaid.org.

Although the project can seem daunting at times, we at FastWeb and FinAid have seen a vast number of students—literally tens of millions—take it on and succeed. We wish you the best of luck and the best of skill as you move on to your college, graduate and/or professional education.

—Mark Kantrowitz and Doug Hardy

Appendix—Saving for College

It is less expensive to save for college than to borrow. Either way, you're setting aside a portion of your income to pay for college. But when you save, the money earns interest, while when you borrow, you're paying the interest. Even if the child has already matriculated, the tax benefits of certain savings plans can save you money and cut down your borrowing.

Paying for college before your child matriculates definitely costs much less than paying for college afterward. The math is compelling: Investing $200 a month for ten years at a 10% return would yield $41,310. Borrowing the same amount at 8.5% interest with a ten-year term would require payments of $512 a month, which is 2.6 times as much. Even if your return on investment were a modest 4%, you'd accumulate $29,548 in ten years. Borrowing this amount at 8.5% interest requires monthly payments of $366; you'd spend 83% more!

Moreover, the sooner you start saving for younger children, the less you'll have to borrow when they reach college age.

College Gold was written primarily for high school-level students and their families, who face imminent college costs, and focuses on financial aid. Families who have saved money for college for many years, however, have greater assets and less need for financial aid (although much of *College Gold* advice is beneficial to them as well).

We could write an entire book about saving for college; this brief introduction is an overview of the most important facts and strategies to help you **start now.**

BOOK TO WEB

You'll find a number of interactive savings calculators
and planning tools at www.collegegold.com.

CODE: 1032

BIG GOALS, SMALL STEPS

The more you can save, the better off you'll be. Saving just $25 a week from birth to age seventeen at a simple 5% interest will yield $34,839, a nice college fund.

Table A below shows the results of saving different amounts per week at different interest rates and various numbers of years to enrollment. The first three columns correspond to a family that begins saving when the child enters high school. The last three columns correspond to a family that begins saving when their baby is born.

Table A: Growth of Weekly Savings					
Weekly Amount	0% 4 years	5% 4 years	10% 4 years	0% 17 years	5% 17 years	10% 17 years
$10	$2,080	$2,304	$2,559	$8,840	$13,936	$23,263
$25	$5,200	$5,759	$6,399	$22,100	$34,839	$58,157
$50	$10,400	$11,518	$12,797	$44,200	$69,679	$116,314
$100	$20,800	$23,036	$25,594	$88,400	$139,358	$232,627

Table B shows how much you'd need to save per week in order to reach various savings goals at 8% interest at different numbers of years to enrollment.

Table B: Weekly Savings Required to Reach Savings Goal					
Goal	1 year	4 years	8 years	12 years	17 years
$5,000	$92.29	$20.38	$8.58	$4.77	$2.66
$10,000	$184.58	$40.76	$17.16	$9.54	$5.32
$25,000	$461.45	$101.92	$42.88	$23.86	$13.28
$50,000	$922.90	$203.84	$85.76	$47.72	$26.56
$100,000	$1,845.82	$407.68	$171.53	$95.42	$53.11
$250,000	$4,614.54	$1,019.20	$428.81	$238.56	$132.78

Table C shows how much of your savings goal comes from interest compounding given various interest rates and different numbers of years to enrollment.

Table C: Percentage of Savings Goal from Compound Interest					
Interest Rate	1 year	4 years	8 years	12 years	17 years
5.0%	2.5%	9.7%	18.7%	27.0%	36.6%
7.5%	3.8%	14.3%	27.1%	36.4%	50.6%
10.0%	5.0%	18.7%	34.8%	48.3%	62.0%

MAKE IT EASIER TO SAVE

The following savings strategies make it easier to save. Even if you use just a few of them, you'll find that savings habits have a cumulative effect—the more you save, the less difficult it seems.

1. **Save early and often.** Start saving the day the baby is born, if not earlier, and save as often as you can. The sooner you start, the more you can take advantage of compounding to watch your savings grow. It will also help you get into the habit of saving. The longer you save, the more you can take advantage of higher-return/higher-risk investments.

2. **Save as much as you can.** If you don't think you can afford to save, start small. You will find that you will adjust your spending habits, and

can gradually increase the amount you save. Don't worry too much about starting small, since the compounding of interest over time will help your savings grow. The first step is to get into the habit of saving.

3. **Save regularly.** Rather than save money at random intervals, try to save a little every month. The more frequently you can save, the better, but at the very least save once a year. If you can save with the same frequency as you receive your paycheck, you will find it easier to get into the habit of saving.

4. **Make saving automatic.** Sign up for payroll deduction or ask your bank to automatically move money from your checking account to your savings account every month. Many state section 529 college savings plans and prepaid tuition plans have options where you can have money transferred from your checking account every month. If the money isn't in your checking account, you'll be much less likely to spend it.

5. **Earmark savings for college.** Use a special account designated for college (but in the parents' name, not the child's). This will help you save, because it will motivate you to save.

6. **Take advantage of "save as you spend" plans.** Services such as Upromise (www.upromise.com) credit a small percentage of spending to college savings accounts. Similar plans are available from investment firms that contribute to Section 529 plans through credit card purchases (e.g., 2% of every purchase goes into a 529 plan, up to a yearly limit). On a dollar basis, you're likely to get more value out of these cards than from a typical frequent-flyer mileage plan, for example.

7. **Establish a goal.** Decide how much you need to save by the time the child will reach college age. If you specify a goal, you'll be able to measure your progress toward that goal. Use the calculators at www.collegegold.com. We recommend using the full cost of four years of college the year the student was born as your savings goal. This works out to be about one-third of anticipated college costs.

8. **Invest windfalls, don't spend them.** If you should get a windfall, such as an inheritance, winning the lottery, a large income tax refund or a bonus at work, put it in the college savings fund. It is better to save than to spend.

9. **Increase the amount you save each year.** Increase the total amount you save each year by at least 5%. So if you save $100 a month this

year, you should save at least $105 a month next year. When you get a raise, increase the amount of money you save.

10. **Ask relatives to help.** Set up a section 529 plan, and ask relatives (especially the grandparents) to contribute money to the plan. Sixty percent of grandparents say that they would contribute to a section 529 plan if asked, especially since they know the money will be spent on the child's education.

11. **Redirect old regular payments toward the savings goal.** Whenever you have a regular payment that stops, try shifting the money you were previously paying into college savings. Since you were already used to spending that amount, saving it should be relatively painless. For example, when your children enter kindergarten, redirect the money you were previously spending on day care and diapers to college savings.

12. **Review your living expenses.** Create a monthly budget that reflects your actual spending habits, and try to identify living expenses you can cut. Any time you cut your expenses, redirect the money toward savings. For example, if you turn down your thermostat to save on heating costs, put the money you save in the college savings fund.

13. **Use it as an opportunity to teach your children.** Involve your children in the investment decisions. For example, you could allow them to manage a small portion of the investment portfolio and track its growth. Some parents will even set up a "matching" plan, where money the child saves for their education is matched by additional money from the parent. Delayed gratification is a hard concept for younger children (and even some adults) to appreciate, so encouraging it early will help establish good habits. You will also find that acting as a role model for your children will make it easier for you to save as well.

14. **Get the rest of your finances in shape.** Pay off your credit cards (and get rid of them if you'll be tempted to run up the balances again) and maintain a cash reserve equal to six months' salary as a cushion against job loss. Be sure to save for your retirement as well, maxing out the employer's matching contribution.

MYTHS ABOUT SAVINGS

There are myths and misunderstandings about the impact of savings on the actual cost of college, so before you think, "Yeah, savings are good, *but* . . ." let's see the role clearly in this brief review:

Because a portion of a family's assets (including savings) is counted in determinations of financial need, many families mistakenly believe that they are penalized for saving. However, the federal government does not count all of the assets, just a fraction. The bottom line is the more money you save, the more options you'll have and the less you'll need to borrow.

Many parents mistakenly believe that if they don't save for college, they'll be able to shift the costs to their children through loans, or that the federal government and the schools will pick up the tab. Student loans only go so far in covering college costs, and the government and schools consider parents to have the primary responsibility in paying for their children's education. Furthermore, children have to begin paying most loans soon after graduation, when their incomes are generally lower.

Some count on their IRA or 401(k) plan to fund their children's college. We do not recommend taking an early distribution from a retirement plan. Between the taxes, penalties and the negative impact on financial aid, such a move offers only short-term relief while hurting the parents' retirement savings. Even borrowing from a retirement fund is not a good option. What are you going to live on when you retire?

Some families notice that credit card debt isn't considered by the federal need analysis formula, while savings, as an asset, is counted. They accumulate debt in lieu of savings, thinking they will get more financial aid. This strategy tends to backfire for three reasons: First, the financial aid you acquire in this way will still be loans, so you're doubling up on your debt. Second, credit card debt tends to be high—you're paying about 18% on that debt. By paying off the credit card debt and saving, you're realizing a tax-free difference in money of up to 14% to your advantage on the interest you're no longer paying to the credit card issuer. Third, by paying off credit card debt with savings, you are actually reducing the amount of assets counted when the time comes to calculate your EFC.

SECTION 529 SAVINGS PLANS

We like Section 529 College Savings Plans, which are among the most tax-advantaged savings vehicles available. They offer substantial federal income tax benefits, as well as gift and estate tax advantages. They are sponsored by states, and there are some differences among the states in the plans' fees and state tax treatments. (In most cases, you do not need to be a resident of a state to take advantage of its Section 529 College Savings Plan.) If your state allows you to deduct contributions on your state income tax return, use your state's section 529 college savings plan. Otherwise, focus on the state plans with the lowest fees. Some of the section 529 college savings plans have very high sales charges—as much as 5% or 6%—and expenses, while others may be very low.

Section 529 college savings plans are similar in many ways to retirement plans, such as 401(k) and IRAs, although with much higher contribution limits and more favorable tax status. The money in the plan is controlled by the account owner, not the child. So if the child decides to not go to college, they do not have access to the funds as they would with a typical trust. The money in a section 529 college savings plan is treated as a parent asset by the need analysis formulas, so they have a minimal impact on financial aid eligibility.

Contributions to Section 529 College Savings Plans may be made by anyone, subject to standard gift limitations ($12,000 for an individual donor; $24,000 for married donors making a joint gift). The five-year gift tax averaging option lets you use your gift tax exclusion for the next five years to give up to $60,000 per donor and $120,000 per couple now.

They allow your money to grow in a tax-deferred fashion, and qualified withdrawals are exempt from federal income tax. Many states also exempt section 529 plans from state income tax, and may even give you a tax deduction for your contributions.

Many state section 529 college savings plans offer age-based asset allocation portfolios (similar to those described in investing, below). Such portfolios base their asset allocation according to either the age of the child or the number of years until matriculation, gradually shifting the funds from more aggressive to more conservative investments. They tend to divide the ages into four to seven age ranges. Some plans offer both a regular age-based portfolio and a conservative age-based portfolio, where the conservative portfolio starts off with moderate risk investments instead of more aggressive investments.

If you are nervous about investing in stocks and bonds, and just want to preserve the principal while earning a modest amount of income, you should seriously consider using a section 529 college savings plan or a section 529 prepaid tuition plan. Most section 529 college savings plans offer a money market fund or a protected principal fund, and some even have a guaranteed option which protects the principal and guarantees a minimum rate of return (typically at least 3%).

Contributions to a 529 plan not only earn money on a tax-deferred basis (like a 401(k) or IRA retirement plan), but under current law distribution are also tax exempt when used to pay for qualified higher education expenses. (See chapter 15 for more on education tax benefits.)

Every parent should consider investing in a 529 college savings plan for their children.

INVESTING

Simple savings accounts, delivering about 4% interest as of this writing, have not kept pace with college cost-of-attendance inflation, and so families with a few years to save might wish to invest a portion of their college savings in a more aggressive way. Here are general guidelines for investing with a goal of having more money saved when the time comes to pay for college:[84]

1. **Begin with an aggressive strategy, and switch to a more conservative strategy when college comes closer.** Choose your investments according to the number of years until enrollment and your tolerance for risk. For example, you might start with high yield high risk investments when the child is young, and gradually shift the college savings to lower risk investments as college approaches.

2. **Be aware of the risk associated with your investments.**
    *   Higher risk investments include individual stocks and mutual funds. (We recommend avoiding extremely high risk investments, such as stock options, hedge funds, futures and other derivatives, unless you are an extremely experienced investor and are familiar with all the risks of such investments.)
    *   Lower risk investments include bonds and bond mutual funds, state prepaid tuition plans, short-term U.S. Treasury Zero Coupon Bonds (such as U.S. Treasury STRIPS), U.S. Series EE Savings

For long-term savers, here is a model of changing risk strategy over an eighteen-year period:

- When the baby is born, put 75% of the money in high-risk investments and 25% in low-risk investments. (Age 1–5)
- When the child enters the first grade, put 50% of the money in high-risk investments and 50% in low-risk investments. (Age 6–10)
- When the child starts the seventh grade, put 25% of the money in high-risk investments and 75% in low-risk investments. (Age 11–15)
- When the child reaches the middle of the junior year in high school, put almost all of the money in low-risk investments. It is important to realize any capital gains by December 31 of the junior year in order to not have them count as income during the financial aid need analysis. (Age 15–18)

Bonds, Treasury Inflation-Indexed Securities and FDIC insured savings accounts and certificates of deposit.

3. **Evaluate investment vehicles carefully before investing.** Carefully evaluate all the various investment vehicles before deciding where to invest. For example, you might be told to invest in tax-free municipal bonds in order to minimize the tax bite. But you might be able to find a mutual fund that isn't tax-exempt but which has a higher yield after taxes. Although life insurance and annuity products are sheltered from financial aid need analysis, using them as an investment vehicle is not your best option, since the rate of return, after subtracting fees, commissions and other loads is often very low. Always compare investments based on the net return after all expenses including taxes are subtracted, and consider the impact on need-based financial aid. It pays to shop around.

4. **Reevaluate your investments at least once a year.** If you find that the assumptions behind your investment strategy are not correct or your risk tolerance has changed, you may want to change your investment allocations.

5. **Diversify your investments.** You may want to invest in a mix of stocks and bonds, so that your money isn't all in stocks, and keep some portion of the money in a money market account or savings account. If

you invest some portion of college savings in stocks, for example, we believe it is better to invest in mutual funds, since mutual funds spread out the risk over many different individual investments. You should choose approximately four to six different types of investments in order to minimize your downside risk. (This is a strategy called *asset allocation*, and you can learn more about it at financial advice resources such as Kiplinger's, *Money Magazine*, Morningstar, *Smart Money*, Bloomberg, or the Motley Fool.)

6. **Invest regularly.** Investing a fixed amount of money at regular intervals (e.g., once a week, once a month) gets you the benefit of *dollar cost averaging*, a good investment technique. It also gets you in the habit of planning for your future. If possible, have it done automatically through payroll deduction or bank drafting (EFT), so that the money is taken out of your bank account before you have a chance to spend it.

7. **Save in the parent's name, not the child's name.** This will minimize the impact of the fund on need-based financial aid. See chapter 14 for more details about saving in the child's name vs. the parent's name.

8. **Save in tax-advantaged savings vehicles.** Too many parents use taxable savings accounts and CDs as their primary college savings vehicle, letting taxes diminish the return on investment. Section 529 plans offer many tax advantages (see below). Don't plan on tapping into your IRA to pay for college expenses. Although you can do so without paying a 10% penalty if the money is used for qualified tuition expenses, you will still be paying income tax on the withdrawal, and the inclusion in income will affect next year's financial aid eligibility. Using your IRA will also limit your ability to take advantage of the tax credits for education (Hope Scholarship and Lifetime Learning) and the education tax deductions.

9. **Avoid capital gains starting at least one calendar year before enrolling in college.** When college is two years away, move most of the money into safe investments, such as FDIC insured certificates of deposit or a money market fund. You need to realize the capital gains early enough so that they don't affect eligibility for financial aid. (If you did realize significant capital gains the tax year before applying for financial aid, ask the college's financial aid administrator for a "profes-

sional judgment" review, on the grounds that the one-time capital gains is not reflective of award year income and that the formula is effectively double-counting them.) You also don't want to be forced to sell stocks at a loss in order to pay tuition, so sell them sooner, rather than waiting until the last minute. When putting money in CDs, time the maturity dates to occur when you'll need the money to pay bills, such as the beginning of the semester, so that you won't have to pay an interest penalty for early withdrawal.

FINANCIAL AID IMPACT OF SAVINGS VEHICLES

The following table lists the current financial aid treatment of the most common savings vehicles. For the purpose of assessing the impact on financial aid eligibility, we assume that the beneficiary is the child and the account owner is the par-

Savings Vehicle	Financial Aid Treatment	Comments
Coverdell Education Savings Account (formerly Education IRA)	asset of account owner (high impact if student owner; low impact if parent owner)	You may contribute up to $2,000 per year to a Coverdell account, and they may be owned by the student or the student's parent. If the child is the account owner, it counts as a child asset. If a parent is the account owner, it counts as a parent asset. In most cases the child is the account owner. Distributions do not affect eligibility (i.e., distributions do not count as income or a resource).
Section 529 College Savings Plan	asset of account owner (low impact)	Distributions do not affect eligibility (i.e., distributions do not count as income or a resource). Note that nonqualified distributions (i.e., distributions that are subject to federal income tax) do count as income to the distributee. Starting on July 1, 2006, custodial 529 college savings plans will be treated as a parent asset if the account owner is a dependent student.

continued

Savings Vehicle	Financial Aid Treatment	Comments
Section 529 Prepaid Tuition Plan	asset of account owner (low impact)	Starting on July 1, 2006, all prepaid tuition plans are treated as assets. Custodial versions are treated as parent assets, even if the account owner is a dependent student. (Previously, prepaid tuition plans were treated as resources, which reduced financial aid eligibility dollar for dollar.) Noncustodial versions are also treated as parent assets.
UGMA/UTMA Custodial Account	asset of beneficiary (high impact)	The income from a custodial account must be reported on the child's tax return and is taxed at the child's rate, which is usually higher. Neither the donor nor the custodian can place any restrictions on the use of the money when the minor becomes an adult. At that time the child can use the money for any purpose whatsoever without requiring permission of the custodian, so there's no guarantee that the child will use the money for his or her education. Also, since UGMA and UTMA accounts are in the name of a single child, the funds are not transferable to another beneficiary (as 529 plans are)
For financial aid purposes, custodial accounts are considered assets of the student. This means there is a high impact on financial aid eligibility.
Effective July 1, 2006, the custodial versions of 529 college savings plans, prepaid tuition plans and Coverdell Education Savings Accounts are treated as the asset of the parent for federal student aid purposes when the student is a dependent student. So if you roll over a custodial account into one of these three types of accounts you will shift its financial aid treatment from a student asset to a parent asset.

Savings Vehicle	Financial Aid Treatment	Comments
Series I and EE Savings Bonds	asset of registered owner (low impact)	A savings bond registered in the parent's name counts as a parent asset (low impact). A bond registered in the child's name as a single or co-owner counts as a child asset (high impact). If the bond was registered in the child's name, but parent's (owner's) funds were used to purchase the bond, the parent may change the beneficiary.
Regular Taxable Investments	asset of account owner (low impact if owned by parent, high impact if owned by student)	[none]
Variable Life Insurance	not reported on FAFSA (low impact)	Generally, the cash value of life insurance and assets in retirement plans are not reported on the FAFSA.
Traditional IRA	asset value not reported on FAFSA (low impact)	Withdrawal will count as taxable income, affecting next year's financial aid. Current year taxpayer contributions to IRAs, SEP, SIMPLE, Keogh, 401(k), 403(b) and other retirement plans are reported as untaxed income on the FAFSA.
Roth IRA	asset value not reported on FAFSA (low impact)	If Roth IRA owner hasn't been invested for five years, withdrawal will count as taxable income, affecting next year's financial aid.
401(k)	asset value not reported on FAFSA (low impact)	Withdrawal counts as taxable income, affecting next year's financial aid. If you borrow from the 401(k) instead of withdrawing funds, amount received does not count as income.
2503(c) Minor's Trust	asset of beneficiary (high impact)	If trust restrictions prevent liquidation, trust will continue as an asset in subsequent years, continuing to hurt need-based financial aid eligibility.

continued

Savings Vehicle	Financial Aid Treatment	Comments
Other Trust Funds	asset of beneficiary (high impact)	Generally speaking, voluntary restrictions on uses of the trust will backfire, hurting financial aid eligibility. Only court-ordered involuntary trusts, such as those established to pay future medical expenses, are omitted from the FAFSA. All other trusts will generally count as an asset of the beneficiary. If the trust assigns ownership of the income to one party and the principal to another, you may need to do a net present value calculation to determine the value of the asset. If ownership of the trust is contested and the trust is frozen, it is not reported on the FAFSA.

ent (except where specified otherwise). Generally speaking, if the account owner has the ability to change the beneficiary at any time, the savings are treated as an asset of the account owner, not the beneficiary. Note that Congress may decide in the future to change the treatment of assets in the federal need analysis methodology to stop distinguishing between student and parent assets, replacing it with a uniform treatment of family assets.

PREPAID TUITION PLANS

Prepaid tuition plans are college savings plans that are guaranteed to increase in value at the same rate as college tuition. For example, if a family purchases shares worth half a year's tuition at a state college, these shares will always be worth half a year's tuition—even ten years later, when tuition rates may have doubled.

The main benefit of these plans is that they allow a student's parents to lock in tuition at current rates, offering peace of mind. The plans' simplicity is also attractive and most offer a better rate of return on an investment than bank savings accounts and certificates of deposit. The plans also involve no risk to principal, and often are guaranteed by the full faith and credit of the state. Since public college tuition tends to increase faster when the stock market is not performing well, a prepaid tuition plan can be a useful hedge against market downturns, which can decrease the value of invested savings.

Until recently, prepaid tuition plans were counted as a resource by the need analysis methodology, which caused a high impact on financial aid eligibility. Starting July 1, 2006, prepaid tuition plans are treated as assets on the FAFSA,[85] receiving the same favorable treatment as Section 529 College Savings Plans.

Section 529 prepaid tuition plans allow you to lock in future tuition rates at in-state public colleges at today's prices, and are often guaranteed by the full faith and credit of the state.

Prepaid tuition plans are exempt from federal income tax, and are often exempt from state and local income taxes. Favorable state tax status may be limited to the state's own plan. Some states offer a full or partial tax deduction for contributions to the state's plan. Most plans require that either the account owner or the beneficiary be a state resident when the account is opened.

Anybody can contribute to a prepaid tuition plan, including grandparents and friends of the family. The money in the plan is controlled by the account owner, not the child. If the child dies or decides to not go to college, the plans can be transferred to another member of the family.

Before investing in a prepaid tuition plan, parents should carefully evaluate the plan and their other investment options. From an investment perspective, a prepaid tuition plan is a low-risk, tax-advantage investment vehicle, with earnings indexed to the average increase in tuition.

SAVINGS PUT SIMPLY

Finally, here are five good rules of thumb for deciding how much to save:

- A good rule of thumb is the **one-third rule.** This rule states that you should expect to save one-third of the expected college costs, pay one-third from current income and financial aid during the college years and borrow one-third using a combination of parent and student loans. In effect, this spreads college costs across your past, present and future income.

- Try to save at least 10% of your paycheck (per child), starting the day the child is born. (If you wait until the child enters first grade, you will need to save 18% of your salary per child). This figure assumes a median household income.
- Try to save 10% to 15% of each year's college costs (per child), starting the day your child is born.
- Try to save at least $2,500 per child per year from birth. That's about $50 a week or about $210 a month.
- Base your savings goal on paying full freight at a public college in your state. This should be a little less than half the cost of an expensive private college, offering you a more reasonable goal. This is a good proxy for what your net costs after financial aid will be at a more expensive college.
- Set a savings goal of the cost of four years of college the year your child was born. Since college costs increase by a factor of 3-4 over any seventeen-year period, this meshes well with the one-third rule.

Saving now for college is not only cheaper than borrowing later; it's a lot easier on your peace of mind. As you see your savings grow over months and years, you'll know that college will be much easier to afford and your child will have more flexibility in his or her choice of a college. If you can do a little less spending now, and a little more saving, the payoff will be more than worth the effort. So once again—get started (and good luck)!

Acknowledgments

The authors would like to thank all their colleagues at FastWeb who contributed their time and expertise to *College Gold*. Baird Johnson and Stacey Dolnick have given tireless attention to the project from the beginning. Special thanks also to Stephen Borkowski, Jean Danielson, Clay Johnson, and Joshua Kell. Rich Coleman, a student, and Karen DeGrout Carter, a parent, added their comments to the manuscript as well.

Donna Gullmette Brown, Alan Hoffman and Marcel Legrand, as well as Chris Michael (founder and president of Military.com), also gave early help and support for the project. Thanks, as always, to our agent, Peter Ginsberg of Curtis Brown, Ltd., for his advice, support and counsel.

Special thanks to David Levy, Assistant Dean and Director of Financial Aid at the California Institute of Technology, who reviewed the manuscript. David is a member of the FastWeb Advisory Board, and all other members provided expertise, advice and anecdotes. Many are quoted in this book. They are: William Elliott, Vice President for Enrollment Management, Carnegie Mellon University; Scott Friedhoff, Vice President for Enrollment Management at Allegheny College; Barbara Fritze, Vice President for Enrollment and Educational Services, Gettysburg College; Michael Holland, Vice President, Administrative and Student Affairs, Linn-Benton Community College; Lori Johnston, Counselor, Hastings (MI) High School; Patricia Ross, Vice President, Coca-Cola Scholars

Foundation, Inc.; James Sumner, Dean of Admission and Financial Aid, Grinnell College; Cathy Thomas, Associate Dean of Enrollment Services, University of Southern California; Linda Zimring, Director, College & Gifted/Talented Programs, Los Angeles Unified School District, District C.

College financial aid administrators, high school guidance counselors, scholarship sponsors and other education professionals all played a role in the development of *College Gold*, and we're grateful for their contributions. They are: Daniel Barkowitz, Director, Financial Aid, MIT; Carla Bender, Associate Director of Financial Aid, Hope College; Michael J. Bennett, Director of Financial Aid, Brookdale Community College; Kevin Byrne, Director of Scholarships, Michael and Susan Dell Foundation; Louis Fraulo, Supervisor of Counseling and Guidance Services at Clifton (NJ) High School; Ellen Frishberg, Director of Student Financial Services and the University Financial Aid Officer, Johns Hopkins University; David Gelinas, Director of Financial Aid, Sewanee: The University of the South; Perri Green, Contest Coordinator, American Foreign Service Association; Tom Holcombe, Holland & Knight Charitable Foundation; Jeff Hollingsworth, Assistant Secretary of the Phillips Foundation; Melissa Ibanez, Director of Financial Aid, University of Pittsburgh, Bradford Campus; Debbie Kahler, Programs Manager, Elks National Foundation; Leo Kornfeld, President of Kornfeld and Associates; Brian Lindeman, Director of Financial Aid, Macalester College; Liz Kerr, Patrick Kerr Skateboard Scholarship; Tom Mortensen, Senior Scholar, Federal Pell Institute for the Study of Opportunity in Higher Education; Vincent Pecora, Director of Financial Aid, Towson University; Alison Rabil, Director, Office of Financial Aid, Barnard College; Joseph A. Russo, Director of Student Financial Strategies, University of Notre Dame; Anne Sandoval, Guidance Counselor, Detroit Country Day School; Bob Shorb, Director of Student Aid and Family Finance, Skidmore College; Cathy Simoneaux, Director of the Office of Scholarships and Financial Aid, Loyola University New Orleans; Wells Singleton, Nova Southeastern University; Frank Valines, Senior Associate Director, Office of Student Financial Aid, University of Maryland; and Steve van Buskirk, Director of Programs, Veterans of Foreign Wars National Headquarters.

Many students also contributed to the book; a few wished to remain anonymous, and the others are quoted by name in the text. Thanks to them for setting a great example and sharing their well-earned experience with financial aid and scholarships.

About the Authors

Mark Kantrowitz is the Publisher of FinAid.org, the leading source for unbiased and clear financial aid information, the Director of Advanced Projects at Fast-Web, the most popular and complete scholarship resource available, and is the President of MK Consulting Inc.

As a recognized financial aid expert for more than two decades, Mark has been called to testify before Congress about financial aid on several occasions and is interviewed regularly by news outlets, including the *Wall Street Journal*, *New York Times*, MSN, CNN, NBC, ABC, CBS, *USA Today*, the Associated Press, Bloomberg, *Money* magazine, *SmartMoney*, *Kiplingers*, *US News & World Report* and *Newsweek*. Additionally he is consulted by financial aid administrators, professional associations, and federal agencies nationwide and is on the editorial board of Regulatory Advisor, a publication of the Council on Law in Higher Education.

Mark's work in financial aid has been recognized by many awards, including a Meritorious Achievement Award from the National Association of Student Financial Aid Administrators, a Special Award from the College Board, the President's Award from the National Association of Graduate and Professional Students and the Jefferson Medal from the American Institute for Public Service.

Mark is an ABD on a Ph.D. in computer science from Carnegie Mellon University (CMU), has a Masters degree in Computer Science from CMU and

Bachelor of Science degrees in mathematics and philosophy from the Massachusetts Institute of Technology (MIT) and is an alumnus of the Research Science Institute Program established by Admiral H. G. Rickover. He was able to pay for his undergraduate education through scholarships and summer employment and his graduate education entirely through scholarships and fellowships. Some of the major scholarships, fellowships and education awards Mark has been awarded include: National Science Foundation Graduate Fellowship, Hertz Foundation Research Fellowship Grant, MIT Karl Taylor Compton Prize, MIT William L. Stewart Jr. Award, Courant Institute Prize for Mathematical Talent, Westinghouse Science Talent Search, Massachusetts State Science Fair First Award (four-time winner), USA Mathematical Olympiad, Massachusetts State Math Olympiad, New England Math League and Continental Math League. Mark is a member of Phi Kappa Phi and Sigma Xi honor societies, and a national member of the Alpha Epsilon Lambda honor society of graduate and professional students. He is a cancer survivor, the author of three books and holds five patents, with several additional patents pending.

Doug Hardy is General Manager/Editor-in-Chief of Monstercareers.com, authoring three books with Monster founder Jeff Taylor (*Monster Careers; Monster Careers: Interviewing* and *Monster Careers: Networking*). He manages the marketing of books through Monster. He also creates and presents multiday workshops based on the Monster Careers job search program to students, job seekers and others. Doug has worked as an editor, writer and editorial manager for more than twenty-five years at major media companies, including Random House, The New York Times Magazine Company, and AT&T New Media. He has built and managed large content organizations in book, magazine and Web publishing. Doug was VP Product/Editor-in-Chief of Monster.com from 1999 to 2002, prior to starting Monster's book program.

Notes

1. www.census.gov/apsd/www/statbrief/sb94_17.pdf
2. The characters described in this book are fictional. Any resemblance to any person, living or dead, is purely coincidental.
3. There are proposals to rename this the Student Aid Index (SAI), but a name change will not affect the role it plays in student aid.
4. Its formal name is "Federal Need Analysis Methodology."
5. Trends in Student Aid 2005, College Board.
6. For undergraduate students, these include Federal Pell Grants, Federal Supplemental Educational Opportunity Grant, Federal Work-Study, Federal Perkins Loan, Federal Stafford Loan, Federal PLUS Loan, Direct Loan, Direct PLUS Loan and SSIG. There are also graduate student awards, like Byrd, Javits, NSF, NDSEG, GANN, etc.—it's a long list.
7. The College Board lists 588 participating colleges and scholarship programs as of April 2006.
8. The prior year's contributions, however, are counted as untaxed income.
9. The rationale for front-loading is that some students matriculate in college only to discover that it isn't the right path for them. If they drop out, they'll be burdened with less debt and less likely to default on that debt. (Dropping out is a high probability predictor of default on student loans.) Unfortunately, it does feel a little like "bait and switch," since most families consider the award letter when choosing which college to attend, and a college that practices front-loading of grants will seem to provide a more generous aid package.
10. Early Decision = commitment to attend. Early Action = no commitment to attend.

Early Admission = collective term for Early Decision and Early Action, where the student is admitted early.

11. Consider adding the e-mail address cpsnotify@cpsemail.ed.gov to your e-mail program's white list to avoid having your SAR blocked or sent to a junk mail folder.

12. If you listed the school on your FAFSA (see chapter 5), it will automatically get a copy of your SAR. But it doesn't hurt to check that they have it. If you want to send it to more than six schools, wait until you receive your SAR, and then go online at www.fafsa.ed.gov to replace the existing set of six schools with a new set of (up to) six schools.

13. The worksheet is based on broad historical trends. Tuition inflation and inflation rates for such expenses as transportation, books and living expenses vary year by year. Where the forward-looking data are in doubt, we've used conservative (e.g., higher) numbers.

14. Also keep in mind that not all colleges will be able to meet that need. In some cases your family may have to pay more than the EFC.

15. For students enrolled in a bachelor's degree program, the ratio of total aid (including loans) to the student budget was 57.7%. Overall value was 52.1%. If we look at just grants (not including work-study) as a percentage of the student budget, the figures are 31.5% for bachelor's degree candidates and 30.4% overall.

16. The Stafford and PLUS loans don't have any such credit restrictions, so if you already have a mortgage and other consumer debt close to the 37% figure, you'll still be able to add education loans. You just won't be able to get a home equity loan. Nevertheless, if your loan payments exceed this threshold, you should think carefully about how much you can afford in additional monthly loan payments.

17. "The Big Payoff: Educational Attainment and Synthetic Estimates of Work-Life Earnings," U.S. Census Bureau, July 2002. www.census.gov/prod/2002pubs/p23-210.pdf

18. *Ibid.* Measured in constant 1999 dollars.

19. The results can lead to negative feelings among families. In the 2006 *College Gold* survey, only 41% of respondents believed they had received their fair share of financial aid.

20. Although one must file a FAFSA to apply for the unsubsidized Stafford loan and the Graduate and Professional Student PLUS loan, a FAFSA is not required for parents of undergraduate students to obtain a PLUS loan.

21. This is encouraged but not required. We strongly recommend you get a PIN.

22. Quoting from section 479A(a) of the Higher Education Act of 1965: "Special circumstances may include tuition expenses at an elementary or secondary school, medical or dental expenses not covered by insurance, unusually high child care costs, recent unemployment of a family member, the number of parents enrolled at least half-time in a degree, certificate, or other program leading to a recognized educational credential at an institution with a program participation agreement under section 487, or other changes in a family's income, a family's assets, or a

student's status." They are not limited to these circumstances—these are just the ones explicitly mentioned in the law.

23. If you file your income tax returns on a fiscal year basis, as opposed to a calendar year basis, pick the fiscal year that overlaps the most with the prior calendar year. Even if your fiscal year ends before December 31, you still can't file the FAFSA before January 1.

24. The Asset Protection Allowance (APA) shelters parent assets up to a certain amount. The exact amount is determined by the age of the older parent and is sensitive to the current inflation rate. In practice, only about 10% of families of dependent students have any contribution from parent assets, given that the value of the primary residence and retirement savings are both sheltered, a portion of the rest is sheltered by the APA, and most lower income families have assets disregarded entirely.

25. Whether parents are counted as enrolled in college is a professional judgment item. The school will want to see documentation that the parent is genuinely seeking a degree. Many schools will reduce income by the amount the parents are spending for their own education, instead of increasing the number in college figure.

26. Effective July 1, 2006, plans owned by a dependent student are treated as though they were a parent asset for financial aid need analysis purposes.

27. Dependency status may be updated at any time if it changed for a reason other than a change in the applicant's marital status. Household size and number in college may be updated if they changed for a reason other than a change in the applicant's marital status, but only if the FAFSA is selected for verification. If so, the updated figures must be accurate as of the verification date. Most colleges will cooperate in selecting a student for verification if it increases their financial aid eligibility.

28. Like any government hotline, the accuracy of the information provided by 1-800-4-FED-AID depends on the experience and training of the staff answering the phones. If the person you speak with seems unsure of himself or herself, we suggest using a best 2-out-of-3 approach, calling again to see if the answer is consistent. Also, get the name of the person with whom you spoke. If a college financial aid administrator says that the information you were given is wrong, they will want to refer the person who provided the incorrect information for further training.

29. You may need to delete a few of your previously listed colleges before you can add new colleges. Don't worry about this, as they will have already received a copy of the school equivalent of your SAR.

30. 2003–04 National Postsecondary Student Aid Study (NPSAS:04).

31. Eligible statuses include: U.S. citizen or national, U.S. permanent resident, Citizens of the Freely Associated States, Federated States of Micronesia and the republics of Palau and the Marshall Islands, and certain other eligible non-citizens. Note that U.S. citizens include all fifty states, Puerto Rico, District of Columbia, U.S. Virgin Islands, Guam and Northern Mariana Islands. Natives of American

Samoa and Swain's Island are not U.S. citizens, but they are U.S. nationals and so are eligible.

32. See www.sss.gov. Men are required to register within thirty days of their eighteenth birthday. Male students who fail to register with Selective Service before turning age twenty-six are ineligible for federal student loan and grant programs, including Pell Grants, Federal Work-Study and Stafford Loans. (Parents who want to borrow a PLUS loan do not have to satisfy the registration requirement.) Several states have also made Selective Service registration a prerequisite for state financial aid and for matriculation at public colleges and universities.

33. 2003–04 National Postsecondary Student Aid Study (NPSAS:04).

34. Longer terms can be obtained by consolidating the loans. See below.

35. Only one parent needs to be denied PLUS, so long as neither parent has been approved for a PLUS loan, for the student to be eligible for increased Stafford loan limits. Since Stafford loans have a lower interest rate, many parents prefer for the student to have higher Stafford loan limits. Thus, parents who think they may be denied a PLUS loan should consider having just the parent with the adverse credit history apply for only one PLUS loan, in order to obtain a denial. The school will then use this denial to increase the student's Stafford loan limits.

36. You might also wish to consult the federal government's "Collections Guide to Student Loans" at www.ed.gov/offices/OSFAP/DCS/index.html.

37. The first $850 in income for children is tax free. The next $800 in income is taxed at the child's rate. If the child is under age fourteen, then all income above $1,700 is taxed at the parent's marginal rate. If the child is age eighteen or over, all income above $1,600 is taxed at the child's rate.

38. National Center for Education Statistics, *The Condition of Education 2003*, Indicator 42: Federal Grants and Loans: "During this same period [1999–2000], the percentage of undergraduates enrolled full-time for the full academic year who had federal student loans increased from 31% to 44% and the average amount they borrowed per year grew (in constant 1999 dollars) from $4,000 to $4,800 (see table 42-1). About 30% of undergraduates received federal grants in both 1992–93 and 1999–2000, but the average amount of these grants grew from $2,400 to $2,500. The average percentage of federal aid received as loans increased from 54% to 64%."

39. The LIBOR index is a one- or three-month average of the interest rates that large international banks charge each other to borrow money. It represents the bank's short-term cost to borrow capital. The LIBOR index tends to be slightly higher than the Federal Funds Rate or 91-day T-Bill rate. The Prime Lending Rate is the interest rate that lenders charge to their most creditworthy customers. The Prime Lending Rate tends to be about 2.8% higher than the LIBOR index. Prime + 0% may sound better than LIBOR + 2.8%, but the rates are similar. Moreover, the spread between the Prime Lending Rate and LIBOR has been growing, so a loan that is pegged to the LIBOR index will generally have a lower interest rate over time than one that is pegged to the Prime Lending Rate. Thus it is usually better for the borrower to have

a loan that is pegged to the LIBOR index than one that is pegged to the Prime Lending Rate.

40. Most lenders advertise only the rate they charge during the in-school period to customers who have excellent credit. The rates charged during repayment are 1% to 2% higher, and the rates charged for lower credit scores can be as much as 4% higher.

41. You can check your credit history at a government-sanctioned free web site that is a joint venture of the three major credit reporting bureaus (Equifax, Experian and Transunion). Go to www.annualcreditreport.com.

42. Per 34 CFR 682.201(b)(2) and HEA Section 428B(a)(1)(A), if a parent has an adverse credit history, they are not eligible for the PLUS loan. In such a circumstance the student will be eligible for increased Stafford loan limits. Note that an adverse credit history is not based on credit scores, but rather on bankruptcy or default on federal education debt.

43. For a subsidized Stafford loan, the federal government pays the interest on the loan while the student is in school and during the six-month grace period after the student graduates (or drops below half-time enrollment). For an unsubsidized Stafford loan, interest accrues while the student is in school. The student may either pay the interest as it accrues, or defer it by capitalizing it. Capitalizing interest adds it to the principal, increasing the size of the loan. Capitalized interest does not affect the loan limits.

44. Some lenders have introduced features that allow one to defer repayment on the PLUS loan while the student is in school. Note that if the parents are enrolled at least half time in college, the repayment of the PLUS loan is deferred, although interest continues to accrue.

45. Itemizing deductions may affect the ability to qualify for the simplified needs test or automatic zero EFC. On the other hand, since simplified needs requires an income of less than $50,000, those who take advantage of it are not likely to be itemizing, since the standard deduction is usually a better deal.

46. A student would have to borrow approximately $38,000 at 6.8% with a ten-year term in order to pay $2,500 in interest during the first year after entering repayment. The amount of interest paid drops with each successive year, the same as with any other amortized loan.

47. Society of Human Resources Management spokeswoman Jen Jorgensen, quoted in CareerJournal, August 31, 2005.

48. For secondary math/science teachers, and elementary/secondary special ed teachers, the amount increased from $5,000 to $17,500 on October 30, 2004. It remains at $5,000 for the others.

49. Note that the employee must provide the services exclusively to the high-risk children from low-income communities. In other words, an employee of such a facility who isn't dedicated full-time to providing such services doesn't qualify for loan forgiveness. See http://ifap.ed.gov/dpcletters/GEN0515.html.

50. *Perkins Repayment, Forbearance, Deferment and Cancellation* Department of Education; Federal Student Aid Handbook 2005–2006, vol. 6, p. 6–87.

51. But if no income tax return was filed, then these figures should be reported only in income earned from work and not in Worksheet B, since the federal processor uses income earned from work as a proxy for AGI when AGI is $0. Including it also in Worksheet B in such a situation would lead to double-counting. Tricky, eh?

52. SLRP is $65,000 for Army ($20,000 for reservists) or Navy, $10,000 for Air Force.

53. We'll use the general term Financial Aid Administrator in this chapter, although these college personnel occasionally have different titles, such as Financial Aid Advisor, Director of Financial Aid and Financial Aid Counselor.

54. Not her real name.

55. Some schools will award a set amount of grants first, then fill in with self-help, followed by any remaining need covered by additional grants.

56. I've often argued that colleges should focus more of their discretionary student aid budgets on low-income families (earning in the bottom quintile of family incomes), since the tradeoff between grants and loans has a bigger impact on success in college in that population than among middle-income students.

57. See their web site: www.nationalmerit.org/nmsp.php.

58. On the other hand, if you start your search early enough, you might be able to improve your grades enough so that you qualify. With scholarship databases like Fast-Web, it is sometimes helpful to run the search again with a slightly higher GPA or SAT/ACT score, to see what might be available if you improve your academic performance.

59. The FastWeb scholarship database is particularly thorough about listing small local awards, and encourages all scholarship sponsors to submit information. FastWeb can code those awards to show them only to students who qualify.

60. Just seeing yourself "um" and "ah" and ramble is one of the best ways to improve your interview presence.

61. Examples of financial aid seminars that provide free financial aid information and advice without a sales pitch for products or services include Monster.com's Making It Count and NASFAA's College Goal Sunday.

62. This assessment rate will be changing to 20% on July 1, 2007.

63. Remember that contributions in the prior year will be counted as untaxed income.

64. The age at which the trust ends and assets are transferred to the child. This is not necessarily the traditional age of majority (18–21 years of age).

65. If ownership of income and principal are split, one must generally perform a net present value calculation to determine the present value of the beneficiary's future proceeds from the trust.

66. 270 days for federal education loans.

67. Scholarship money is counted as part of your contribution to college, so if you don't use it for that, you'll have to find the same amount from somewhere else.

68. If the college uses the Institutional Methodology for awarding its own aid, there may be differences in the EFC from college to college. But generally the institutional EFC figures should be pretty close to one another.

69. The amount of the Pell Grant and subsidized Stafford loan will exhibit some sensitivity to college costs, especially at very low cost institutions. But generally they should be in the same ballpark.

70. This can occur because you submitted financial aid applications to one school later than the other, or because one school asks for information related to unusual circumstances on its institutional aid application and the other doesn't.

71. Colleges that practice gapping will often count the PLUS loan as part of the financial aid package, in part to mask the fact that there's a gap. Be sure to exclude the PLUS loan and unsubsidized Stafford loan when comparing financial aid packages.

72. One of the main reasons why students drop out of college is money. Be realistic in assessing whether the more expensive college is too much of a stretch. You will also perform better in college if you aren't constantly worrying about finances.

73. Students who graduate from undergraduate school with no debt are much more likely to go on to graduate or professional school than students who graduate with heavy debt loads. See www.press.jhu.edu/books/title_pages/3353.thml.

74. According to a 2006 Integrated Postsecondary Education Data System (IPEDS) report, 64% of students at private nonprofit colleges, 53% at public colleges and 25% at private for-profit colleges graduate in six years.

75. Note that education tax benefits were not considered in our net cost and out-of-pocket cost analysis of the financial aid award letters. Education tax benefits can help defray the difference in out-of-pocket costs, typically by about 20% of the difference.

76. Parking on college campuses can be extremely expensive, in part because many colleges use this and other methods to discourage students from bringing a car to school.

77. Or IRS Publication 970 (www.irs.gov/pub/irs-pdf/p970.pdf).

78. For example, if the student's parents are divorced and the student has been living with the mother, but the mother dies, normally the father would become responsible for completing the FAFSA. But if the student has not had any contact with or financial support from the father in many years, the school could perform a dependency override to make the student independent. Any financial support the student receives from his guardian or other relatives would then be reported on Worksheet B.

79. The actual adjustment will take into account the fact that the federal need analysis formula already includes an allowance for typical medical costs. The amount of the family's unreimbursed medical expenses will be reduced by this allowance, as well any amounts already subtracted from AGI (e.g., the self-employed health insurance

deduction) and any related tax credits (e.g., the Health Coverage Tax Credit), before family income is adjusted by the result.

80. During the acceptance period, many colleges keep a list of students who are not yet accepted, but might be admitted if accepted students decline to attend.

81. A recent trend is for students to maintain "portfolios" of the work they have performed during the school year. At some colleges, they maintain this in a password-protected web page that parents and other relatives can visit.

82. This will only combine the consolidated loans. If you still have unconsolidated loans, you still have multiple payments.

83. If you used up your three-year forbearance before consolidating, consolidating can get you a new three-year forbearance. Such tricks are mainly exploited by medical school students.

84. Disclaimer: Historical performance of any investment is no guarantee of future results. The tax code and investment market is complicated enough that we recommend professional help for all but the simplest investment vehicles. Our goal here is to show you a range of ways to invest for college; we don't endorse any individual investment strategy or investment company. If you are investing for the long term, it's wise to learn about investment markets and risk, and to enlist the services of a financial advisor such as a Certified Public Accountant or Certified Financial Planner. Before selecting a financial adviser, test their knowledge by asking them about the impact of college savings on eligibility for financial aid. But keep in mind that the 529 college savings plans with the highest sales charges and other fees were often the advisor-sold versions. An index fund, like a S&P 500 mutual fund, may offer a higher after-tax return on investment than some of the plans with the highest fees.

85. The asset value is defined as the refund value of the prepaid tuition plan.

Index

Index

Index

Index

interest on, 80, 81, 82–83, 84, 85, 87–88, 89, 95, 96, 101, 104, 105, 231–32, 254–56, 257, 263
  limits on, 83
  military repayment program for, 119–20
  parent, 80, 84–85
  repayment of, 85–89, 95, 97, 112, 113, 114, 243, 251, 253, 254–57, 263
  scams involving for, 198–99
  student, 80–83, 89, 204, 231–32
  subsidized vs. unsubsidized, 82
  see also specific loans
Graduate and Professional Student Federal PLUS Loans, 263
Graduated Repayment plan, 88
graduate students, 260–66
  fellowships and scholarships for, 264–65
  government loans for, 262–64
  research grants for, 265–66
grants, xii, 5, 6–7, 9, 10, 11, 18, 20, 33, 38, 59, 67, 69, 128, 131, 132, 133, 146–47, 191, 204, 218, 223, 234, 239, 240, 251
  comparison of, 219, 220–21
  definition of term, 72
  front-loading of, 21
  government, *see* government grants
  merit-based, 8, 11, 72, 128, 129, 147, 261
  need-based, 8, 11, 16, 17, 72, 129
  research, 139–40, 265–66
  see also scholarships
Green, Perri, 176
Grinnell College, 132–33
guidance counselors, scholarship information and, 158–59

Hagen, LaNice, 110, 157
Harvard University, 139, 147
Head Start Act, 114
Heart of America Christopher Reeve Award, 139
Higher Education Act (1965), 73
Holcombe, Tom, 137, 145–46, 158
Holland & Knight Charitable Foundation, 137, 145–46, 158
Holocaust Remembrance Project, 137
home equity, 17, 20–21, 46
home equity loans, 96, 102–4, 222
Hope Scholarship, 76, 230, 231, 232, 278
Horatio Alger Association, 151
Humana Foundation Scholarship, 144

Ibanez, Melissa, 76, 84, 209, 229
Income Contingent Repayment (ICR), 88–89

Income Sensitive Repayment (ISR), 88, 89
independent students, 18, 41, 65, 83, 103, 127, 129, 236–37, 241, 249, 259
in-school deferments, 104
"Institutional Methodology," 121, 128, 214
Institutional Student Information Report (ISIR), 72
Intel, 139
Intel International Science and Engineering Fair (ISEF), 163
Intel Science Talent Search (STS), 144, 158, 162–63, 172, 188
interest tax deductions, 103–4
Internal Revenue Service (IRS), 110, 114, 205, 207, 231
  Publication 78 of, 200
international fellowships, 264
internships, 109, 111–12, 157
interviews, scholarship, 170, 176, 186–90, 192
investing, 46, 47, 276–79, 281
IRAs, 103, 176, 206, 235, 274, 275, 278, 281
Ivy League schools, 2, 19, 45

Jack Kent Cooke Foundation Undergraduate Transfer Scholarship Program, 163, 261
JNS College Scholarship, 144
John F. Kennedy Profiles in Courage Essay Contest, 138, 163–64
Johnston, Lori, 34, 52, 197, 237
Juniata College, 141
junior year, admissions process and financial aid timetable in, 25–26, 51

Kachelski, J., 10
Kahler, Debbie, 170
Katrina, Hurricane, 112
Kerr, Liz, 170–71
Kiplinger's, 278
Kiwanis, 144
Klingon Language Institute, 141
Kohl's Kids Who Care Program, 153
Kor Memorial Scholarship, 141
Kornfeld, Leo, 80–81

letters of recommendation, 27, 28, 184–86
Leveraging Educational Assistance Partnership (LEAP), 75
Levy, David, 16, 109, 130, 147, 169, 228, 242
"LIBOR," 101
libraries, 160
life insurance, 281
Lifetime Learning Tax Credit, 230–31, 232, 278
Lindeman, Brian, 14, 132, 236

Index

Index

Index